Testing Global Interdependence

GLOBAL DEVELOPMENT NETWORK SERIES

Series editors: Natalia Dinello, *Principal Political Scientist, Global Development Network*

Meeting the challenge of development in the contemporary age of globalization demands greater empirical knowledge. While most research emanates from the developed world, the Global Development Network series is designed to give voice to researchers from the developing and transition world – those experiencing first-hand the promises and pitfalls of development. This series presents the best examples of innovative and policy-relevant research from such diverse countries as Nigeria and China, India and Argentina, Russia and Egypt. It encompasses all major development topics ranging from the details of privatization and social safety nets to broad strategies to realize the Millennium Development Goals and achieve the greatest possible progress in developing countries.

Titles in the series include:

Testing Global Interdependence
Issues on Trade, Aid, Migration and Development
Ernest Aryeetey and Natalia Dinello

Testing Global Interdependence

Issues on Trade, Aid, Migration and Development

Edited by

Ernest Aryeetey

Director, Institute of Statistical, Social and Economic Research, University of Ghana, Legon

Natalia Dinello

Principal Political Scientist, Global Development Network, New Delhi, India

GLOBAL DEVELOPMENT NETWORK

Edward Elgar
Cheltenham, UK • Northampton, MA, USA

Published by
Edward Elgar Publishing Limited
Glensanda House
Montpellier Parade
Cheltenham
Glos GL50 1UA
UK

Edward Elgar Publishing, Inc.
William Pratt House
9 Dewey Court
Northampton
Massachusetts 01060
USA

A catalogue record for this book
is available from the British Library

Library of Congress Control Number: 2006937961

ISBN: 978 1 84542 878 5

Printed and bound in Great Britain by MPG Books Ltd, Bodmin, Cornwall

Contents

vi *Testing Global Interdependence*

Notes on the Contributors

ERNEST ARYEETEY is Director of the Institute of Statistical, Social and Economic Research at the University of Ghana, Legon. His research focuses on the economics of development, with a particular emphasis on the role of institutions. His holds a doctorate in economics from the University of Dortmund, Germany.

JEAN-CLAUDE BERTHÉLEMY is Professor of Economics at the Sorbonne, Paris, where he obtained his doctorate. He is also an associate member of the French Academy of Social Sciences, Vice-chair of the European Development Research Network and resource person for the African Economic Research Consortium. He previously was a senior staff member of the Organization for Economic Cooperation and Development and is a consultant for various international organizations.

CARLOS CASACUBERTA holds an M.Sc. in economics from the London School of Economics and Political Science. He is a researcher at the Department of Economics, School of Social Sciences, Universidad de la República, Uruguay.

SATISH CHAND is director of the Pacific Policy Project and Associate Professor in Economics at the Australian National University. He has a Ph.D. from the Australian National University and has published on international trade, aid and economic growth. Being from Fiji, his geographic interests are in the island states of the South Pacific.

JAMES K. CHIN is a Research Fellow at the Center for Asian Studies at the University of Hong Kong. He has published more than 40 journal articles and book chapters on Chinese international migration and diaspora, Sino-Southeast Asian relations and the maritime history of Asia.

RICHARD N. COOPER is the Maurits C. Boas Professor of International Economics at Harvard University. His primary fields of interest include both international trade and international monetary economics, international environmental and energy issues.

NATALIA DINELLO has earned doctoral degrees from the University of Pittsburgh and the Soviet Academy of Science. As Principal Political Scientist at the Secretariat of the Global Development Network, she designs and implements strategies and programs for building research capacity in developing and transition economies. She also has an extensive publication record for her own research.

CHANTAL DUPASQUIER holds a master's degree in economics from the Université du Québec and is currently officer-in-charge of the Policy Planning and Coordination Section in the Office of Strategic Planning and Programme Management, United Nations Economic Commission for Africa (UNECA) in Addis Ababa. Prior to joining UNECA she was an assistant chief at the Bank of Canada. She has also been a monetary operations adviser to the IMF and has written papers on a broad range of issues related to monetary policy as well as economic and social development.

GABRIELA FACHOLA holds an M.Sc. in economics from the School of Social Sciences, Universidad de la República, Uruguay, where she is affiliated as a full-time instructor and researcher.

NÉSTOR GANDELMAN is director of the Department of Economics at Universidad ORT Uruguay. He holds a doctorate in economics from the University of Rochester. His research has focused primarily on applied industrial organization and labor economics.

ADAMA KONSEIGA joined the African Population and Research Center in August 2005 as a post-doctoral fellow. He received a Ph.D. in Economics through a unique collaboration between the University of Bonn in Germany and the University of Auvergne in France. He has previously worked at the Ministry of Economic Development and Finance as a Project Manager assigned to the European Development Fund Projects for Burkina Faso. Konseiga won the 2005 Global Development Medal for Outstanding Research on Development.

PATRICK N. OSAKWE holds a doctorate in economics from Queen's University, Canada, and is currently the officer-in-charge of the Financing

Development Section in the Trade, Finance and Economic Development Division of the U.N. Economic Commission for Africa (UNECA) in Addis Ababa. Before joining UNECA, he was a senior analyst with the Bank of Canada. He has conducted extensive research in international and development economics.

ISIDRO SOLOAGA is coordinator of the doctoral program in economics at the Universidad de las Américas, Puebla, Mexico. He previously was a researcher with the World Bank Developmental Research Group.

DHANANJAYAN SRISKANDARAJAH is an Associate Director of the Institute for Public Policy Research, a leading progressive think-tank based in London. His current research examines the economic, social and political impacts of migration. He has been consultant to various international organizations and is a regular media commentator on migration issues. He holds a Ph.D. from the University of Oxford, where he was a Rhodes Scholar.

ERNESTO ZEDILLO was president of Mexico from 1994–2000 and is currently director of the Yale Center for the Study of Globalization and Professor of International Economics and Politics at Yale University. He also serves as co-coordinator of the Task Force on Trade for the U.N. Millenium Project. He earned Master's and Ph.D. degrees in economics from Yale University, where he studied the issue of public indebtedness in Mexico and its link to future growth of petroleum exports.

Foreword

Independence and Interdependence: Mutual Reinforcement

Ernesto Zedillo

One of the most popular adventure novels in the history of world literature, *Robinson Crusoe*, was first published in 1719, but its message of independence, self-reliance and self-sufficiency still fascinates minds and spirits. However, the fictional story of an English castaway who spent 28 years on a remote island before being rescued by compatriots stirs the reader's imagination largely due to the improbability. Indeed, the real-life castaway, Scottish sailor Alexander Selkirk, who is often considered to be Crusoe's prototype, was rescued after only four years on an uninhabited island. Writer James Joyce interpreted Crusoe as the true example of the British colonist whose mission is expansion rather than seclusion. As if acknowledging the growing interdependence of the eighteenth-century world ruled by the exploration and colonization impulse, Daniel Defoe's novel ends with its protagonist's return to the same island, which has since been discovered.

In the twenty-first century, distances have become largely irrelevant, the remaining uninhabited islands have been discovered, if not populated, and 'Robinsons' on remote islands hardly lack connection with the rest of the world in the era of an information technology revolution. Moreover, man-made barriers to the exchange of goods and ideas and to travel have been lowered or removed. Global interconnectedness is now manifested in terms of trade, capital flows and migration. With the colonial past left behind us, modern national sovereignties celebrate their independence. However, in light of the promise of a better life through globalization, they can gain more from their independence if they capitalize on interdependence. In reference to developing countries, I have said elsewhere that 'We are now independent to the extent that we are interdependent'.[1]

Sure, there still remain 'castaway' nations existing at the margins of the global economy and polity. Millions of people are living in abject conditions on the fringes of the interdependent world. The dilemma of whether to embrace or reject globalization continues to face many countries. And the way in which this dilemma is addressed by nation states and civil societies will have a decisive influence on the character of modern times. Depending on the resolution of this dilemma, the twenty-first century will be remembered in history as an arena of great success or great failure.

My deep persuasion is that interdependence among countries can be beneficial for all parties and that global integration is part of the solution to the problems of poverty and inequality. The biggest present-day challenge is inclusion of the have-nots in the process of globalization. Time and again it has been shown that when people lack education; adequate training; good health; basic human, political and property rights; security; and elementary infrastructure, they cannot take advantage of the tremendous opportunities presented by the market economy. Two billion people, including a high proportion of the world's poor, live in countries which have scant involvement in the global economy. These countries, many in Africa, have minimal participation in world markets, exporting a few commodities and importing negligible quantities of goods, and many had negative economic growth throughout most of the 1980s and 1990s. Within other developing countries, extreme poverty is found precisely in those regions and communities which contemporary globalization has left largely untouched. For example, the problem for subsistence peasants in any developing country is not that globalization has reached them, but rather the opposite: they remain outside the world market.

The formally independent but marginalized nations risk losing their sovereignty because of their economic weakness and political instability. Every country – poor as well as rich – needs other countries' markets, capital and in some cases population flows in order to support its own economic expansion. Therefore, interdependence is indispensable for the pursuit of prosperity, peace and security. It is also critical for preservation and strengthening of true independence.

I do not tire of emphasizing that global integration is not a given. It is not irreversible, as some claim, based on the wrong belief that the phenomenon is essentially driven by technological change in transportation and telecommunications. Contemporary interdependence urged by political decisions can also be overturned, with a resultant dislocating, and even destructive, effect on global integration. Promoting a globalization which would offer opportunities to all involved requires effective political decision making at both national and international levels.

The developed countries can no longer insulate themselves in a cocoon of prosperity, while many developing countries linger in misery. Rich nations are responsible for world development, and this is reflected in their engagement in the international arena to facilitate trade, provide aid for development and address the issues of migration. This pro-development agenda should empower the disadvantaged to participate, with a credible chance of success, in the global market economy. However, the primary responsibility for achieving growth and equitable development lies with the developing countries themselves. It is at the national level that sovereign states make decisions to foster the market economy by opening it to foreign trade and liberalizing financial markets. It is through solid national policies that the countries' independence can be further advanced and their positions in the interdependent world improved.

True, global integration, like any economic and social process, has downsides. Although economic and political openness is expected to generate global gains that far exceed the losses, the benefits of globalization are not distributed equally across countries and populations. But it is also true that effective policies and strong institutions at the local, national and international levels can significantly limit the negative aspects of interdependence and strengthen its potential to be a force for good. Apart from an altruistic sentiment, addressing the challenges of globalization is in the self-interest of all countries – both poor and rich, weak and powerful.

The project *Global Trade and Financial Architecture*, that I had recently the honor of leading, has been driven by the aspiration for equity in governing globalization. In our report of the project results, we acknowledge that there will be losers from multilateral liberalization of access to markets – and suggest the means to compensate for the losses and assist the disadvantaged groups.[2] We also recognize that the poorest developing countries cannot benefit from economic openness unless they build physical, human and institutional capacity to trade. Therefore, a significant increase in well-targeted 'aid for trade' is proposed. Finally, we recommend moving away from providing exceptions from international rules to developing countries in favor of helping them meet development goals and advocate establishing a global program on policy transparency.

The project ideas and proposals are consistent with the letter and spirit of this book. The contributors to this volume – all of whom are associated with the Global Development Network, which fosters high-quality socio-economic research in and about the developing world – are also concerned about costs and benefits of global interdependence. They specifically address the question of countries' adjustment to the perils of globalization, that I consider to be central for attracting developing countries into the global economy. Indeed, any scheme of compensation to the losers from trade liberalization should take into account the adjustment costs and the fact that these costs are incurred before one can take advantage of new trade opportunities. In devising such schemes, assigning different roles to bilateral and multilateral development assistance – contemplated by some contributors to this volume – can prove helpful.

It is no wonder that this publication addresses a diversity of issues on trade, aid and migration: these issues are interconnected in their relation to development. 'Aid for trade,' to which I attribute much importance, testifies to this interconnectedness. Migration also enters the development field, particularly as a result of internationalization of the services sector. This collection of articles also brings to mind that the rationale for global integration is not only economic. Contacts generated by trade, investment and migration may serve to sensitize a country's population to the values, cultures and customs of other countries. Whenever people believe that economic interdependence serves their own self-interest – by giving them better opportunities to improve their well-being – these contacts encourage a convergence of values that reduce the risk of violent conflict among interdependent nations. For these and many other reasons, constructive interdependence must not be allowed to falter.

We are reminded by many accounts – academic, literary and journalistic – that it takes much courage, will, intelligence and endurance to be independent. But no less courage, will, intelligence and endurance are needed to embrace interdependence and extract dividends from it. While it is rather difficult nowadays to be left alone, many nations and groups are still left behind. To lift them from their 'castaway' status, international cooperation is imperative. The experiences of countries, such as those analyzed in this book, can serve as useful reference points in policymakers' efforts to make the global economy more inclusive and receptive to the newcomers.

NOTES

1. Ernesto Zedillo (2001), 'Globalization and the Changing Roles of States'. Remarks at the 2001 annual meeting of the Trilateral Commission, London, 10 March 2001, available at http: //www.trilateral.org/annmtgs/trialog/trlgtxts/t55/zed.htm.
2. 'Strengthening the Global Trade Architecture for Economic Development: An Agenda for Action'. Policy brief of the project on 'Global Trade and Financial Architecture', spearheaded by the Department for International Development and the Yale Center for the Study of Globalization, New Haven, Connecticut, 2005, available at http://www.ycsg.yale.edu/focus/ index.html

Preface: Social Science Tests of the 'Butterfly Effect'

Ernest Aryeetey and Natalia Dinello

More than ever before, we live today in an interdependent world. Peter Peterson (2003), the chairman of the U.S.-based Council on Foreign Relations, acknowledged that even a military, economic and geopolitical superpower depends on the rest of the world. In his 2001 Nobel lecture, United Nations Secretary-General Kofi Annan suggested that the world of human activity has its own 'Butterfly Effect'. Nature, he remarked, 'is so small and interdependent that a butterfly flapping its wings in the Amazon rainforest can generate a violent storm on the other side of the earth'. As noted by Paul Streeten (2001), the founder of the multidisciplinary international journal *World Development*, 'Interdependence exists when one country by unilateral action can inflict harm on (or provide benefits to) other countries. Competitive protectionism, devaluation, deflation or pollution of the air and sea beyond national boundaries are instances'.

The growing global interdependence is reflected not only by the huge expansion in world trade over the last two decades, but also by the massive expansion of capital flows, the easier access to foreign technologies, the growing use of foreign resources for development through international assistance and the changing scope and growth of migration. These expansions have created major opportunities for countries to use resources which were previously not available to them for their own development. Thus it has been possible for the U.S. government to rely on the savings of other economies to finance its huge budget deficits at little cost. But the opportunities have been accompanied by new risks which countries must address. Many economists have wondered whether growing external trade poses any threat to the rural environment, particularly in poor countries, as natural resources are tapped to support growing world demand. There is evidence that stronger economies have been better able to deal with the risks than more fragile ones.

While the external trade opportunities arising from global interdependence are huge, the extent to which these reach all parts of national economies has been the subject of debate. Killick (2002) discusses the potential benefits with a look at the static efficiency benefits arising from the classical 'gains from trade' arguments. These are based on the advantages of economies of scale and specialization and competition following international exposure. While the potential benefits may be large at the national level, they diminish as they move to the communities where the poor live. There are far too many structural constraints making it difficult for the poor to take advantage of whatever opportunities may be available to the national economy. A major constraint is, of course, the infrastructure difficulties associated with all poor economies.

In the area of technology transfer, both risks and opportunities accompany the introduction of foreign technologies into poor communities. In general terms, foreign technologies are expected to facilitate production and consumption in ways which were previously inconceivable. And this has been achieved in many places. Farm productivity is expected to rise enormously as a result of major improvements in the resilience of various seed varieties and their capacity to multiply, even under marginal conditions. In terms of consumption, poor rural households are expected to increase their consumption as a result of the newfound ability to grow food over longer cycles and store it using improved methods. But there has always been risk associated with the introduction of new seed varieties. For example, old crop varieties may be destroyed as new technology is not adapted to produce food items with the same attributes as the older varieties in terms of taste and appearance. The possible 'wiping out' of traditional foods as a result of new technologies is well known in many developing countries.

Increased flows of foreign private capital can be easily associated with rapid growth in a number of countries, particularly in Southeast Asia. But it is difficult to find similar cases in other parts of the developing world, and this discontinuity leads to a debate about the conditions under which private capital may boost growth and development. In the same vein, the debate about whether aid does actually lead to economic transformation continues with no end in sight. In more recent times, however, the biggest challenge, as suggested in the globalization literature, has come from the responses to international migration. Increasingly the benefits from migration to both developed economies and the less developed ones are being recognized in terms of the productivity gains acquired from new skilled labor where there was a deficit, and the new remittance flows which facilitate income enhancement in poor countries. In Ghana, for example, the regions which experienced the largest reductions in poverty between 1992 and 1998 were those with the greatest increases in remittances as a share of household receipts. But the benefits and costs of international migration are extremely difficult to measure in a way that is free from passion, particularly as the distinction between 'brain drain' and 'brain gain' has acquired wide circulation. In any case, it is difficult to justify the movement of highly skilled health professionals from poor to richer countries by any sound economic arguments when health institutions in developing countries can no longer function as a result of this migration.

In light of these contentious issues, it is no wonder that one of the most critical questions today is whether global interdependence – in its current shape and form – is beneficial or harmful for development. Consequently, one of the most vexing dilemmas facing developing countries is whether to embrace or reject globalization. Although much ink has been spilled by academics debating these issues, their resolution is a matter of practice. And it largely depends on specifics – specific means of integrating into the global economy, specific contexts of exercising openness, specific areas of engaging at the international level and specific mechanisms of adjusting to the challenges of globalization. Some developing countries have chosen to distance themselves from key players in the global arena, but most have ventured to test the benefits and disadvantages of global interdependence. Introducing perspectives on a variety of subjects related to trade, foreign aid, migration and development, this volume seeks to translate a general theme about accepting globalization and gaining from deeper integration of various economies and societies into practical questions about the effect of particular trade policies and agreements on poverty, consequences of government actions to reduce migration and the rationale and implications of foreign aid.

This book is organized in three parts: trade, aid and migration. Based on diverse narratives of multiple countries' experiences in the context of globalization, the study highlights both motivations and results of participation in the process of global integration. These narratives reflect multiple tests of global interdependence – the social science incarnation of the Butterfly Effect – which may ultimately suggest how to limit globalization's negative aspects and how to ensure that it is a constructive phenomenon. Addressing a broad range of questions, the book chapters nevertheless overlap in highlighting three major themes: first, the interrelationship among trade, aid and migration as engines of development; second, the importance of conditional acceptance of globalization, that connotes an adjustment to the new global reality depending on specific contexts; and third, the need for effective means of building on global interdependence to maximize its benefits and minimize its costs.

The chapters in this volume were presented at the Sixth Annual Global Development Conference, that took place in Dakar, Senegal, in January 2005. Held under the theme *Developing and Developed Worlds: Mutual Impact*, the conference was organized by the Global Development Network (GDN), an organization with the dual mission of building research capacity in social science and bridging research and policy. Most of the authors of the book chapters represent GDN's network partners in the developing and developed worlds; some of them are the finalists from the annual Global Development Research Medals competition. (Only scholars from developing and transition economies are eligible to participate in this competition.) This book follows another GDN-sponsored publication, *Globalization and Equity: Perspectives from the Developing World* (Dinello and Squire 2005), which included a set of papers delivered at the Fourth Annual Global Development Conference, held in Cairo, Egypt, in January 2003. The 2005 book highlighted the countries' disparate experiences in globalization and equity but nevertheless maintained that there is a fledgling consensus on the benefits of the developing world's entry into a global universe and the necessity for prudent adjustment to the perils of this endeavor.

INTERRELATIONSHIP AMONG TRADE, AID AND MIGRATION: IMPLICATIONS FOR DEVELOPMENT

Trade, aid and migration are the important indicators of mutual impact between developing and developed countries. Their strong interrelationship provides a rationale for assembling research findings on trade, aid and migration in one book. It also implies that the tests of the Butterfly Effect should be comprehensive and multifaceted in order to capture the full costs and benefits of global interdependence.

The theme of interconnectedness among various vehicles of development has acquired prominence in the recent literature on globalization (see, for example, Faini and Venturini 1993). As argued by George Cho (1995), there exists a complex interrelationship among trade, aid and development. As developing countries become more and more aware of the limitations and insufficiency of aid alone as a factor of economic growth, they increasingly seek *both* international trade and aid alone. Not denying the role of aid as a means of promoting development, William Cline (2004) claims that free international trade promises greater benefits to developing countries than aid. According to his estimates, while assistance from rich to poor countries amounts to about $50 billion per year, total long-term income gains to developing countries from global free trade could reach $200 billion annually. Migration is also considered as an aspect of global integration which evolves together with international trade and capital markets (Kapur and McHale 2005). Some periods are marked by greater mobility of goods and capital, while others may be characterized by more intensive migration (Hatton and Williamson 2003, 1–2).

This book begins with an essentially optimistic message articulated by Richard Cooper. In his overview chapter Cooper writes: 'Relative to expectations at the dawn of global development policy, the world economy performed outstandingly well during the second half of the 20th century' (1). The evidence he cites ranges from historically unprecedented worldwide growth in average per capita income to declines in poverty and infant mortality, as well as improvement in diets, rising human longevity and the containment or even disappearance of many diseases. Consistent with the notion of interrelationship between trade and foreign aid to developing countries, Cooper attributes successes in extending general welfare to *both* factors. According to him, world exports grew more rapidly than output in the last 50 years, often leading the way and supporting the conventional wisdom that openness – that is, some form of serious engagement with the world economy – is a significant contributor to growth (5). At the same time, national economies became interdependent in terms of capital. The movement of aid funds and private capital confirmed one of the advantages of engagement with the world economy – the possibility of gaining investment funds not only from domestic savings but also from savings elsewhere in the world (11).

Several articles in this collection continue this theme. The chapter on trade capacity building in Sub-Saharan Africa by Chantal Dupasquier and Patrick Osakwe demonstrates a logical link between trade and aid, showing how aid can help create necessary prerequisites for fair and effective international trade. The authors refer to the high implementation costs of the African countries' acceptance of the Uruguay Round (1986–94) multilateral trade agreements as evidence of these countries' lack of capacity to negotiate effectively on trade issues, to exercise the rights of World Trade Organization membership without jeopardizing important development goals, to formulate effective trade policies, to exploit trading opportunities and to fulfill commitments to the multilateral trading system (78). The authors do not 'doubt that trade, if well managed, could play a very important role in the economic development of African countries. It provides easy access to foreign exchange, new technology and more consumer choice. It also increases efficiency in the use of resources through increased competition and allows the exploitation of economies of scale associated with enlarged market size' (102). However, the poorest countries are unable to take advantage of international trade without building sufficient trade capacity.[1] Trade-related technical assistance offered by rich countries under the recent Doha Development Agenda (DDA) (since 2001) is one element in a capacity-building program which, according to the authors, should be closely integrated into broader means of creating an enabling environment for development.

Working from the perspective of migration and development, another contributor to the book, Dhananjayan Sriskandarajah (see Chapter 6), contends that international migration can add to increased trade flows between sending and receiving countries and stimulates investment in domestic education and individual human capital investments. Sriskandarajah is not alone in emphasizing the link among migration, trade and capital: he follows in the steps of Robert Lucas (2005, 3) who similarly argued that migrants could promote both trade and investment in their country of origin. Lucas substantiated his thesis by referring to the migrants' better knowledge about trading and investment opportunities and by their ability to enforce contracts through a network of contacts at home, a strategy particularly important in countries with no legal framework for conducting business (117). Furthermore, Adama Konsiega (see Chapter 8) further applies the conventional wisdom about interconnectedness among various factors of development to skilled migration. In the era of globalization,' Konsiega writes, 'Highly talented workers are essentially becoming more globally mobile as goods, services and capital have become more globally mobile over time' (212), thus reinforcing the notion of intellectual circulation as inseparable from trade and capital flows.

This interrelationship among trade, aid (as part of capital flows) and migration also suggests the interconnectedness of economic and political perspectives, a view projected by several contributors to this book. Writing primarily about economic parameters of world development during the last 50 years, Cooper nevertheless goes beyond economics, arguing that civil and political liberties (which also have a significant influence over migration) also spread during this period (13). In Chapter 4 Jean-Claude Berthélemy explores commercial interests as a motive for aid and as a counterpoint to donors' geopolitical interests which also affect decisions about assistance to developing countries. As another example of addressing both economic and political viewpoints, Satish Chand analyzes a remarkable turn in Australian aid policy – from serving primarily commercial interests to expressing political security-related concerns (see Chapter 5).

The existence of an interrelationship among international trade, aid and migration – as documented in this book – may have implications for development in terms of gradually becoming aware of and gaining from global interdependence. A state's entry into a larger world may begin within a single dimension of global integration, which would allow testing of the costs and benefits of being incorporated in the global economy. However, the first access to international resources and opportunities may launch a series of initiatives resulting in a more profound integration. This gradualism can get further impetus if an economic rationale for the integrating strategy is reinforced by political reasons and vice versa.

EMBRACING GLOBALIZATION: ACCEPTANCE AND ADJUSTMENT

As a case in favor of embracing globalization, Isidro Soloaga writes in Chapter 1 about the likely impact of trade reforms and implementation of the DDA[2] on various types of Cambodian households, including the poor. Based on simulations using household expenditures, he comes to the conclusion that although changes in prices expected as a result of the DDA's implementation will have on average an almost nil effect on poverty, the change of the tariff structure to a 7 per cent flat rate would produce an average positive impact on households' income of about 3.7 per cent, almost all of it coming from a reduced tariff on foodstuffs (34). Also, noticeable improvements in the livelihoods of poor Cambodians are expected as a result of employees switching to the industrial sector from both agriculture and services as well as from advances in two key elements of rice production technology. These findings are broadly consistent with conclusions of other studies on possible implications of the DDA. For example, Thomas Hertel and Alan Winters (2005) found, using a global modeling framework, that world poverty will likely reduce under the core DDA scenario, that this reduction will be more pronounced in the longer run, and that complementary domestic reforms are needed to take advantage of the new market opportunities.

As another case in favor of trade liberalization, that is part and parcel of global integration, Carlos Casacuberta, Gabriela Fachola and Néstor Gandelman examine how exposing the Uruguayan manufacturing sector to international trade flows affected employment, capital and productivity (see Chapter 2). Uruguayan market-oriented reforms, launched in the 1970s along with tax structure modernization, trade liberalization and full convertibility of the capital account, form the background of their study. Based on their analysis of data from the Uruguayan Manufacturing Survey for the period 1982–95, Casacuberta, Fachola and Gandelman show that trade liberalization had a strong positive impact on productivity levels: the capital-to-labor ratio must have increased, produced by a switch towards more capital-intensive technologies; the reallocation of factors of production and the adoption of new production technologies generated an important increase in total factor productivity (72–73).

Notably, this rise in productivity happened in Uruguay under very specific conditions. First, unions still maintained significant power in Uruguay, and reforms were often negotiated with them directly. Second, most industries displayed high concentration levels, which gave firms considerable market power, particularly in setting prices (53). According to the authors, highly unionized sectors experienced larger employment creation rates and lower employment destruction rates while maintaining their higher productivity over less unionized sectors. At the same time, more concentrated sectors have experienced lower capital destruction levels than less concentrated sectors, which means that the market power derived from concentration was translated into higher capital net creation rates (68).

In both the Uruguayan and Cambodian case studies in this book, the tests of global interdependence yielded (or are expected to yield) positive results which are consistent with other evidence on the benefits of globalization (Srinivasan and Bhagwati 1999; World Bank 2002; Dollar and Kraay 2001, 2002a, 2000b, 2004; Bhagwati 2004). Nevertheless, broad generalizations from these cases are somewhat risky because the advantages of global integration are registered in very specific contexts, accounting for specific adjustments to the challenges of globalization. For example, in Uruguay high levels of industry unionization and concentration may have mitigated any negative effects of trade liberalization for local workers.

Chapter 3 by Dupasquier and Osakwe also highlights the dangers of perceiving international trade as an unconditionally 'good thing'. As confirmed by authoritative observers of the international trade negotiations (Stiglitz and Charlton 2004, 9), the African countries' trade commitments have diverted resources from important development projects, with dire consequences for poverty reduction. However, Dupasquier and Osakwe suggest that performing the same test of global interdependence under conditions of Africa's increased trade capacity – as a result of the set of adjustments – could produce very different results. This cautious, differentiating approach is welcome, considering the results of some influential studies which have shown that there is no simple generalizable conclusion about the impact of trade liberalization on poverty, although the benefits appear to increase over the long run (Winters et al. 2004).

Similarly, Konsiega's message in Chapter 8 is that broad generalizations are not always helpful: much depends on the context. Based on data on skilled migration from seven countries of the Western African Union, he provides evidence of the benefits of migration between capital-rich and capital-poor countries as a powerful factor of growth and income convergence, yet this finding does not stand when migration occurs between developing countries of the Union. Following Anthony Venables (1999), Konsiega concludes, 'An African country should prefer a "North–South" type of integration agreements' (222) in order to extract gains from its participation in the world economy. Furthermore, extending this theme to migration in general, Sriskandarajah stresses, 'Whether the impacts of migration are positive or negative depend[s] very much on the context and how the situation is managed' (180). Believing that not one set of policies is universally applicable, he proposes a matrix of policies which might be appropriate for particular contexts (see Chapter 6).

The only chapter in this collection that highlights *un*conditional acceptance of globalization is that by James Chin in Chapter 7, who presents the views of prospective illegal migrants from China. Consistent with the book's message, his study nevertheless shows the excruciating consequences of this unconditional acceptance. Chin's interviews reveal that the migrants see the world outside China, the West in particular, as an epitome of upward mobility, quick enrichment and personal satisfaction. Their dreams for a better life in the global economy include dazzling images of 'a decent life with [their] own villas and cars,' high income, less competition for jobs and other opportunities, hefty remittances and luxurious houses built at home with money earned abroad (199). Although these dreams are inspired by the success stories of some of their compatriots, they neglect the high costs of illegal migration: enormous monetary payments to 'human cargo' smugglers (up to $55,000, according to Chin); complex, potentially fatal journeys to the land of their dreams and the bleak reality of toiling overseas. Blinded by their desires and fantasies, the prospective migrants even idealize so-called snakeheads (organizers or brokers of illegal migration), calling them 'good guys' (192–93) or even 'ministers of nongovernmental labors' and 'directors of nongovernmental bank' (202). This sentiment reflects an inherent aspiration for a world without borders and an infatuation with opportunities associated with globalization. Testing these opportunities with one's own lives constitutes a contemporary drama of migration.

The underlying message, as it is reiterated by several contributions to this volume, is therefore two-fold. Foremost, as manifestations of the Butterfly Effect in international human activity become more and more tangible, practical experience with global interdependence highlights both the glory and anguish of globalization. Therefore, to achieve a smooth and relatively painless integration in the global economy, policymakers should consider specific conditions of entering the larger world and contemplate necessary adjustments.

BUILDING ON GLOBAL INTERDEPENDENCE

Global interdependence obliges both developed and developing countries to seek a mutual accommodation. Aid offered by rich countries to poor ones is not an expression of benevolence; it is imperative for all parties involved in global integration, to build on interdependence. The articles by Berthélemy and Chand explore motivations behind foreign assistance. Berthélemy provides empirical evidence that rich countries' development assistance results from a combination of self-interest and altruism; Chand documents the specific case of Australian assistance to its island neighbors, highlighting the recent shift in emphasis to security as the rationale for aid and interventions.

The official purpose of aid is usually to help lift developing countries out of poverty and stimulate their development, while not substituting local capital investment. However, developing countries' dependence on aid has become a notorious unintended consequence in past decades (van de Walle 2005, Lancaster and Wangwe 2000; Sobhan 1982). Trying to understand the origin of this dependence, Berthélemy highlights the previous research findings on vested interests in maintaining the aid system in *recipient* countries (Svensson 2000). His contribution, however, consists of providing evidence of the influence of such vested interests on aid-allocation decisions by *donor* countries. Based on the estimate of an aid-allocation equation, using a yearly panel of bilateral aid commitments granted by 22 bilateral donors – members of the Organization for Economic Cooperation and Development – to 137 developing countries over the 1980s and 1990s, Berthélemy demonstrates that trade-related business interests in the donor countries heavily influence their aid policies.

Complementing the findings on the key role of geopolitical interests in donors' aid decisions, Berthélemy confirms that foreign aid is directly beneficial to donors and their close business partners from the developing world. At the same time, the neediest aid recipients are likely to lose whenever aid is granted for reasons other than poverty alleviation. Having uncovered the motives behind aid allocation, Berthélemy proposes a new architecture for international aid, that takes account of the existing global realities and difficulties in changing them. Specifically, he suggests sharing responsibilities between the bilateral and multilateral donors: the bilateral donors would take care of the most promising economic partners, while the multilaterals would concentrate their assistance on the neediest countries. The rationale behind this proposal would be to find incentives for non-altruistic bilateral donors to increase their aid budgets (122). Moreover, this aid architecture should satisfy various players in the global political and economic system and enable them to reap benefits from their interdependence.

Berthélemy's proposal also makes sense in light of the fact that the bilateral donors have been increasingly advised to consider aid effectiveness as a prerequisite of assistance (Hansen and Tarp 2000; Tarp and Hjertholm 2000). For example, Steven Radelet insists that donors be much more goal- and results-oriented in their aid programs and allocate aid to poorer countries with strong and moderate governance (Radelet 2004). The message of Nicolas van de Walle's (2005) recent book – namely, that aid combined with 'bad governance' hurts poor countries in general and the poorest people in those countries in particular – implies that only well-governed countries should qualify for aid, while they need it least.

In this collection of articles Cooper refers to the 'apparent ineffectiveness of aid' (the lack of its association with higher economic growth) unless it is given to 'well-managed countries' (12). Dupasquier and Osakwe observe that assistance for building trade capacity is primarily channeled toward those countries of Sub-Saharan Africa which 'tend to have more effective government, better regulatory framework and more exports' (93). Chand also notes the concerns about the impact and cost-effectiveness of Australian aid and pressures to improve aid effectiveness. However, if aid is provided only to well-managed countries, the poorly governed countries – those that particularly need a relief from a 'poverty trap' to launch the engine of growth (Sachs et al. 2004) – will be excluded, with disastrous consequences for them and the world at large. Berthélemy's proposal that the multilaterals concentrate their efforts on assisting the neediest recipients, instead of targeting the good performers, could therefore correct the bias of bilateral aid (123) and thus help build on global interdependence.

The chapter by Chand supplies some illustrations for Berthélemy's theoretical arguments and their empirical testing. At the same time, it provides an interesting twist on the theme of global interdependence, demonstrating how Australia's aid for development reflects current anxieties about global and regional security. It also reminds that globalization refers not only to economic interdependence but also to political interdependence and mutual security. The latter concern is now located at the center of political thinking in many countries.

Chand's chapter is also intriguing because it reveals a curious reversal of aid policy goals – from the primary goal of 'poverty reduction through sustainable development' which has been officially pursued by Australia since 1997, to the earlier 1984 view that aid policy should be driven by multiple mandates, including humanitarian, strategic and commercial goals (14). Furthermore, it analyzes the latest shift of Australian aid policy toward 'interventionism,' that entails a greater direct involvement on the part of the Australian security forces and other public servants in the neighboring region. This shift represents a rather controversial 'experiment' – reflecting the tensions between the 'altruistic' aid policy and 'self-interest' in aid addressed by Berthélemy's chapter – that may have lessons for the broader donor and recipient communities (122). Similar to Berthélemy, Chand does not lament non-altruistic motives but rather seeks an international aid architecture which would accommodate these motives and rely on compensatory multilateral aid to ensure dividends from global interdependence.

Writing on the issue of migration, Sriskandarajah also emphasizes the significance of a proactive, although realistic, policy. Considering that the very poor countries stand to lose the most and gain the least from migration (due to brain strain, low return migration potential, poor environment for the productive use of remittances etc.), achieving global poverty reduction requires coordinated efforts on the part of policymakers worldwide (180). Sriskandarajah's proposals include creating an environment for more effective dialogue between those arms of governments which do not traditionally work together – for example, departments responsible for home or immigration affairs and those responsible for international development. Sriskandarajah also emphasizes the need for a 'robust supranational framework' for managing migration. Admitting that this framework cannot be built overnight, he advocates more productive partnerships between developed and developing countries and action on shared development objectives as a relatively easy step forward.[3] Sriskandarajah's concluding statement expresses well the spirit of other book chapters: 'Given the global and interdependent scope of the challenges, it would seem wise to have global and interdependent approaches to tackling them' (181). Continuing this theme and having found that brain gain happens only when the Western African Union countries choose an industrialized country (such as France) as a target destination (222), Konseiga in fact suggests that building on global interdependence may be even more beneficial than building on regional interdependence.

Whenever global and interdependent approaches to tackling challenges of globalization are missing or ineffective, informal and clandestine structures fill this void. This is the message of Chin's article, that contends, 'Human migration including irregular migration is a natural human flow which cannot be forcibly stopped by governmental administrative means' (204). Based on his conversations with prospective illegal migrants from China, Chin shows that his interviewees question 'why governments, either the Chinese government or any foreign government, do not provide them with a legal channel to go overseas and to reunite with their families' (198). Given the lack of legal channels, migrants build on the existing international human trafficking networks founded on the principles of 'kinship, local ties and dialect groups' (190) to go around the remaining barriers among countries. As suggested by Chin, irregular migration can be transformed into managed migration if the developed and developing countries find the will to honestly evaluate global labor demand and supply and to negotiate the movement of laborers. As a result, regulation of migration will dispel many illusions and thrills prompted by globalization, but it will also decrease the perils and pitfalls associated with global interdependence.

In sum, to benefit from global interdependence, policymakers must actively manage the globalization process. But there is no 'silver bullet' for making this process instantly advantageous to all parties involved. Building on global interdependence requires constructive international dialogue, patience, experimentation and constant retooling of the available arsenal of adjustment. There is no easy way to satisfy all participants in global integration, but as suggested by the contributors to this book, it is possible to correct the existing biases and to articulate the commonly accepted international policies.

* * *

As implied by the articles in this book, the existence of the Butterfly Effect in reference to the world of human activity is no longer disputed: it is taken for granted. Indeed, an improvement in rice production technology in Cambodia can have implications for the world prices on rice, affecting not only poor Cambodians. And changing aid flows to Sub-Saharan Africa can influence both international trade and migration patterns, creating effects which can be felt well beyond the African continent.

In a separate study Peterson (2003) calls global interdependence a 'sobering reality'. Meanwhile, the costs and benefits of this 'reality' and the means of adjusting to and building on it in specific contexts remain contentious subjects. We hope this collection of articles will contribute to the better understanding of the dilemmas and struggles associated with global integration. We also hope that this volume will enhance the message of GDN's 2005 book *Globalization and Equity: Perspectives from the Developing World*. There is indeed a broad consensus that the developing world's entry into a global universe offers both 'roses and thorns'. Practical steps toward mutual accommodation – or at least consideration – between developing and developed countries, discussion of which runs through this book, can prevent huge crises and extend the 'freedom from want'. Any lessons from disparate experiences of various countries in addressing the challenges of globalization should therefore be helpful.

NOTES

1. The unfavorable balance between benefits and costs for developing countries as a result of the Uruguay Round was indicated by several authors (Croome 1998, Nogues 2005).
2. The Doha Development Agenda is interpreted as a step towards greater globalization of the world economy. For instance, as noted by Soloaga, the framework for agriculture seeks to reform global agricultural trade by the elimination of all forms of exports subsidies as well as

all export measures with equivalent effect (e.g., exports credits, insurance programs) and by substantial reduction in tariffs.

3. Other researchers have proposed more specific practical steps to compensate developing countries for the loss of their human capital. They refer to tying development aid to human capital recruitment, sharing payroll and income tax revenues with poor-country providers of human capital, U.S.-style continuing post-emigration tax obligations to countries of origin, conditional education grants that are repayable on emigration, sharing the proceeds of visa fees or the revenues of visa auctions (Kapur and McHale 2005).

BIBLIOGRAPHY

Annan, Kofi (2001), Nobel Lecture, text available at http://nobelprize.org/nobel_prizes/peace/laureates/2001/annan-lecture.html.

Bhagwati, Jagdish (2004), *In Defense of Globalization*, New York: Oxford University Press.

Bhagwati, Jagdish and T.N. Srinivasan (2002), 'Trade and Poverty in the Poor Countries', *American Economic Review*, **92** (2), 180–83.

Cho, George (1995), *Trade, Aid and Global Interdependence*, New York: Routledge.

Cline, William (2004), *Trade Policy and Global Poverty*, Washington, DC: Institute for International Economics, Center for Global Development.

Croome, John (1998), 'The Present Outlook for Trade Negotiations in the World Trade Organization', Washington, DC, World Bank, Policy Research Working Paper No. 1992.

Dinello, Natalia and Lyn Squire (eds) (2005), *Globalization and Equity: Perspectives from the Developing World*, Cheltenham, UK: Northampton, MA, USA, Edward Elgar.

Dollar, David and Aart Kraay (2001), 'Globalization, Inequality and Poverty Since 1980', World Bank: Washington, DC, available at http://worldbank.research/global.

——(2002a), 'Growth is Good for the Poor', *Journal of Economic Growth,* **7** (3): 195–225.

—— (2002b), 'Trade, Growth and Poverty', *Economic Journal*, **114** (493), F22–F49.

Faini, Riccardo and Alessandra Venturini (1993), 'Trade, Aid and Migrations: Some Basic Policy Issues', *European Economic Review*, **37** (2 – 3), 435–42.

Faini, Riccardo, Jaime De Melo and Klaus F. Zimmermann (1999), *Migration: The Controversies and the Evidence*, New York: Cambridge University Press.

Hansen, Henrik and Finn Tarp (2000), 'Aid Effectiveness Disputed', *Journal of International Development*, **12** (3), 375–98.

Hatton, Timothy and Jeffrey Williamson (2003), 'What Fundamentals Drive World Migration?', Helsinki, World Institute for Development Economics Research, Discussion Paper No. 2003/23.

Hertel, Thomas and L. Alan Winters (2005), 'Estimating the Poverty Impacts of a Prospective Doha Development Agenda', a paper available at http://www.gdnet.org/impact/Resource_Centre/Hertel_Winters_WorldEconomy.pdf.

Kapur, Devesh and John McHale (October 2005), 'The Global Migration of Talent: What Does it Mean for Developing Countries?', *CGD Brief*, available at www.cgdev.org/content/publications/detail/4473.

Killick, Tony (2002), 'Inequality Briefing', London, UK Department for International Development, Briefing Paper No. 3.

Lancaster, Carol and Samuel Wangwe (2000), *Managing a Smooth Transition from Aid Dependence in Africa*, Washington, DC: Overseas Development Council.

Lucas, Robert (2005), *International Migration Regimes and Economic Development*, Lyme, CT: Edward Elgar.

McCulloch, Neil, Alan L. Winters and Xavier Cirera (2001), *Trade Liberalization and Poverty: A Handbook*, London: Centre for Economic Policy Research.

Nogues, Julio J. (2005), 'Unequal Exchange: Developing Countries in the International Trade Negotiations', Economics Working Paper Archive, International Trade Series, No. 0502011.

Peterson, Peter (2003), 'Global Interdependence: A Sobering Reality,' Annual Essay, The Conference Board 2003 Annual Report, available at http://www.conference-board.org/pdf_free/annualessay2003.pdf.

Radelet, Steven (April 2004), 'Aid Effectiveness and the Millennium Development Goals', Washington, DC, Center for Global Development, Working Paper No. 39.

Sachs, Jeffrey, John McArthur, Guido Schmidt-Traub, Margaret Kruk, Chandrika Bahadur, Michael Faye and Gordon McCord (2004), 'Ending Africa's Poverty Trap,' *Brookings Papers on Economic Activity*, No. 1, 117–240.

Sobhan, Rehman (1982), *The Crisis of External Dependence: The Political Economy of Foreign Aid to Bangladesh*, Dhaka, Bangladesh: University Press.

Srinivasan, T.N. and Jagdish Bhagwati (1999), 'Outward Orientation and Development: Are Revisionists Right?' festschrift for Anne Krueger, Columbia University, New York, 19 September 1999, available at http://www.Columbia.edu/~jb38/Krueger.pdf.

Stiglitz, Joseph E. and Andrew Charlton (2004), *The Development Round of Trade Negotiations in the Aftermath of Cancun*, Report of the Commonwealth Secretariat and the Initiative for Policy Dialogue.

Streeten, Paul (2001), 'Integration, Interdependence and Globalization', *Finance and Development*, **38** (2).

Svensson, Jakob (2000), 'Foreign Aid and Rent-Seeking', *Journal of International Economics*, **51** (2), 437–61.

Tarp, Finn and Peter Hjertholm (eds) (2000), *Foreign Aid and Development: Lessons Learned and Directions for the Future*, London: Routledge.

van de Walle, Nicolas (2005), *Overcoming Stagnation in Aid-Dependent Countries*, Washington, DC: Center for Global Development.

Venables, Anthony J. (1999), 'Regional Integration Agreements: A Force for Convergence or Divergence?', Washington, DC, World Bank, Country Economics Department Working Paper No. 2260.

Winters, L. Alan, Neil McCulloch and Andrew McKay (2004), 'Trade Liberalization and Poverty: The Evidence So Far', *Journal of Economic Literature*, **42** (1), 72–115.

World Bank (2002), *Globalization, Growth, and Poverty: Building an Inclusive World Economy*, New York: Oxford University Press.

Acknowledgments

This book is the result of the Global Development Network's efforts to promote policy-relevant social science research on development. Published as part of the GDN Series, it assembles papers from the 2005 Annual Global Development Conference and the Global Development Research Medals competition. The editors and contributors to the book owe their gratitude to GDN President Lyn Squire as both reviewer and adviser and to the GDN Secretariat staff for general support. Their thanks also goes to Ann Robertson who was invaluable in supervising the copyediting process and preparing the text for publication. Finally, they are indebted to the staff of Edward Elgar Publishing Ltd. whose extraordinary receptivity and tactful advice make preparation of the GDN Series a continually rewarding experience.

Introduction: Growth and Poverty in the World Economy, 1950–2000

Richard N. Cooper

Relative to expectations at the dawn of global development policy, the world economy performed outstandingly well during the second half of the 20th century. Economists had, of course, been concerned with the causes and consequences of development since Adam Smith and earlier, and a number of countries in the nineteenth century, attempting to emulate Britain, strove for industrialization, what contemporaries considered to be 'development'. But development as a global objective for improving the economic well-being of ordinary people, reflecting Franklin Roosevelt's stated desire in 1941 to extend 'freedom from want' throughout the world, was first embodied in the United Nations Charter, that called for 'economic and social progress and development'. It is reflected in the formal name of the World Bank, the International Bank for Reconstruction *and Development* (IBRD), put there at American insistence over initial British reservations (Kapur et al. 1997, 57–62). It is necessary to recall here, in view of some revisionist history, that this was done in 1943, at the height of World War II and well before the emergence of the Cold War, which is usually dated from 1946–48.

EXPECTATIONS

When people embraced economic development as a desirable objective of post-war economic policy in the late 1940s, what exactly did they have in mind, and what were their expectations? It turns out to be difficult to answer these questions in quantitative terms.

'Development' was not precisely defined, but it was taken to mean improved economic opportunity by increasing production of goods and services in a lasting way, through capital formation (e.g., the provision of infrastructure, the early post-reconstruction emphasis of the IBRD) or through improved productivity. In short, it was associated with economic growth. In particular, it did not include simple income transfers from one country to another; somehow the recipient country should increase its productive capacity. It was assumed, however, that economic growth would improve nutrition, reduce mortality and morbidity, increase longevity and generally increase living standards, as has indeed generally proven to be the case.

It is worth recalling that while gross domestic product (GDP) these days has entered the lexicon of the man-in-the-street, national accounts were invented only in the 1930s and were still a relatively new idea beyond specialists in the late 1940s. Quantitative historical work, mainly on the 1920s and 1930s, on aggregate economic output – economic growth – was still in its infancy. People felt they could identify some useful things that needed to be done without attempting to quantify them.

I have found only four relevant quantitative projections to indicate at least some specialists' expectations about future growth. Using a base of the late 1930s, Colin Clark (1942) made projections of the world economy to 1960, implying an annual growth in per capita income of 1.5 per cent. The Paley Commission (1952) projected U.S. growth in per capita income to 1975 of 1.8 per cent, and implicitly less for the rest of the world. Woytinsky and Woytinsky (1953) offered quantitative projections of world population and energy use which implied a growth in world per capita income of 0.8 per cent a year to the year 2000. Finally Lewis (1955) offered expected per capita economic growth in less-developed countries of about 0.5 per cent a year.

OUTCOME

Using the figures to be discussed below, gross world product over the half century 1950–2000 rose by 3.9 per cent a year, of which 1.9 per cent was population growth and 2.1 per cent growth in output per person.

Compared with the expectations of Lewis, Clark, Woytinsky and Woytinsky and the Paley Commission, the increases both in population and in per capita output turned out to be significantly higher than contemporaries expected in the late 1940s. When we allow for the fact that infant mortality declined, longevity increased, nutrition improved, and literacy increased (see Table I.1), we can conclude that the actual performance of the world economy over the past half century has been nothing short of spectacular relative to expectations at the beginning of the period.

(Indeed, in the long stream of history, three features of the second half of the twentieth century stand out: rapid economic growth; the sharp increase in population, from 2.5 billion in 1950 to over 6 billion at the end of the century; and extensive inflation, with the U.S. GDP deflator increasing by a factor of

Table I.1 Selected Indicators of the Human Condition in Developing Countries

Indicator	1960	1980	2000
Infant Mortality[a]	140	80	52
Life Expectancy[b]	43	59	64
Illiteracy[c]	53	43	28

Notes:

a.   Deaths per 1000 births.

b.   Years from birth.

c.   Per cent of adults.

Source: World Bank, World Development Indicators (multiple years).

six, or 3.7 per cent a year. The increase in population was made possible by improvements in material well-being, and in turn contributed to growth insofar as productive lives were both more numerous and longer. It remains an open question to what extent the inflation, at least at modest rates, may also have contributed to growth.)

Of course, the spectacular success was not spread uniformly, either over time or across countries. World per capita income (Maddison 2001, 2002), grew by 2.8 per cent a year in the 1950s, rose to 3.0 per cent in the 1960s, fell to 1.9 per cent in the 1970s, fell further to 1.3 per cent in the 1980s, and rose to 1.5 per cent in the 1990s and through 2001. (See Table I.2.) Thus, while early performance far outshone early expectations, expectations presumably get revised on the basis of experience; and against the experience of the 1950s and 1960s, the last three decades have been disappointing.

There were also regional differences. The richest economy, the United States, saw per capita income grow by 2.2 per cent a year over the half century. Western Europe grew more rapidly, at 2.8 per cent, while Asia grew more rapidly still, at 3.3 per cent from a much lower base (see Table I.2). However, Latin America grew 'only' at 1.6 per cent a year, while Africa grew only 1.0 per cent annually – high by historical standards, but low by the standards we have learned are possible and some analysts have come to expect. Moreover, during the period 1990–2001 per capita income in Africa grew at only 0.2 per cent, and Latin America 1.3 per cent a year (Maddison 2002).

For the world as a whole, apart from measurement errors, growth in output must equal growth in income. For an individual country, the two may diverge because of changes in the country's terms of international trade. As we shall

Table I.2 Annual Increase in Per Capita GDP (per cent)

Region	1950s	1960s	1970s	1980s	1990s	Average
U.S., Canada, Australia	1.7	2.9	2.1	2.2	2.0	2.2
Western Europe	4.2	4.0	2.5	1.9	1.7	2.8
Eastern Europe	3.8	3.4	3.0	−0.6	0.7	2.0
Former USSR	3.3	3.5	1.5	0.7	−3.5	1.0
Latin America	2.2	2.4	3.0	-0.7	1.3	1.6
Asia	3.8	4.1	2.9	3.2	3.0	3.3
Africa	1.9	2.5	1.2	−0.7	0.2	1.0
World	2.8	3.0	1.9	1.3	1.5	2.1

Sources: Calculated from Maddison (2001, 330) and (2002, 39).

see, this factor was especially important for oil-exporting countries, whose real income rose more rapidly than their output.

CONVERGENCE?

A question of general interest is whether, during this half century, countries have converged in their standards of living. This would provide evidence of the 'catch-up' hypothesis, whereby those countries which were initially far from the technological frontier and from best economic practices could, in principle, grow more rapidly than those closer to those frontiers. An extensive econometric literature has developed on this topic, essentially testing whether countries that were relatively poor in 1960 grew more rapidly than those which were relatively rich. This is not the place to review that literature, except to note that the general finding is one of 'conditional convergence'. That is, initially poor countries grew more rapidly than rich countries, conditional on a number of other factors, such as life expectancy (as a proxy for general health) or educational attainment (see e.g., Barro 1997).

But I would not have expected to see, over a period as short as 35 years (the rough time frame of these studies), convergence in the sense sought. Many human and indeed biological processes follow a logistics curve, that does imply ultimate convergence but only after initial divergence – and only if the most advanced parties stand still once they have made the adjustment. But the technological frontier, so far anyway, has been constantly expanding, so 'best economic practice' is constantly changing – manifested concretely in the

Figure I.1 Country Distribution of Growth in Per Capita Income, 1950–1998

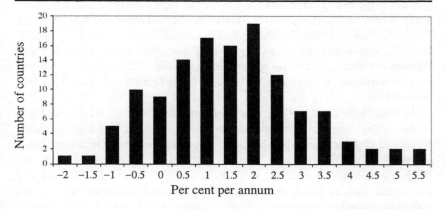

fact that real per capita income in the United States, the richest large country, continues to grow. Thus the 'convergence target' is not static, but is constantly moving. This poses severe challenges for any country trying to 'catch up,' even though the potential for catch-up is present. Initially poor countries could still be expected to grow more rapidly, but the catch-up period might indeed be a very long one.

Figure I.1 presents the distribution of national growth rates in per capita output from 1950 to 1998 for 128 countries or groupings of small countries. Per capita income in the United States, initially the wealthiest country (at $9561 in 1990 international dollars), grew at 2.2 per cent a year. That can be regarded as a benchmark. Many countries grew more rapidly than the United States, but more grew more slowly. Growth in GDP would show more countries growing more rapidly than the United States because of more rapid population growth, but our main concern here is with improvements in material well-being, proxied by growth in per capita output. The growth rates broadly reveal a bell shape, with growth concentrated in the 2.0–2.5 per cent interval, and tapering away both below and above. Eighteen countries actually showed a decline in per capita income, although the sharpest declines were for Qatar and Kuwait, that experienced large increases in real income due to improvements in their terms of trade and large growth in population through migration. If we leave aside the oil-exporting countries, the declines are led by Cuba (−0.9 per cent a year), Niger (−0.9), Djibouti (−0.7), Madagascar (−0.7), Haiti (−0.5) and Afghanistan (−0.5). If we leave aside the oil exporters, fourteen countries experienced some decline in per capita income, most of which were in sub-Saharan Africa. Most of these countries experienced considerable internal conflict, sometimes outright civil war.

At the other end of the scale, four economies recorded an extraordinary increase in per capita output in excess of five per cent a year over half a century: South Korea (6.0), Taiwan (5.9), Botswana (5.3) and Oman (5.3), all very poor countries in 1950. Indeed, Botswana was the world's poorest country in 1950, with a per capita income of $349 (in 1990 international dollars), followed by Tanzania, Burma and the behemoth China (Maddison 2001). But per capita income growth for most countries is clustered in the 1.0–3.0 per cent intervals.

As noted above, growth rates declined in the later decades of the twentieth century. The distribution of growth rates across regions also shifted. In the 1950s and 1960s it was mainly Northern European countries which grew more rapidly than the United States; thereafter their relative growth slowed. By the 1970s the rapid growers shifted to Southern Europe and to East Asia, starting with Japan, then to Southeast Asia, China and more recently to India. A few high growers were spread more widely, including Israel and Palestine, Tunisia and Saudi Arabia (to 1980) in the Middle East and Mauritius and Swaziland in Africa. Puerto Rico holds the record in the Western hemisphere, followed by Trinidad and Brazil (mainly to 1980). A host of other countries, such as Mexico, Egypt, Pakistan, Turkey and many smaller countries have made steady, if less spectacular, progress. Eastern Europe and the Soviet Union grew respectably, although at declining rates, in 1950–80, but then experienced declining output for a period as their economies were transformed from central planning and control to market-oriented, with a major transformation in the composition of output.

Thus on these figures, there has been both convergence (on the United States, the benchmark) and divergence. Many countries, especially those in Western Europe and East Asia, have reduced greatly the (geometric) gap in GDP per capita. Too often we forget how poor some currently rich countries were 50 years ago. Japan in 1949 had a lower per capita income than India did in 1998, and Greece, Spain and Portugal were only modestly richer (Maddison 2001). South Korea had a per capita income equivalent to that of India in 1965, and only 24 per cent higher than India in 1950.

On the other hand, many countries have fallen further behind than they were in 1950. Indeed, African countries, while poor in 1950, were on average nearly twice as rich as East and South Asian countries (excluding Japan). But their low average growth rates have seen them recede considerably, such that by 1998 their per capita output, while 60 per cent higher than in 1950, was less than half that of the East and South Asian countries on the same comparison (Maddison 2001, 305, 327). Haiti was 36 per cent richer than South Korea in 1950; by 1998 South Korea was 16 *times* richer than Haiti.

Figure I.2 records the distribution of national growth rates in per capita

Figure I.2 Per Capita Growth Weighted by Population

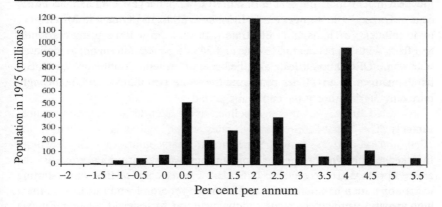

income, but weighted by population in 1975 rather than simply by number of countries. There it can be seen that again growth rates averaging between 2.0 and 2.5 per cent per annum are the most common, but the distribution is trimodal, due mainly to China and the Soviet Union, with the preponderance of growth taking place at rates higher than the modal interval.

Using countries as observations and weighting by population, the income of the median world citizen has risen significantly relative to the income of those at the 90th percentile. But those at the 20th percentile have fallen further behind both (Cooper 2002, 133–34). This calculation, however, is crude compared with those which allow for distribution of income within as well as between countries, as discussed below. To compare the average income in the 20 poorest countries with that in the richest 20 countries, as is sometimes done, is of course deeply misleading, since both groups substantially change in composition over long periods of time. As noted above, both Botswana and China were among the ten poorest countries in 1950, but neither would be included in that list today.

At a very fundamental level, development is moving people out of agriculture into socially more productive activities, as productivity in agriculture also increases. In the poorest countries, near subsistence, over 80 per cent of the labor force is engaged in agriculture, including fishing. In the richest countries, less than five per cent is engaged in agriculture (under 2 per cent in the United States), and sometimes even that low share produces a surplus for export. In this simple but fundamental dimension the past half century also experienced great change. Twenty to 30 per cent of the (rising) labor force moved out of agriculture between 1965 and 2000 in most developing countries for which data are available. For example, the share of the labor force in agriculture declined over this period from 84 to 63 per cent in Bangladesh (a country of low growth); 49 to 21 per cent in Brazil; 81 to 47 per cent in China; 55 to 29 per cent in Egypt; 71 to 43 per cent in Indonesia; 50 to 18 per cent in Mexico; 82 to 49 per cent in Thailand, to illustrate with some large developing countries, and from 47 to 17 per cent in Greece and 26 to 5 per cent in Japan, to illustrate with some OECD countries. That paragon of growth, South Korea, reduced its share from 55 to 11 per cent over the same period, even while strongly protecting agriculture at the end of the period.

Poverty

In a sense, the whole point of economic growth is to reduce poverty – to create opportunities to develop individual interests and talents which simply cannot operate when nutrition and health are poor, and when one's dominant preoccupation is with providing sufficient food for oneself and family. Yet comparisons of 'poverty' across countries, or even over time within countries, are fraught with both conceptual and practical difficulties. What exactly do we mean by 'poverty', and how sensitive should it be to the general economic and social conditions of the society in which one lives? Having decided on a working definition, how do we measure it accurately?

In terms of international discourse, the conceptual problem has been 'solved' by the suggestion by the World Bank in 1990 that poverty in developing countries should be defined as income below $1 a day per person, measured in purchasing power parity (ppp) dollars of 1985 – drawing on the national experience of India, that along with the United States had pioneered the official measurement of poverty in the 1960s. Research was subsequently devoted to discovering what poverty in many countries was under this standard, how much it had changed over time and what were the principal determinants of those changes.

Much controversy surrounds the many technical aspects of these comparisons. I will draw heavily on work by Surjit Bhalla (2002, 2003), an Indian economist who once worked at the World Bank, who reviews the history and the technical controversies and provides his own, comprehensive estimates of poverty, based on the World Bank definition, by region over the period 1950–2000. A key feature of Bhalla's work is that he focuses (appropriately) on people rather than countries. To do this he needs data on the distribution of income or (preferably) consumption within each country and changes in such distribution over time. He then aggregates these people-oriented data across regions and the world for a number of years to discover trends in world poverty.

Table I.3 sets out poverty rates in what today we call the developing world, as calculated by Bhalla (2002, 148), by region for the turn of each decade from

1950 to 2000, along with a headcount of the people who live below the poverty line. The poverty line Bhalla uses is $1.50 a day in 1993 ppp dollars (= $547 a year, or roughly the equivalent of $505 in Maddison's international dollar of 1990), to allow both for the inflation which occurred after 1985 and to allow for some undercounting of consumption (or income) of high income families in the national surveys on which everyone relies for information on income distribution.

Table I.3 shows that poverty dropped substantially, even dramatically, over the half century, from 63 per cent of the population of the developing world in 1950 to 13 per cent in 2000. The drop was particularly significant, 30 percentage points, over the last two decades, the period of so-called globalization. Significant declines occurred in every region except Sub-Saharan Africa, and even there a modest decline occurred, although an increase was registered after 1980. Furthermore, the *number* of people living in poverty was roughly halved, from 1.223 billion to 647 million, despite a more than doubling of the world population. Again, the number declined in most regions, except for a modest increase in the Middle East and North Africa, and a dramatic increase to over 300 million in Sub-Saharan Africa, where population growth was especially rapid.

The drop from 67 per cent in 1980 to 6 per cent in 2000, shown in Table I.3, for East Asia is dominated by China. Given their huge populations and initially high poverty, the rapid growth in China and India since 1980 virtually assures a world-wide reduction in poverty, even with widening income distribution in each country. To focus on countries rather than people, and on the poorest countries alone, is deeply misleading for what has been happening in the world at large.

A reduction in poverty is generally associated with economic growth, not just in China and India. In fact, it is difficult to find examples of a significant reduction in poverty which are not associated with economic growth, and it is difficult to find significant growth that does not reduce poverty (see Dollar and Kraay 2002a, 2002b).

What is quite separate from the issue of poverty, although remotely related, is the claim that inequality in the world distribution has increased significantly in recent years. It is usually simply assumed that greater inequality is undesirable, and therefore an increase in inequality should be a cause for concern. Yet it is difficult to imagine economic growth starting from a stationary condition that does not for a while, perhaps a long time, increase inequality. As noted above, many human activities follow a logistic pattern, that implies an increase in inequality (of whatever), followed by an eventual decline. The circumstances surrounding any increased inequality are all important in evaluating whether it is desirable or undesirable.

Table I.3 Poverty in the World, 1950–2000

Region and Measure	Poverty line (PPP, US$1.50 per day)					
	1950	1960	1970	1980	1990	2000
Head count ratio (per cent)						
East Asia	86.6	77.5	71.1	67.2	31.3	6.0
South Asia	44.3	37.2	32.1	34.4	18.5	7.8
Sub-Saharan Africa	59.3	53.2	52.2	49.9	55.3	54.8
Middle East/North Africa	26.3	24.3	13.4	4.3	5.2	7.8
Latin America	22.0	16.0	9.4	3.6	5.3	5.2
Eastern Europe	17.8	9.2	3.3	1.7	0.0	0.0
Developing world	63.2	52.5	46.4	43.5	25.4	13.1
Number of poor people (millions)						
East Asia	830	729	833	955	521	114
South Asia	208	209	229	310	207	105
Sub-Saharan Africa	104	118	150	188	279	362
Middle East/North Africa	27	32	23	10	16	29
Latin America	36	35	27	13	23	27
Eastern Europe	49	29	12	7	0	0
Developing world	1223	1131	1262	1479	1056	647

Note: PPP = purchasing power parity.
Source: Bhalla (2002, 148).

Bhalla's work on poverty also permits him to address the issue of inequality, focusing again on people rather than countries. He gets results which sharply contradict the conventional findings, based on countries, of growing world inequality. Using Gini coefficients as a measure of inequality (ranging between zero, perfect equality, and one, extreme inequality), Bhalla (2002, 178) finds that between 1960 and 1980, when rich countries were growing rapidly, world inequality increased, but between 1980 and 2000 world inequality decreased to below where it was in 1960. This occurred despite an increase in inequality in the industrialized world, as Europe and Japan slowed relative to the United States. If China and India are excluded, inequality was virtually unchanged between 1980 and 2000 in the developing world, but with China and India included, as they should be, inequality declined sharply. This could occur even if, as is usually assumed, income inequality increased within China and India.

On a regional basis, inequality was highest in Sub-Saharan Africa, and unchanged in 1980–2000, whereas it declined in East Asia, the Middle East (including North Africa) and Latin America, while increasing modestly in South Asia and sharply in Eastern Europe.

An alternative measure of inequality is to compare the median (50th percentile) income in the United States, as the world's richest large country, with median income in the developing world. According to Bhalla's calculations (2002, 179) that ratio declined almost steadily from 24.1 in 1950 to 11.7 in 2000. In short, the median person in the developing world, while still much poorer than his U.S. counterpart, is nonetheless catching up, having more than halved the (geometric) gap over the half century. A similar result holds if the comparison is made between those at the 20th percentile in the United States and in the developing world.

Capital Inflows

Arthur Lewis (1955) concluded that the main requirement for raising growth is a sharp increase in the rate of capital formation, both physical and human. Investment ratios did rise in developing countries, but they crept rather than leapt up, rising from 20.6 per cent of GDP in the 1960s to 22.8 per cent in the 1970s, 25.6 per cent in the 1980s and 26.3 per cent in the 1990s. During the same period of time they declined modestly in the industrialized countries, from 23.7 per cent in the 1960s to 20.8 per cent in the 1990s.

One of the advantages of engagement with the world economy is being able to draw on savings elsewhere in the world for investment; a country no longer has to rely on domestic savings alone. The transfer of real resources to any country can be measured through the current account in its balance of payments. In fact, the current account deficit for developing countries as a group, as defined in the 1980s, exceeded one per cent of their GDP (measured in 1990 international dollars) only in 1982, a year of world recession, and even approached one per cent only in a few other years (e.g., 1978, 1991, 1993), and a few additional years if the large surpluses of OPEC members in those years are excluded. It was well under 0.5 per cent in most years. As a share of domestic investment, these percentages must be increased four- to five-fold, but still remain remarkably small.

Of course, there were large variations from country to country, and even for the same country over time. Net capital inflows were significant, for example, for Israel and South Korea in the 1960s and 1970s, and represented 2 to 10 per cent of GDP for Costa Rica, Chile and a number of smaller countries in the 1980s and 1990s, and 0.5 to 2.5 per cent of GDP for India. Moreover, by virtue of the international capital market a country could engage in intertemporal reallocation of large foreign earnings in some years.

The contribution of foreign capital inflows to development is still a source of uncertainty and controversy (some evidence is summarized in Cooper 2002). Foreign direct investment (FDI) seems to be the most potent in its impact, and even then seems to work best when local education is high. By 2001 FDI to all developing countries exceeded ODA by nearly five times (World Bank, *Global Economic Prospects* 2004, 292).

Foreign aid has been the most visible vehicle used by rich countries to help developing countries over the past four decades. It is therefore worth asking what we can say about the impact of such assistance on economic growth. A World Bank team supervised by Lyn Squire addressed this issue in *Assessing Aid* (1998). The study correctly observes that aid is fungible, in that it may finance a project or activity which the government would have undertaken with its own funds, so the true marginal expenditure from aid need not be the designated expenditure. Only about 35 per cent of aid, on average, increased the investment ratio in a study of 56 countries (42 of which were in Africa or Latin America) over the period 1970–93. None, however, seemed to finance tax reductions, and some aid is initially targeted on government consumption items such as education, agricultural extension or public health. After controlling for other variables, the study suggested that foreign assistance as a per cent of each recipient's GDP had *no* discernable impact on its economic growth over this period, an appalling result even after allowing for the fact that some aid was not targeted for development. However, aid interacted with economic management (measured as a weighted average of trade openness, inflation, budget surplus and institutional quality) in such a way that growth in well-managed countries benefited from aid: on average an increase in aid by one per cent of GDP increased a well-managed country's growth rate by 0.5 percentage points. And in some well-studied cases foreign assistance was extremely important in launching economic reform and subsequent economic growth (see e.g. Haggard et al. 1993, on South Korea in the 1960s).

It is understood these days that much, perhaps even most, of the benefits of foreign assistance and FDI arise from the technical and managerial knowledge they convey rather than from the provision of capital as such.

Growth, Development and Freedom

'Development' was earlier associated with increases in per capita GDP, as a rough proxy for improvements in material well-being. A case can be made that this is a necessary – or at least a strongly facilitating – condition, but not a sufficient one. If we conceive, as Sen (1999) does, of 'development' as increasing the capability of all human beings to achieve those things they most value, then development must also cover the ability of citizens to express themselves and to have some voice in the policies which affect them – that is, development involves civil and political liberties as well as improvements in material well-being.

One of the remarkable trends of the past half century was the extension of functioning democracy to a wider fraction of mankind, including not just Northwestern Europe and North America, but Germany and Japan early in the period, Spain and Portugal in the mid-1970s, and by 2000 included Eastern Europe, Russia, most of Latin America, much of East, South, and Southeast Asia and parts of Africa. The major remaining gaps were in the Arab world, Central Asia, China and Sub-Saharan Africa (where the situation has deteriorated significantly since independence in the 1950s and 1960s). The extension of democracy during the 1980s was what Samuel Huntington called the 'third wave', suggesting that the phenomenon is episodic, not linear, and occasionally even involves reversals.

There has been extensive scholarly discussion over the years on the relationship between freedom, of which functioning democracy is a major manifestation, and economic development. Is development a precondition for a functioning democracy, and is democracy a serious impediment to economic development? Political scientist Huntington (1991, 311) is a strong proponent of the first view: 'Poverty is a principal and probably the principal obstacle to democratic development. The future of democracy depends on the future of economic development. Obstacles to economic development are obstacles to the expansion of democracy.' Barro's empirical analysis (1997, Chapter 2) supports Huntington's view. Modern India, with a functioning, indeed raucous, democracy since its beginnings in 1947, of course stands out as a leading exception to this generalization, as do a few Latin American countries, but a generalization does not have to be universal to have some validity.

Has democracy been an impediment to economic growth? In a study of 18 developing countries during the 1970s and 1980s, Little et al. (1993) found no relationship between economic performance and democracy or the Freedom House ranking on freedom for each country. Helliwell (1994) supports that conclusion on the basis of wider country coverage over a longer period of time. Barro (1997, Chapter 2) finds a weak curvilinear relationship, with growth depending positively on what he calls an 'index of political rights' up to the level achieved by Malaysia and Mexico in 1994, and negatively for higher levels of rights.

While it is true that examples can be found in which an authoritarian government seems to facilitate economic reform and subsequent economic growth – South Korea in the 1960s and 1970s comes to mind – it is also true that many authoritarian governments have neither the desire nor the capacity to undertake economic reforms leading to higher economic growth. Democracies are usually more hesitant and less comprehensive in adopting economic reforms, but also steadier in responding to various forms of turbulence in the process.

LESSONS LEARNED FROM 1950 TO 2000

What conditions are especially conducive to growth, and what conditions are especially detrimental? Geography, institutions, openness, market-orientation, rule of law, government micro-engagement, heavy taxation, corruption and macroeconomic management have all been put forward as serious explanations for inter-country differences in economic growth. Often the debate has focused on dichotomies (e.g., market versus planning, or inflation versus price stability), whereas reality was full of grays which suggest the coarse dichotomies of public debate offer little practical guidance.

Being 'geographically disadvantaged' has been advanced as a reason for poor economic performance, especially countries that are land-locked, such as Bolivia, Laos, Nepal, Paraguay and many African countries. But Botswana, far the most rapid grower in Sub-Saharan Africa, is also land-locked, as are Austria, Czechoslovakia, Hungary, Switzerland – and indeed Chicago, if the U.S. Midwest were treated as a separate economy. Perhaps being land-locked creates some modest disadvantage – although being on the sea does not ensure good natural ports – but it can be overcome through human agency. Chicago can now entertain ocean-going ships (although not the largest) through the St. Lawrence seaway, that once presented huge natural obstacles, such as Niagara Falls.

Note also that the Dominican Republic and Haiti share an island, a climate, equal access to foreign markets and in 1950 they had equal per capita income of around $1050 (in 1990 international dollars). By 1998, in contrast, income in the Dominican Republic had increased by a factor of three, while Haiti's had fallen by 20 per cent. Institutions and policies played a major role in the difference.

The best performing economy in Latin America was Puerto Rico, with a growth in per capita income of 3.9 per cent a year over 50 years. It started in 1950 with a per capita income somewhat greater than that of many of the smaller Latin American countries, but lower than that of all the larger Spanish-speaking countries. It may be dismissed as being part of the United States, yet it grew much more rapidly than the United States did. And while it is part of the U.S. currency area and customs zone, it has wide autonomy in framing its local policies, including education and taxation. Its superior performance calls for explanation. Neighboring Cuba, once among the richest countries in

Latin America, is now one of the poorest, exceeding only Nicaragua and Haiti. Anti-growth policies governed the country. The U.S. embargo of 1960 was an immediate blow, but it can hardly explain four decades of poor performance, despite Castro's continuing use of it as an excuse, not least because no other country supported the embargo. Pairwise comparisons between East and West Germany, and between North and South Korea, make the same point. Political stability prevailed for decades in both pairs. What differed was the incentives for individual effort and risk-taking, the mainstays of continuing economic growth.

One important dimension of geography is the presence of disease, for agricultural products as well as for humans. While small children can be replaced, high child mortality involves a serious opportunity cost to the mothers, and of course any education of the child is lost. Debilitating diseases, representing equilibrium between parasite and host, may be worse than fatal disease from the perspective of economic growth, because of its deleterious effects on productivity. Again, human agency can overcome or greatly mitigate the impact of disease; southern Europe was once malarial, as was Singapore. Smallpox was once endemic in Europe, resulting in high mortality. The Panama Canal could not have been built before learning that yellow fever-bearing mosquitoes had to be kept at bay. But the obstacles to be overcome are surely higher in some places than in others.

Hong Kong and Singapore both registered outstanding growth, over 4.5 per cent a year for half a century. The relevance of their experience is often dismissed, as mere 'city states'. But Hong Kong has a population greater than that of many European countries, such as Denmark, whose experience is not casually dismissed; and Hong Kong's GDP registers at 22nd in the world, with the vast majority of economies being far smaller. Their main differentiating feature is that agriculture (apart from fishing) was not a dominant part of either economy even when they were poor. There are however other potential 'city states', such as Djibouti, which would be much better off if they had performed only half as well. And while the transformation of agriculture is an important part of development, it is not the only important part; lessons can be learned even from city states.

It has become conventional wisdom that openness – that is, some form of serious engagement with the world economy – is a significant contributor to growth. Barro (1997) could not find such a relationship for the limited measures he used, and Rodrik and Rodriguez (2000) have criticized on methodological grounds the several studies usually cited in support of this conclusion, including Sachs and Warner (1995). Cooper (2002) argues that there is little theoretical ground for expecting a priori that openness would contribute to *growth*, as opposed to a once-for-all increase in income, but that in the actual post-1950 world it would be implausible if continuing trade liberalization, in particular, had not contributed significantly to growth. Warner (2003), responding to the methodological criticisms of Rodrik and Rodriguez, has demonstrated persuasively that relative openness, measured in a variety of different ways and formulated with a variety of specifications, was strongly conducive to growth, at least for the 61–86 countries he studied over the period 1970–90. Put another way, those developing countries (with per capita income under $5,000) which remained relatively closed grew far more slowly, on average, than those which engaged more actively with the world economy. GDP growth in the latter group averaged 4.8 per cent a year, versus only 0.8 per cent in the more closed group. There were no countries in the open group which experienced negative growth, in contrast to the relatively closed economies. After controlling for many other variables, Warner registers the judgment that being 'open' rather than 'closed' is worth 3–4 percentage points of growth in GDP – a tremendous impact. Even if one accepts this general dichotomous result, each country is different, and the practical details are all important.

Inflation is said to be inimical to economic growth (e.g. Fischer 2004, Chapter 10, especially 336; also Barro 1997, Chapter 3). That conclusion is shown by much cross-country empirical analysis, and at least for high rates of inflation poses no mystery: those are usually cases in which the budget has gotten out of control and inflation is the residual equilibrator; high inflation is also closely associated with highly variable inflation, rendering forward-looking financial planning – a key and necessary feature of all modern economies – practically impossible.

But it does not follow from these correct observations, as is often assumed, that moderate and controlled inflation, e.g., in the low double digits, is also inimical to growth. For a country without a well-developed financial market, inflation may in fact be less distorting than many other taxes the government might impose to generate needed revenues, including high taxes on imports, and the 'inflation tax' can reach parts of the population which are not otherwise reachable by the tax authorities. Whether this is good or bad for growth of course depends, *inter alia*, on what is done with the revenue. South Korea's annual inflation rate averaged 14 per cent during its take-off period (1966–79), for instance. It would require much higher confidence in one's theories than I have to argue that Korea would have grown even more rapidly had it forced its inflation rate into low single digits, as seems to have become the accepted norm, even for developing countries, in official financial circles.

Most analyses of growth, as here, have been based on examination of aggregate economic statistics and their possible determinants. Since 1990 the McKinsey Global Institute has undertaken a series of 'bottom up' industry studies in selected developing countries – mainly Brazil, India, Korea, Mexico and Russia – as well as developed countries, focusing on the detailed obstacles to achieving best practice productivity in the use of labor and capital, recognizing that best economic practice will be sensitive to relative factor prices.

These studies provide the basis for the unsurprising finding (Lewis 2004) that there is no single impediment to adoption of best practice, enhancing productivity and hence living standards; rather a host of often-interacting obstacles is found. Lewis argues, however, that serious competition in domestic markets is usually a necessary condition for adoption of improved techniques, and that serious domestic competition is unlikely to occur without a national mindset which accords high value to consumers as opposed to producers. Adoption of improved techniques is also unlikely to occur without significant engagement with the world economy, where best practice is typically generated and where it is constantly changing, both with regard to cost and price and with regard to product quality. He further argues that an economically intrusive government is all-but-inevitably captured by special (producer) interests and hence is typically a serious impediment to competition, hence advancing productivity.

CONCLUSION

The performance of the world economy in the period 1950–2000 can only be described as 'fantastic' in terms of the perspective of 1950. If someone at that time had forecast what actually happened, he would have been dismissed by contemporaries as living in a world of fantasy. One would not get this impression from recent discussion, that (properly) focuses on unfinished business, but in so doing erroneously gives the impression that actual performance has been poor. Humans are chronically dissatisfied; expectations rise with success. And some individuals and institutions have a stake in down-playing good performance. There is, to be sure, much work to be done, since too many people still live in poverty. But it is also necessary to note success when there has been success in order to avoid drawing erroneous conclusions. The post-1945 international economic system has, in general, served mankind well.

Countries require a stable social environment to grow and to reduce poverty, because civil disorder shortens horizons and inhibits investment. Countries must find the right incentives to encourage effort, saving and risk-taking and to facilitate engagement with the world economy, where price and quality standards must be met. While the details differ, an increasing number of economies have met these conditions and have seen the material well-being of their people improve enormously.

BIBLIOGRAPHY

Barro, Robert (1997), *Determinants of Economic Growth*, Cambridge, MA: MIT Press.

Bates, Robert and Anne O. Krueger (eds) (1993), *Political and Economic Interactions in Economic Policy Reform: Evidence from Eight Countries*, Cambridge, MA: Basil Blackwell.

Bhalla, Surjit S. (2002), *Imagine There's No Country: Poverty, Inequality, and Growth in the Era of Globalization*, Washington, DC: International Institute of Economics.

——(2003), 'Crying Wolf on Poverty: Or How the Millennium Development Goal for Poverty Has Already Been Reached', Washington, DC, International Institute of Economics Discussion Paper.

Braga de Macedo, Jorge, Colm Foy and Charles P. Oman (2002), *Development is Back*, Paris: OECD Development Centre.

Clark, Colin (1942), *The Economics of 1960*, London: Macmillan.

Cooper, Richard N. (1975), 'Resource Needs Revisited', *Brookings Papers on Economic Activity*, 1, 238–45.

—— (2002), 'Growth and Inequality: the Role of Foreign Trade and Investment', in Boris Pleskovic and Nicholas Stern (eds), *Annual World Bank Conference on Development Economics 2001/2002*, Washington, DC: World Bank, pp. 107–37.

——(2005), 'A Half Century of Development', in François Bourguignon and Boris Pleskovic (eds), *Annual World Bank Conference on Development Economics 2005: Lessons of Experience*, New York: Oxford University Press, pp. 89–118.

Dollar, David, and Aart Kraay (2002a), 'Growth is Good for the Poor', *Journal of Economic Growth*, **7** (3). 195–225.

—— (2002), 'Growth and Inequality: the Role of Foreign Trade and Investment', in Boris Pleskovic and Nicholas Stern (eds) *Annual World Bank Conference on Development Economics 2001/2002*, Washington, DC: World Bank, pp. 107–37.

——(2002b), 'Spreading the Wealth', *Foreign Affairs*, **81** (1), 120–33.

Dollar, David et. al (1998), *Assessing Aid: What Works, What Doesn't, and Why*, New York: Oxford University Press.

Fischer, Stanley (2004), *IMF Essays from a Time of Crisis*, Cambridge, MA: MIT Press.

Haggard, Stephan, Richard N. Cooper and Chung-in Moon (1993), 'Policy Reform in Korea', in Bates and Krueger (eds), *Political and Economic Interactions in Economic Policy Reform: Evidence from Eight Countries*, pp. 294–332.

Helliwell, John F. (1994), 'Empirical Linkages between Democracy and Economic Growth', *British Journal of Political Science*, 24, 225–48.

Huntington, Samuel (1991), *The Third Wave: Democratization in the Late Twentieth Century*, Norman, OK: University of Oklahoma Press.

International Monetary Fund, *International Financial Statistics*, multiple years.

Kapur, Devesh, John P. Lewis and Richard Webb (1997), *The World Bank: Its First Half Century*, Washington, DC: Brookings Institution Press.

Lewis, W. Arthur (1955), *The Theory of Economic Growth*, Homewood, IL: R.D. Irwin.

Lewis, William W. (2004), *The Power of Productivity: Wealth, Poverty, and the Threat to Global Stability*, Chicago, IL: University of Chicago Press.

Little, I.M.D., Richard N. Cooper, W. M. Corden and Sarath Rajapatirana (2003), *Boom, Crisis and Adjustment: Macroeconomic Management in Developing Countries*, New York: Oxford University Press.

Maddison, Angus (1998), *Chinese Economic Performance in the Long Run*, Paris: OECD Development Centre.

——(2001), *The World Economy: A Millennial Perspective*, Paris: OECD Development Centre.

—— (2002), 'The West and the Rest in the International Economic Order', in Braga de Macedo et al. (eds), *Development is Back,* Paris: OECD Development Centre.

President's Materials Policy Commission [Paley Commission] (1952), *Resources for Freedom*, Washington, DC: Government Printing Office.

Rodrik, Dani and Francisco Rodriguez (2000), 'Trade Policy and Economic Growth: A Skeptic's Guide to the Cross-National Evidence', in Ben Bernanke and Kenneth S. Rogoff (eds), *Macroeconomics Annual, 2000*, Cambridge, MA: MIT Press, pp. 261–325.

Sachs, Jeffrey D. and Andrew M. Warner (1995), 'Economic Reform and the Process of Global Integration', *Brookings Papers on Economic Activity*, 1, 1–118.

Sen, Amartya (1999), *Development As Freedom*, New York: Alfred A. Knopf.

Warner, Andrew M. (2003), 'Once More into the Breach: Economic Growth and Global Integration', Washington, DC, Center for Global Development, Working Paper No. 34.

World Bank (1998), *Assessing Aid: What Works, What Doesn't, and Why*, New York: Oxford University Press.

World Bank, *World Development Report*, multiple years.

World Bank, *Global Development Finance*, multiple years.

World Bank, *Global Economic Prospects*, multiple years.

Woytinsky, Wladimir S. and Emma S. Woytinsky (1953), *World Population and Production*, New York: Twentieth Century Fund.

PART ONE

International Trade and its Implications

1. Trade Reforms and Poverty: The Case of Cambodia

Isidro Soloaga

The linkages between trade policies and poverty have been addressed at length in several well-known publications (e.g., World Bank 2001a; WTO 2001; Anderson and Martin 2005), and there is a consensus that changes in trade policies can affect an economy in various ways, creating opportunities for the poor as well as risks. Moreover, the current round of multilateral trade negotiations, known as the Doha Development Agenda (DDA), is intended to enhance the relevance of the World Trade Organization (WTO) for development issues. The DDA covers most of the core elements of the WTO: agriculture, services and non-agricultural market access.

The DDA is truly a step towards greater globalization of the world economy. For example, the framework for agriculture seeks to reform the global agricultural trade by eliminating all forms of export subsidies as well as all export measures with equivalent effect (e.g., exports credits, insurance programs). Member countries are to substantially reduce trade-distorting domestic support measures. Additionally, the DDA framework calls for a reduction in tariffs to improve market access for all products. In particular, the DDA calls for substantial tariff reductions that are expected to be made from bound rates with deeper cuts in higher tariffs and for reductions or elimination of nontariff barriers (Newfarmer 2006). In 2004 Hoekman, Nicita and Olarreaga estimated how the successful conclusion of the DDA would affect international prices, imports and exports. One of their main findings is that welfare gains from a successful Doha process would increase with GDP per capita, casting doubts about the DDA's ability to deliver a 'development' round, since trade liberalization per se is likely to increase income inequality across countries: high-income countries would gain more than developing countries. But, this is not inevitable in every country.

This study assesses the likely impact of trade policies in general – and those coming from implementation of the DDA in particular – on household income and expenditures in Cambodia. The chapter also explores other avenues which may affect Cambodian households, specifically reforms in the rice market sector. The empirical methodology is an extension of that used in Nicita, Olarreaga and Soloaga (2002), where changes in the prices and quantities of goods and factors are mapped to individual household consumption and income structures. The price and quantity effects of DDA adopted here are estimated in Hoekman, Nicita and Olarreaga (2004).

This assessment is conducted in a partial equilibrium setting and provides a proxy of the magnitude of the first-order impact on poverty as a result of changes in key prices and quantities. Specifically, I assess the likely impact on household income and expenditure due to:

*   changes in world prices derived from implementation of the DDA;
*   changes in Cambodia's tariff structure to a flat 7 per cent rate;
*   a reduction in transaction costs ('unofficial taxes' and/or transportation costs);
*   technological improvements in rice production (reduction in post-harvest losses and increases in the milling yield of paddies); and
*   increased demand for labor in the industrial sector.

The chapter begins with a summary of the poverty profile of Cambodia, highlighting key issues related to the measurement of poverty in Cambodia. It then identifies who the poor people are in terms of consumption patterns and in terms of sources of income. Next, the chapter presents the framework used to assess different plausible impacts coming from the DDA, followed by the results of various statistical simulations.

POVERTY IN CAMBODIA

Poverty in Cambodia has several distinct features. First, poverty rates are highest in rural areas and among people living in households headed by farmers. Second, poorer households tend to be larger, younger and have more children. Third, the poor are more likely to live in households where the head is illiterate and has few years of schooling. Poverty is much lower for those households where the household head has a secondary or advanced education.

Knowing how the poor obtain and spend their income is crucial for understanding how economic policies affect poor people. Trade policies should affect the poor's income sources more than their consumption bundle, because that trade reform will affect many relative prices, some of which will move in offsetting directions, thereby creating scope for adjusting the consumption bundle. In contrast, as the poor generally have limited assets – typically low-skilled labor or small quantities of low-quality agricultural land – which do not cushion the effect of big changes, the impact on the sources of income is generally more important (World Bank 2001a). The study outlined in this chapter relies heavily on locating the poor in terms of patterns of expenditures and sources of income. The rest of this section presents a description of the main expenditures of Cambodia's people, ordered by deciles of adult equivalent per capita expenditures, and then a description of their main sources of income.[1] The data used come from the 1999 Cambodia Socio-Economic Survey (CSES), that sampled 6000 households in 600 villages and which was the most suitable data set available when this report was written.

Consumption Patterns

Table 1.1 shows the share of some key consumption aggregates in total expenditure. Expenditures on food take about 75 per cent of total expenditures for the first five deciles, and are lower than 70 per cent only in the highest two deciles. As expected, expenditures on rice (all varieties) are by far the most important single cost for the poorest deciles: this share is 28.4 per cent in the poorest decile, about 23 per cent in the second and third deciles, and still above 20 per cent for the fourth and fifth deciles. Thus, any policy with a high impact on rice prices should also have a high impact on poor households' consumption. A simple exercise can show that, keeping the other prices and sources of income constant, a reduction of 10 per cent in the price of rice would imply an extra 3 per cent of disposable income for people in the poorest decile (10 per cent of 28.7 per cent) and 0.6 per cent for people in the richest decile (10 per cent of 5.7 per cent). Ranking second in importance among food items is 'fish and fish products', comprising between 9.2 and 11.1 per cent of total household expenditure in deciles one through nine and only 5 per cent in the tenth decile. Regarding non-food expenditures, the major differences between deciles seem to be concentrated in 'housing, fuel and transportation', which captures 46.7 per cent of the total expenditures in the richest decile and only 15.7 per cent in the poorest one.

Figure 1.1 shows the share of food expenditures in total expenditures for households in Phnom Penh (the main urban center and capital city of Cambodia), in other urban areas and in rural areas. In rural as well as in urban areas other than the capital the share of food in total expenditures is higher than 70 per cent for the first eight deciles, while in Phnom Penh this share is below 55 per cent for all deciles, and as low as 18 per cent for the tenth decile.

Table 1.1 Expenditure Shares, by Decile of Per Capita Consumption (percentage per decile)

Consumption item	1	2	3	4	5	6	7	8	9	10	Avg.
Food total	75.7	76.3	76.0	73.7	73.7	72.6	72.0	70.3	64.4	38.6	63.5
Rice, all varieties	28.4	23.3	22.7	20.7	20.6	18.9	17.5	15.1	12.5	5.8	15.6
Fish and fish products	9.9	11.1	10.6	10.5	10.9	10.8	10.0	10.0	9.2	5.0	8.9
All other consumption items	37.4	41.9	42.7	42.5	42.2	43.0	44.5	45.2	42.7	27.8	39.0
Non-food total	24.4	23.8	24.1	26.4	26.3	27.5	28.0	29.7	35.6	61.4	36.5
Housing, fuel and transportation[a]	15.7	15.5	15.2	17.1	17.3	17.4	17.5	19.4	24.1	46.7	25.5
Clothing[b]	2.9	2.8	3.0	3.0	2.8	3.4	3.4	3.2	2.9	2.3	2.9
Other expenditures[c]	5.8	5.4	5.9	6.2	6.1	6.6	7.1	7.1	8.6	12.4	8.2

Notes:

a. Includes house rent (rental value of subsidized housing, rental value of owner-occupied housing, hotel charges), house maintenance and repair, water and fuel, medical care, transportation and communication, and personal care.

b. Clothing and footwear (tailored clothes, ready-made clothes, shoes, etc.).

c. Includes furniture and household equipment and operation, expenditures in recreation, education, personal effects and miscellaneous items.

Source: CSES 1999, Round 2 data.

Figure 1.1   Share of Food Expenditures in Total Expenditures (in percentage by consumption decile)

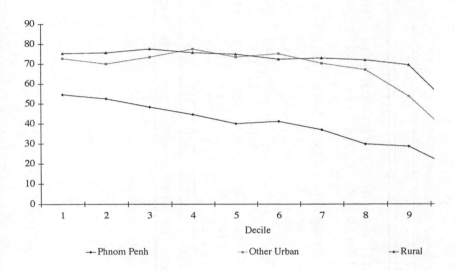

—•—Phnom Penh   —•—Other Urban   —•—Rural

Source: CSES 1999, Round 2 Data.

Sources of Income

Table 1.2 shows the sources of income by per capita adult equivalent consumption decile. Earnings from self employment are on average equal to 60.9 per cent of total income, two-thirds of which come from activities related to cultivation (22.4 per cent of total income), most of which comes from rice cultivation (16.3 per cent), livestock (9.4 per cent), fish growing (5.6 per cent) and forestry and hunting (5.7 per cent). Income from wage employment was on average only 20.5 per cent, slightly higher than the 16.5 per cent coming from rental income, interest received and imputed value of houses. Income from remittances represents on average only about 2.1 per cent of total income. Table 1.2 also shows a pattern similar to that of consumption: the composition of income by sources is similar for deciles one to eight, and only for the ninth and tenth deciles are the shares different. The two top deciles show a higher importance of non-farming activities in self employment sources of income (above 25 per cent), a higher importance of wage income, and, for the tenth decile, a higher proportion of income coming from other sources such as rental

Table 1.2 Contributions to Income from Different Sources (by decile)

Source of income:	1	2	3	4	5	6	7	8	9	10	Avg.
Self-employment	67.8	71.4	71.7	70.3	73.6	68.5	71.2	70.7	63.3	36.3	60.9
Cultivation	27.8	29.7	31.1	30.3	31.9	32.1	30.6	32.3	19.8	3.2	22.4
Rice cultivation	21.4	24.3	25.3	23.6	25.7	25.0	22.7	20.4	9.7	2.1	16.3
Other crops	6.4	5.4	5.8	6.7	6.2	7.1	7.9	11.9	10.1	1.1	6.1
Livestock	16.6	14.3	14.2	13.0	12.4	11.9	11.6	12.0	8.3	1.5	9.4
Fish growing, etc.	6.1	7.1	5.5	8.7	6.9	6.8	8.7	7.1	5.2	2.1	5.6
Forestry/hunting	8.3	10.2	9.7	7.3	7.7	7.9	8.1	6.1	4.9	0.6	5.7
Non-farming activities	8.9	10.0	11.2	10.9	14.7	9.8	12.2	13.2	25.1	29.0	17.7
Other sources	32.2	28.6	28.3	29.7	26.4	31.5	28.8	29.3	36.8	63.9	39.1
Wages	19.0	15.0	15.9	14.5	14.3	18.5	17.6	16.5	21.0	30.2	20.5
Remittances	1.2	1.9	1.6	2.8	1.3	2.4	1.6	1.7	2.3	2.6	2.1
Other (rent, dividends, etc.)	12.1	11.7	10.9	12.4	10.8	10.6	9.6	11.1	13.4	31.0	16.5
Total	100	100	100	100	100	100	100	100	100	100	100

Source: CSES 1999, Round 2 data.

28

income, interest received and imputed value of houses, which reflects higher capital stock ownership.

Figure 1.2 shows the relative importance of wages as a source of income in different regions of the country: for deciles one through eight, wages are about 40 per cent of total income in Phnom Penh and about 20 per cent in the rest of the country.

Figure 1.3 shows the distribution of employment of the household head broken down by industry and gender. Some 75 per cent of Cambodian household heads have 'agriculture, hunting and forestry' as their main occupation, with a slightly higher proportion for female-headed households (78 per cent). Employment in the public, education and health sectors ranks next in importance (9 per cent average for the whole country, 11 per cent for male head of households and 3.5 per cent for females) followed by employment in the wholesale and retail trade sectors (7.3 per cent average for the whole country). The textile sector as well as the hotel and restaurant sector are the main sources of income for only 0.8 of Cambodia's head of households.

DIFFERENT POLICIES, DIFFERENT POVERTY EFFECTS

I begin by assuming a model where the household is the unit of analysis. Total net household income (savings) is defined as the sum of total income minus the sum of total expenditures. Each household has different endowments (for example, land quality, balance of skilled and unskilled laborers) which generate income (from agriculture, from labor etc.) and different expenditure patterns (i.e. expenditures for food versus non-food items). If households have different consumption patterns, they will be affected differently by changes in prices due to DDA, other trade policies (e.g. a fixed tariff rate for all goods) and domestic market reforms. Moreover, since some of the households will also be producing goods (e.g., rice), changes in prices will affect them in direct relationship to their net market position. This means that if the price of rice goes down after the reforms, all net consumers (i.e., consumption > production) would benefit, but net producers (i.e., production > consumption) would see a diminished income. In turn, due to differences in the stock of human resources available in each household, expansion or contraction in export sectors will affect them differently. Households whose members went to school and are currently participating in the industrial labor market will be in a better position to profit from an expansion in exports than rural families.

For interested readers, the exact formulation used in my simulations is presented in an Appendix. To facilitate the understanding of what follows below, I present here a particular formulation for two cases: the rice market

Figure 1.2   Share of Wage Income in Total Income (in percentage by consumption decile)

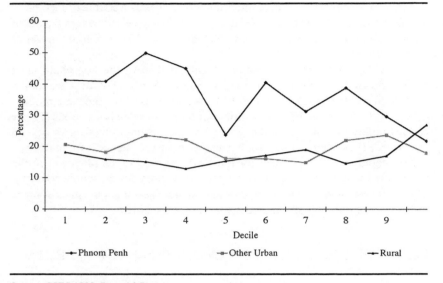

Source: CSES 1999, Round 2 Data.

and wage labor. For rice, I relate each Cambodian household to the following expression:

$$Net\ Income\ from\ Rice = f(X^{Srice}\ P^{Rice},\ X^{DRice}\ P^{Rice}) \qquad (1.1)$$

Here the dependent variable is the net income from rice, determined by the household's net position in the rice market. For a given price of rice (P^{Rice}), if the supply of rice produced by the household (X^{Srice}) is greater than the demand for rice consumed by the household (X^{Drice}) I say that this household is a net producer of rice. The household is a net consumer of rice in the opposite case (X^{Srice} could be zero for households which do not produce any rice). If the household is a net producer of rice, and the price of rice goes up due to a new policy intervention, the net income of the household will also go up. If the price of rice goes down, in a static case where I do not allow the farm household to switch production to other products, these households are going to lose income. If I also do not allow households to change consumption quantities, when the price of rice decreases, all those households with zero rice production would experience an increase in net income, equal to the savings from their (now

Figure 1.3   Employment by Industry, Group and Gender

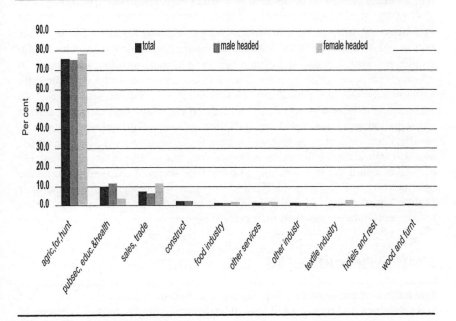

Source: CSES 1999, Round 2 Data.

lower) expenditures on rice: $(P^{RiceNew}-P^{RiceOld})*X^{Drice}$ (where $P^{RiceNew}$ is the new price of rice and $P^{RiceOld}$ is the previous price of rice). The simulations model changes in P^{Rice} coming either from the DDA's impact on Cambodia or from simulated domestic reforms in this sector. This study seeks to identify which households will be affected by those changes and to estimate the impact on poverty.

Using a similar method I have also modeled other effects. In particular, I assess the likely impact on Cambodian households of an expansion in the textile sector, that I assume translates into an increasing demand for labor. The following equation shows my approach:

$$Iflpinda = f(L^{Skilled}\ W^{Skilled},\ L^{Unskilled}\ W^{Unskilled} \tag{1.2}$$

where Iflpinda is the household's income from labor participation in industrial activities and is determined by its stock of labor allocated to this activity ($L^{Skilled}$ and $L^{Unskilled}$) and by its remuneration ($W^{Skilled}$ and $W^{Unskilled}$, respectively). In the simulations I keep wages fixed and change the labor demand. As stated above, differences in the stock of human resources available in each household mean that an expansion in labor demand will affect each household differently. The goal of the simulation for this case is to identify which households will be in a better position to benefit from increased demand for labor in the textile sector. For example, if labor demand for the textile sector expands by 50 000 employees, which household is more likely to have a member switching from whatever he or she is doing now to work in the textile sector? As will be fully explained below, the probability of switching – and increasing household income – is related to two factors: household members' current labor market participation and household human capital. In turn, using available data (age, gender, education, etc.) describing the people currently employed by the textile sector, I can estimate the expected wage which a given person from outside the sector could get by switching to the textile sector. Specifically I simulate how poverty will be affected if 50 000 people switch sectors based on their probability of being hired and whether or not their expected earnings in the textile sector are greater than their current earnings.

SIMULATION RESULTS

The following simulations adopt strong assumptions on quantities demanded and consumed and on price linkages, thus capturing only partial and extremely simplified aspects of the plausible impact of trade policies and DDA implementation on households. Nonetheless, the dimension of the impacts simulated, as well as the distribution across consumption deciles, allows a first approximation for the potential positive or negative effect of different economic policy scenarios derived from the Doha Development Agenda on poor people in Cambodia. The specifications to assess the impacts are flexible enough to capture key avenues identified elsewhere for improving the livelihood of poor households (see equations 1.1A, 1.2A and 1.3A in the Appendix).[2] For example, by introducing tax equivalent parameters for different types of transaction costs and parameters for the milling yield of paddy rice, post-harvest losses and milling costs, the specifications used here allow for the simulation of several different effects which seem appropriate for today's Cambodia, in addition to those coming from trade reforms and from the DDA.

Following common practices in the literature on poverty, I anchor the analysis on household expenditure and express all results as a percentage of household expenditure, ordered by decile of per capita adult equivalent total household consumption. That is, the absolute change in net income of household *i* which is expected to come from a policy change is divided by total household *i* expenditures. The interpretation in terms of poverty is straightforward: a

Table 1.3 Impact of Price Changes on Household Expenditures, by Per Capita-Consumption Decile

	1	2	3	4	5	6	7	8	9	10	Avg.
Cambodia	−0.22	−0.30	−0.33	−0.30	−0.34	−0.34	−0.36	−0.37	−0.39	−0.40	−0.34
From food basket	−0.20	−0.27	−0.30	−0.28	−0.31	−0.31	−0.33	−0.34	−0.36	−0.37	−0.31
From other goods	−0.02	−0.02	−0.03	−0.02	−0.03	−0.03	−0.03	−0.03	−0.03	−0.03	−0.03

Source: Author's calculation, based on CSES 1999, Round 2 data.

simulation identifies a pro-poor strategy if the latter provides extra money for the first five deciles. The size of the impact is measured as a percentage of household expenditure.

Simulation One: Changes in Prices

As indicated above, simulations from Hoekman, Nicita and Olarreaga (2004) provide estimates for changes in world prices coming from successful DDA implementation. What follows assesses the likely impact of those changes on Cambodian household budgets, assuming that changes in tariffs map one-to-one with changes in domestic prices (this is known as 'perfect pass through').[3] The simulation provides an assessment of how a change in prices will affect consumption across all households. For the case of products such as rice, cereals and fish which are also produced in many households, it is assumed that the change in income is given by:

$$\Delta NetIncomechange\_from\_good\_i = P^{goodi}(X_m^{Sgoodi} - X_m^{Dgoodi})\frac{\Delta[P_m^{goodi}]}{P_m^{goodi}}$$

The sign of the impact on a particular household will be given by the sign of $(X^{Supply\ goodi} - X^{Demand\ goodi})$. For example, for net rice-seller households, the impact will be positive, and negative for net rice-buyer households. For all other goods not produced by the household, $X^{Supply\ goodi}$ is set to zero and a rise in prices translates into an income loss for the family.

As shown in Table 1.3, this simulation indicates that, everything else remaining constant (including the amount of rice consumed and produced by each household), the expected changes in international prices due to the implementation of the DDA translates into about 0.3 per cent less income for the average Cambodian household.[4]

Simulation Two: Trade Policy

As noted elsewhere (Olarreaga 2003), the tariff structure has important implications for the government's export-led economic development and poverty-alleviation strategy. Due to high tariffs on semi-processed and consumer goods, Cambodians are required to pay above international prices for basic needs, unless the smuggling of imported goods circumvents these high prices. Table 1.4 shows the current tariff structure for the main categories for which detailed information on household consumption is available. Although for rice (the main single consumption item in household budgets) the tariff is only 7 per cent, for the different types of meat, dairy products and prepared and preserved vegetables, the tariff is above 30 per cent. Regarding non-food items, the average unweighted tariff for clothing and footwear is 28 per cent. For fish the tariff is 18 per cent, which raises the domestic price above international levels, but at the same time there is an export tax of 10 per cent that plays in the opposite direction. Since there is no detailed information on consumption rates for different types of fish, I assumed that there is no change in the tariff rate for fish and fish products.

Simulation number two assesses the impact of a reform which sets all tariffs to 7 per cent. As with simulation number one (change in the price of rice), this model keeps quantities consumed and produced constant. Thus, the results presented in Table 1.5 underestimate instantaneous gains (because demand would increase for those goods which become relatively cheaper) and overestimate instantaneous loses (because production is expected to diminish after price change). That is to say, by applying the framework described in the Appendix, I obtain a lower bound of favorable changes which may affect poor people, and an upper bound for the negative changes. Obviously, there will be other positive or negative income effects which are not considered in this simple formulation. For example, jobs can be lost due to the contraction of an import-competitive sector and for many households this may outweigh the gains from consumption. Moreover, lower tariffs could also mean a decrease in tariff revenues for the government, and this might affect the level of transfers to the poor.

Table 1.5 presents the results for simulation number two. The lower prices due to tariff reduction imply an improvement of 3.7 percentage points in average household purchasing power. Most of this increase comes from reduced prices for food items (3.2 per cent of household expenditure) and a smaller share from reduced prices on clothing and footwear (0.5 per cent of household expenditure).

Table 1.4   Tariff Rates for Main Consumer Items (percentage)

Consumption item	Share in total consumption, average for Cambodia	Current tariff level
Rice (all varieties)	15.6	7
Other cereals and preparations (bread, maize, other grains, rice/wheat flour, noodles, biscuits, etc.)	2.6	19
Fish (fresh fish, shrimp, crab, fermented, salted and dried fish, canned fish, etc.)	8.9	18(*)
Meat (pork, beef, buffalo, mutton, dried meat, offal)	5.0	35
Poultry (chicken, duck, and other fresh bird meat)	3.2	35
Eggs (duck egg, chicken egg, quail egg, fermented/salted egg, etc.)	1.4	33
Dairy products (condensed milk, powdered milk, fresh milk, ice cream, cheese, other dairy products, etc.)	0.9	33
Oil and fats (vegetable oil, pork fat, rice bran oil, butter, margarine, coconut/frying oil, etc.)	1.3	7
Fresh vegetables cabbage, eggplant, cucumber, tomato, green gourd, beans, onion, shallot, chili, etc.)	4.3	7
Tuber (cassava, sweet potato, potato, traov, jampada, etc.)	1.4	7
Pulses and legumes (green gram, dhall, cowpea, bean sprout, other seeds, etc.)	1.0	7
Prepared and preserved vegetables (cucumber pickles, other pickles, tomato paste, etc.)	0.8	34

Table 1.4   continued

Consumption item	Share in total consumption, average for Cambodia	Current tariff level
Spices and seasoning (fish sauce, soy sauce, vinegar, garlic, ginger, coriander, red pepper, monosodium glutamate, etc.)	1.7	16
Tea, coffee, cocoa	0.8	24.5
Non-alcoholic beverages (drinking water, sugar cane juice, syrup with ice, bottled soft drinks, fruit juice, etc.)	0.8	35
Alcoholic beverages (rice wine, other wine, beer, whisky, palm juice, etc.)	1.6	35
Tobacco products (cigarettes, mild tobacco, strong tobacco, etc.)	2.2	26
Other food products (fried insects, peanut preparation, flavored ice, ice, etc.)	1.0	22
Food taken away from home (meals at work, school, restaurants, snacks, coffee, soft-drinks purchases outside home)	2.9	(**)
Prepared meals bought outside and eaten at home	0.8	(**)
Total food	64.0	17
Textiles and footwear	2.9	28

Notes:

*There is also an export tax of 10 per cent on fish.

**The effect is going to be indirect, through the tradable contents of these mostly non-tradable final goods.

Source: World Bank 2004.

Table 1.5   Impact of Price Changes on Household Expenditures Due to Flat Tariff of 7 per cent (by per capita-consumption decile)

	1	2	3	4	5	6	7	8	9	10	Avg.
Cambodia	2.2	2.9	3.3	3.6	3.8	3.9	4.2	4.4	4.5	4.1	3.7
From food basket	1.8	2.5	2.8	3.1	3.3	3.4	3.6	3.9	4.0	3.7	3.2
From other goods	0.4	0.4	0.4	0.5	0.5	0.5	0.5	0.5	0.5	0.4	0.5

Source: CSES 1999, Round 2 Data.

Simulation Three: Growing Industrial Labor Demands

This section assesses the impact of economic growth on household labor income. The simulations of this section suggest which households are expected to benefit from an expansion in the industrial sector and by how much.

If there is an expansion in the industrial sector (e.g., garment and footwear), labor demand in these sectors should grow. Consequently, household income should also grow, either through increased employment, higher wages or both. But how pro-poor is this situation likely to be? It is easy to imagine a situation in which, due to high human capital requirements for labor in the expanding sectors, only households with more formally educated members in the upper brackets of the income distribution would benefit *directly* from growth, while the poor benefit only indirectly through a 'trickle down' effect. This simulation explores whether this situation holds true for Cambodia, assessing the expected impact on poverty of an increase in labor demand by the industrial and non-public services sector. It involves the following steps.

For each household:

1) I identify the income sources of each household according to the sector of principal occupation of all household members and select those household members who work for a wage.
2) I consider that there is surplus labor in the informal labor market and in the subsistence agriculture sector, and that a marginal loss of labor in this labor surplus sector implies minimal or zero loss of output. For a rationale of this approach, see Macnac (1991) and Dickens and Lang (1985).
3) For each person, I estimate the probability of participating in the industrial labor market. This probability is a function of age, education, family composition and location, among other factors. Those persons who are not currently participating in the industrial labor market and whose wages

are lower than those paid in the industrial sector for a person of similar characteristics (i.e., lower than the expected wage in the industrial sector for a person with similar human capital characteristics), are ranked in descending order by their probability of participating in the industrial sector. In other words, I construct a queue of potential entrants to the industrial labor market.

4) As the industrial sector grows, workers from non-industrial sectors are assigned to the industrial labor market according to their probability. The first to be incorporated is the person with the highest probability and so on. This adapts the literature of 'matching methods' to these particular simulations. See, for instance, Cochran and Rubin (1973) and Hechman, Ichimura and Todd (1997).

5) The impact on household income comes from the wage premium paid by the industrial sector calculated as the difference between the actual wage of the person and the expected wage of this person in the industrial sector (i.e., the fitted wage for each individual) times the total number of working days. The econometric estimations used to estimate the probabilities and to impute wages are detailed in Nicita, Olarreaga and Soloaga (2001).

Table 1.6 shows which workers are likely to switch jobs (i.e., that are in the queue), the average amount of the current wage these people are earning, their expected wage when they switch to the industrial sector and the amount of the difference in wages. This exercise indicates that there were about 220 000 laborers (174 439 + 45 536) who would switch to the industrial sector. Almost 80 per cent of them would be people currently working in the service sector (trade, restaurants, hotels, public employees) and the rest would be people working in the primary sector (agriculture, mining and fishing). Women make up the majority of the people likely to switch from the primary sector (57 per cent), although women are a minority of the people switching from the service sector (23 per cent). The average gain for people switching from the primary sector is equivalent to 22 per cent of current wages and it is equivalent to 39 per cent for those switching from the services sector.

Table 1.7 shows how an additional 50 000 or 125 000 workers would affect income in the industrial sector. The first and third panels show the average impact of increasing 50 000 and 125 000 workers in the industrial sector respectively, and consider all households (i.e., including households which are not expected to switch occupations). The second and fourth panels show the simulated impact only on those households which have at least one member who switched to the industrial sector.

Overall, changes in average income are modest: 0.2 and 0.5 per cent for each scenario, respectively. Nonetheless, the results are important for those households which have at least one member switching to the industry sector (see second panel in Table 1.7). If industrial labor demand increases by 50 000 employees, for households with job switchers, the average expected gain from the change is about 8.3 per cent, a bit higher for those laborers coming from rural areas (8.7 per cent versus 8.3 per cent for workers living in urban areas). Results are similar when considering an increase of 125 000 employees.

Simulation Four: Improving Key Elements in the Rice Sector

In Cambodia, most efficiency gains will come from reforming domestic production, processing and trade systems rather than from reforms at the border. This section presents results from simulations in the rice sector that calculates how changing in three production techniques will affect poverty: introducing better varieties of seeds which improve the paddy-to-rice yield, reducing post-harvest losses and reducing transaction costs.

This simulation implies a reduction in post-harvest losses, improved paddy-to-rice milling yields and a reduction in broadly defined transaction costs. The two first elements are key technical components of the rice production system and are often indicated as the leading avenues for improving household revenues (Greenland 1997; JICA 2001). Broadly defined transaction costs were also identified as impediments for development of the rice sector (see IF's sector study on rice in World Bank 2001b). To assess the impact of a change in these three technical components, a useful decomposition of the value of the m quality of paddy rice output, presented in the Appendix, includes measures of the rate of post-harvest losses (currently 10 per cent on average) due to improper handling, lack of storage facilities, rodents, etc); paddy-to-rice milling yield (currently 0.62 on average); and transaction costs (currently about 10 per cent).[5] All of these parameters can be modified through adequate economic policies. The simulation which follows assesses the impact of: reducing post-harvest losses to 5 per cent through improved handling and packaging; increasing milling yield from 0.62 per cent to 0.64 per cent, due to improved rice varieties; and halving transaction costs from 10 per cent to 5 per cent through better infrastructure or reducing other transaction costs.

The combined simulated effect of a 5 percentage point improvement in post-harvest management, a 2 percentage point improvement in milling yield and a 5 percentage point reduction in (broadly defined) transaction costs produced an increment in total value of production of 15 per cent (0.5776 / 0.5022). The gains are directly linked to the amount of rice produced.

To calculate the impact at the household level by decile, the change in the value of rice output was divided by total household expenditure. The average gain in this simulation is 4.6 per cent (see Table 1.8), with net sellers gaining

Table 1.6 Number of Workers Likely to Switch Jobs if Demand for Labor Rises in the Industry Sector (by decile)

	1	2	3	4	5	6
From Primary Sector						
# of workers expected to switch jobs	5171	7218	3821	4108	3672	7407
(% female)	50	74	8	62	74	51
Current wage in sector (Riels/day, average)	3165	2901	4751	3056	3260	3951
Expected wage in industry (Riels/day, average)	4154	3427	5138	3758	3636	5142
Difference	989	526	386	702	376	1191
Difference as % of Current wage	31	18	8	23	12	30
From Service Sector						
# of workers expected to switch jobs	20417	16072	12331	10381	6594	15804
(% female)	29	28	24	25	25	12
Current wage in sector (Riels/day, average)	3734	3583	3676	4288	3499	4642
Expected wage in industry (Riels/day, average)	4994	4654	5306	5834	4975	6005
Difference	1261	1071	1630	1546	1476	1363
Difference as % of current wage	34	30	44	36	42	29

Table 1.6   continued

	7	8	9	10	Total
From Primary Sector					
# of workers expected to switch jobs	4218	3794	3345	2782	45536
(% female)	52	55	54	92	57
Current wage in sector (Riels/day, average)	4435	4390	3895	5834	3818
Expected wage in industry (Riels/day, average)	5463	5347	5178	6948	4671
Difference	1028	957	1283	1114	853
Difference as % of current wage	23	22	33	19	22
From Service Sector					
# of workers expected to switch jobs	1984	11803	31042	35011	174439
(% female)	15	9	26	27	23
Current wage in sector (Riels/day, average)	4345	5065	4335	5340	4394
Expected wage in industry (Riels/day, average)	6251	6972	6221	7492	6087
Difference	1906	1906	1886	2152	1693
Difference as % of current wage	44	38	44	40	39

Source: CSES1999, Round 2 Data.

Table 1.7   Impact on Income of an Increase in Employment in the Industrial Sector (as percentage of total household income)

Impact of Adding 50 000 New Employees to Industrial Sector

All households	1	2	3	4	5	6	7	8	9	10	Avg.
Urban	1.69	0.16	0.17	0.19	0.82	0.21	0.51	0.21	0.33	0.22	0.35
Rural	0.42	0.27	0.11	0.07	0.17	0.14	0.12	0.18	0.21	0.15	0.19
Total	0.52	0.26	0.11	0.07	0.22	0.15	0.15	0.19	0.24	0.19	0.21

Households with at least one member switching to industry	1	2	3	4	5	6	7	8	9	10	Avg.
Urban	16.1	27.5	15.7	6.9	15.0	6.7	17.0	4.5	6.2	4.0	7.2
Rural	12.1	11.3	5.3	9.8	9.4	8.2	6.4	13.6	6.0	4.4	8.7
Total	12.9	11.6	5.8	9.2	10.4	8.0	7.5	10.3	6.1	4.1	8.3

Impact of Adding 125 000 New Employees to Industrial Sector

All households	1	2	3	4	5	6	7	8	9	10	Avg.
Urban	2.5	0.7	0.9	0.2	1.4	0.4	1	0.7	0.9	0.7	0.8
Rural	1.1	0.6	0.4	0.5	0.4	0.5	0.2	0.3	0.4	0.5	0.5
Total	1.2	0.6	0.4	0.5	0.4	0.5	0.3	0.4	0.5	0.6	0.5

Households with at least one member switching to industry	1	2	3	4	5	6	7	8	9	10	Avg.
Urban	15.3	10.8	13.9	5.6	11.6	7.7	10.4	5.8	7.3	4.3	6.8
Rural	15.3	11.3	8.8	12.7	10.2	9.7	6.3	8.4	6.6	6.5	10.0
Total	15.3	11.2	9.4	12.3	10.5	9.6	6.9	7.5	6.9	4.9	9.0

Source: CSES 1999, Round 2 Data.

9.1 per cent and net buyers 1.7 per cent. The average gain for the first five deciles ranges from 5 to 7.2 per cent.

The analysis of how to implement the improvements in key elements of the rice market used for our simulations go beyond the scope of this study. Nonetheless, it is worth mentioning that rice yields can be improved, and that significant achievements in production can be made through increases in rice yield. For example, in Vietnam, Cambodia's neighbor, Minot and Goletti (2000) find that more than 55 per cent of the increase in rice production between 1985 and 1995 came from increments in yields. An International Food Policy Research Institute (Minot 2005) study in Southeast Asia also found that producers need access to well-organized, post-harvest distribution chains which can handle the processing and marketing requirements if they hope to participate in growing formal urban and export markets. Finally, in general poor people are less likely to be able to afford mechanisms which could avoid transaction costs (e.g, low levels of empowerment make them unable to avoid 'unofficial taxes' which a powerful local can impose on them). This implies a negative relationship between transaction costs and income of the poor (Easterly 2001).

CONCLUSION

There are several avenues by which poverty can be reduced – meaning increasing the income of the lowest decile – in Cambodia. This chapter provided an assessment of the likely impact of some trade policies, including those coming from the DDA implementation. Due to the importance of rice for Cambodian households, the chapter also addresses the likely impact of key changes in the rice sector. The assumptions involved in each scenario are strong, but the results go further and provide an indication of *which households* along the income distribution line are more likely to be affected by the different changes and also provide an order of magnitude of the size of the likely impact.

Expected changes in prices as a result of DDA implementation will have scant effect on poverty. With main caveats in place, the change of the tariff structure to a 7 per cent flat rate would produce an average positive impact on household income of about 3.7 per cent, almost all of it coming from reduced tariffs on foods.

The entire non-industrial working population contains a pool of about 220 000 laborers who would most likely be willing to switch jobs and move to the industrial sector. The average gain for people switching from the primary sector is equivalent to 22 per cent of current wages and it is equivalent to 39 per cent for those switching from the services sector. If labor demand in the industrial sector rises by 50 000 employees, households with at least one member switching jobs to the industry sector should see a rise of about 8.3 per cent in income. The rise in income is higher in the first four deciles of the income distribution. If 50 000 laborers switch from agriculture or the service sector to the industrial sector, it would produce an average impact of 0.2 per

Table 1.8 Impact on Households' Expenditures of Improving Key Elements in the Rice Market

	1	2	3	4	5	6	7	8	9	10	Avg.
Total	7.2	5.9	5.4	6.0	5.0	4.8	4.6	4.2	2.6	0.7	4.6
Reduce post-harvest losses by 5%	2.7	2.2	2.0	2.2	1.9	1.8	1.7	1.5	1.0	0.2	1.7
Increase yield by 2%	1.6	1.3	1.2	1.3	1.1	1.0	1.0	0.9	0.6	0.1	1.0
Reduce transaction costs by 5%	2.7	2.2	2.0	2.2	1.9	1.8	1.7	1.5	1.0	0.2	1.7
Total for net-sellers of rice	12.3	11.2	9.9	10.2	8.5	8.7	8.4	7.0	6.4	6.5	9.1
Reduce post-harvest losses by 5%	4.6	4.1	3.7	3.8	3.1	3.2	3.1	2.6	2.4	2.4	3.4
Increase yield by 2%	2.6	2.4	2.1	2.2	1.8	1.9	1.8	1.5	1.4	1.4	2.0
Reduce transaction costs by 5%	4.6	4.1	3.7	3.8	3.1	3.2	3.1	2.6	2.4	2.4	3.4

Source: Authors' calculations based on CSES 1999, Round 2 data.

cent on household income. Finally, improvement in two key elements of rice production technology (paddy-to-rice yield and post-harvest losses) in addition to the lowering of transaction costs should provide a noticeable improvement in the livelihoods of poor Cambodians. Although how to deliver these changes in the rice market goes beyond the scope of this study, recent experiences in other countries show that this can be done and that the gains are huge.

NOTES

1. The population is ordered by per capita household consumption and each decile represents one-tenth of the population. The first decile represents the poorest population, and the tenth decile stands for the wealthiest population. Following Deaton (1997), the deciles were formed by computing the per capita adult equivalent household consumption for each sample household as: total household consumption/(0.5 *number of children + number of adults).
2. A recent example is the chapter on agriculture in the Integrated Framework (IF) study for Cambodia done jointly by the World Bank, UNDP, UNCTAD and the IMF, where a decrease in transaction costs and post-harvest losses are indicated as key avenues for improvement in the rice market, and also the IF's chapter on trade policy, which shows the potential pro-poor effect of some modifications to the current tariff structure (World Bank 2001a).
3. With this assumption, the size of the impact presented here is that of a maximum impact. It is easy to change this assumption to that of partial pass-through taking into account regional variations in price transmissions.
4. Losses are only slightly lower for households that are net-sellers of rice.
5. Transaction costs are loosely defined here. They can capture the impact of bad roads on net revenues, and also bribes necessary to do business, for example.

BIBLIOGRAPHY

Anderson, Kym and Will Martin (2005), 'Agricultural Trade Reform and the Doha Development Agenda', World Economy, 28 (9), 1301–27.
Cambodia Development Resource Institute (2001), *Cambodia's Annual Economic Review 2001*, Phnom Penh.
Cambodia, Ministry of Agriculture, Forestry and Fisheries, Department of Planning and International Cooperation, Statistics Office, *Agricultural Statistics 1999–2000*.
Cambodia, Ministry of Planning (2000), 'Second Five-Year Socioeconomic Development Plan 2001–2005'.
Cambodia, Ministry of Planning, National Institute for Statistics (1999) 'Report on the Cambodia Socio-Economic Survey', Phnom Penh.
Cambodia, National Institute of Statistics (2000), *Yearbook 2000*, Phnom Penh.
Cochran, William and Donald B. Rubin (1973), 'Controlling Bias in Observational Studies', *Sankyha*, 35, 417–46.
Deaton, Angus (1997), *The Analysis of Household Surveys. A Microeconometric Approach to Development Policy*, Baltimore: Johns Hopkins University Press.
Dickens, William T. and Kevin Lang (1985), 'A Test of Dual Labor Market Theory', *American Economic Review*, 75 (4), 792–805.
Dollar, David and Kraay Aart (2000), 'Trade, Growth and Poverty', Paper prepared for the Swedish Ministry of Foreign Affairs, the William Davidson Institute and the World Bank conference 'Poverty and the International Economy', Stockholm, Sweden, 20–21 October.
Easterly, William (2001), *The Elusive Quest for Growth*, Cambridge, MA: MIT Press.
Figueiredo, P. and R. Walraven (2001), 'Cambodia, an Overview of the Land Sector', study commissioned by the Swedish International Development Cooperation

Agency (SIDA).

Gibson John (1999), 'A Poverty Profile of Cambodia', Department of Economics, University of Waikato, Hamilton, New Zealand.

Greenland D.J. (1997), 'The Sustainability of Rice Farming', Manila, International Rice Research Institute.

Group of Eight (2001), 'A Globalized Market Opportunities and Risks for the Poor', Genoa, July.

Hechman, James, Hidehiko Ichimura and Petra E. Todd (1997), 'Matching As an Econometric Evaluation Estimator: Evidence from Evaluating a Job Training Programme', *Review of Economic Studies*, 64, 605–54.

Hoekman, Bernard, Alessandro Nicita and Marcelo Olarreaga (2004), 'Can Doha Deliver a "Development" Round?', mimeo, World Bank, Washington, DC.

International Monetary Fund (2001), *Cambodia: Third Review Under the Poverty Reduction and Growth Facility* (PRGD IMF 2001F), EBS/01/109, 3 July 2001.

Japanese International Cooperation Agency (2001), 'Study on Improvement of Marketing System and Post-harvest Quality Control of Rice in Cambodia', Phnom Penh.

Magnac, Thierry (1991), 'Segmented or Competitive Labor Markets', *Econometrica*, **59** (1), 165–87.

Minot, Nicholas (2005), 'The Development of Post-harvest Systems and Agro-industry as a Strategy to Raise the Income of the Rural Poor', Washington, DC, International Food Policy Research Institute (IFPRI) Working Paper.

Minot, Nicholas and Francesco Goletti (2000), 'Rice Market Liberalization and Poverty in Viet Nam', Washington, DC, International Food Policy Research Institute (IFPRI) Working Paper Number 114.

Nesbitt, Harry J. (ed) (1997), 'Rice Production in Cambodia', Manila, International Rice Research Institute Working Paper.

Newfarmer, Richard (ed) (2006), *Trade, Doha, and Development: A Window into the Issues*, Washington, DC: World Bank.

Nicita A., Marcelo Olarreaga and Isidro Soloaga (2002), 'A Simple Methodology to Assess the Poverty Impact of Economic Policies Using Household Data', Washington, DC, World Bank, mimeo.

Olarreaga, Marcelo (2003), 'The Optimum Tariff for Poverty Reduction', World Bank, mimeo.

Robertson, James and Harold Pohoresky (1997), 'Cambodia: Strengthening the Foundation for Trade and Industrial Development', Paper presented at the Cambodia Development Resource Institute Conference 'Challenges and Options of Regional Economic Integration', Phnom Penh, October.

Sik, Boreak (1999), 'Land Ownership, Sales and Concentration in Cambodia', Phnom Penh, Cambodia Development Resource Institute (CDRI) Working Paper Number 16.

World Bank and International Monetary Fund (2001), *Market Access for Developing Countries' Exports*, April 2001.

World Bank (2001a), *Poverty Reduction Strategy Paper Sourcebook*, chapter on Trade Policy and Poverty; www.worldbank.org.

World Bank (2001b), 'Integrated Framework of Trade Related Technical Assistance: Country Case Study on Cambodia', Washington, DC, World Bank, mimeo.

World Trade Organization (2001), L. Alan Winters, 'Trade and Poverty: Is There a Connection?', available at: http://www.wto.org/English/news_e/pres00_e/pov3_ e.pdf.

APPENDIX 1.1 FRAMEWORK FOR THE ANALYSIS: A HOUSEHOLD MODEL[1]

The household model used for the simulations has the following specifications:

$$NetIncome = \sum_m X_m^{SRice} P_m^{Rice} (1 - t_m^{SRice}) + \sum_i X_i^{SO} P_i^{O} (1 - t_i^{O}) - \sum_j X_j^{I} P_j^{I} (1 + t_j^{I})$$

$$+ \sum_k L_k^{Skilled} W_k^{Skilled} (1 - t_k^{Skilled}) + \sum_l L_l^{UnSkilled} W_l^{UnSkilled} (1 - t_l^{UnSkilled})$$

$$- \sum_m X_m^{DRice} P_m^{Rice} (1 + t_m^{DRice}) - \sum_n X_n^{Oth.Food} P_n^{Oth.Food} (1 + t_n^{Oth.Food})$$

$$- \sum_o X_o^{NonFood} P_o^{NonFood} (1 + t_n^{NonFood})$$

$$+ \sum_p \sum_q T_p^{q} \tag{1.1A}$$

where

X_m^{SRice} = Amount of rice of quality m produced by the household.

P_m^{Rice} = Selling price of rice of quality m produced by the household (gross price). For internationally tradable varieties, this price is the border price.

t_z^{w} = *ad valorem* tax on good z of the w sector. Alternatively, t_z^{w} = is the tax equivalent of a distortion that affects good z of sector w.

X_i^{SO} = Output i (other that rice) produced by the household (for example cattle, handicrafts, services).

P_i^{O} = Selling price of output i produced by the household (gross price). For an internationally tradable output, this price is the border price.

X_j^{I} = Amount of input j used by the household in production(for example, fertilizers, land rented, hired labor, hired animals).

P_j^{O} = Before tax (or before a tax equivalent domestic distortion) price of input j used by the household in production.

$L_{\cdot}^{Skilled}$ = Amount of skilled labor sold by the kth member of the household.

$W_k^{Skilled}$ = Before tax (or before a tax equivalent transaction cost or domestic distortion) wage of skilled labor supplied by the household.

$L_l^{UnSkilled}$ = Amount of unskilled labor sold by the lth member of the household.

$W_l^{UnSkilled}$ = Before tax (or before a tax equivalent transaction cost or domestic distortion) wage of unskilled labor supplied by the household.

X_m^{DRice} = Amount of rice of quality m demanded by the household (including rice produced by the household and not sold in the market).

P_m^{Rice} = Buying price of rice of quality m demanded by the household (gross price)

t_m^{Drice} = Import tariff on rice imports.

$X_n^{Oth.Food}$ = Amount of non-rice food n demanded by the household.

$P_n^{OthFood}$ = Buying price of non-rice food n demanded by the household.

$t_n^{OthFood}$ = Import tariff on non-rice food n.

$X_o^{NonFood}$ = Amount of non-food good o demanded by the household.

$P_o^{NonFood}$ = Buying price of non-food good o demanded by the household (gross price).

$t_o^{NonFood}$ = Import tariff on non-food good o.

T_p^q = Transfer received by household member p from source q (q could be public or private).

In addition, the value of paddy rice output can be expressed as a function of the value of milled rice, as:

$$(1.2A)$$

$$Value\ of\ Rice\ Output = Q_m^{PaddyRice}(1 - phl_m^{PaddyRice})(1 - t_m^{Rice})P_m^{PaddyRice}$$
$$= Q_m^{PaddyRice}(1 - phl_m^{PaddyRice})(1 - t_m^{Rice})(1 - \alpha)\lambda P_m^{Rice}$$

where $phl_m^{PaddyRice}$ denotes the per cent of post-harvested losses due to improper handling, lack of storage facilities, rodents, etc., assumed to be currently about 10 per cent; α denotes milling transformation costs; and λ is the milling yield of paddy-to-rice, assumed to be 0.62 on average (with some regional variation), by the MAFF.

We can consider all quantities in Equation 1.2A as fixed in the short run and simulate what the impact of a change in prices, taxes and/or transaction cost may be. The formulation would be:

$$
\Delta NetIncome \Big/ all\ \overline{q} = \sum_m P_m^{Rice}(1-t_m^{SRice})X_m^{SRice}\frac{\Delta[P_m^{Rice}(1-t_m^{SRice})]}{P_m^{Rice}(1-t_m^{SRice})}
$$

$$
+\sum_i P_i^o(1-t_i^o)X_i^{so}\frac{\Delta[P_i^o(1-t_i^o)]}{P_i^o(1-t_i^o)}
$$

$$
-\sum_j P_j^I(1+t_j^I)X_j^I\frac{\Delta[P_j^I(1+t_j^I)]}{P_j^I(1+t_j^I)}
$$

$$
+\sum_k W_k^{Skilled}(1-t_k^{Skilled})L_k^{Skilled}\frac{\Delta[W_k^{Skilled}(1-t_k^{Skilled})]}{W_k^{Shilled}(1-t_k^{Skilled})}
$$

$$
+\sum_l W_l^{UnSkilled}L_l^{UnSkilled})\frac{\Delta[W_l^{UnSkilled}(1-t_l^{UnSkilled})]}{W_l^{UnSkilled}(1-t_l^{UnSkilled})}
$$

$$
-\sum_m P_m^{Rice}(1+t_m^{DRice})X_m^{DRice}\frac{\Delta[P_m^{Rice}(1+t_m^{DRice})]}{P_m^{Rice}(1+t_m^{DRice})}
$$

$$
-\sum_n P_n^{Oth.Food}(1+t_n^{Oth.Food})X_n^{Oth.Food}\frac{\Delta[P_n^{Oth.Food}(1+t_n^{Oth.Food})]}{P_n^{Oth.Food}(1+t_n^{Oth.Food})}
$$

$$
-\sum_o P_o^{NonFood}(1+t_o^{NonFood})X_o^{NonFood}\frac{\Delta[P_o^{NonFood}(1+t_o^{NonFood})]}{P_o^{NonFood}(1+t_o^{NonFood})}
$$

$$
+\sum_p\sum_q \Delta T_p^q
$$

$$(1.3A)$$

In reality, after changes in prices, producers would switch production to the more valuable crops, consumers would in general switch to cheaper goods and away from the now relatively more expensive ones, and the household would adjust its labor supply to changes in wages. Because Equation 1.3A keeps quantities fixed, this formulation provides a lower bound for any estimated gain and an upper bound for any estimated loss.

IMPACT WHEN ALL TARIFFS ARE SET TO 7 PER CENT

Following Equation 1.3A, households' change in net income after the tariff change is given by:

$$
\Delta NetIncome\Big/_{all\ \overline{q}} = \sum_m P_m^{Rice}(1+t_m^{DRice})(X_m^{DRice} - X_m^{SRice})\frac{[P_m^{Rice}(t_{m1}^{DRice} - t_{m0}^{DRice})]}{P_m^{Rice}(1+t_m^{DRice})}
$$

$$
+ \sum_n P_n^{Oth.Food}(1+t_n^{Oth.Food})(X_n^{D.Oth.Food} - X_n^{S.Oth.Food})\frac{[P_n^{Oth.Food}(t_{n1}^{Oth.Food} - t_{n0}^{Oth.Food})]}{P_n^{Oth.Food}(1+t_n^{Oth.Food})}
$$

$$
+ \sum_o P_o^{NonFood}(1+t_o^{NonFood})X_o^{NonFood}\frac{[P_o^{NonFood}(t_{o1}^{NonFood} - t_{o0}^{NonFood})]}{P_o^{NonFood}(1+t_o^{NonFood})} \qquad (1.4A)
$$

where, t_{ij}^z is the tariff level i of good z (rice, other food, and non-food consumption items), in moment j (0 = before tariff reform, 1 = after tariff reform). Since this simulation does not imply a change in the tariff of rice – it is already at 7 per cent — the first term of the right hand side is zero. The second term of the right hand side captures the fact that although most of the households are net consumer of a given good and benefit from the lowering of tariff, some households could be net producers of the given good and lose from the change in tariff.

IMPROVEMENTS IN THE RICE SECTOR

This simulation implies a reduction in post-harvested loses, improvement in paddy-to-rice milling yields, and a reduction in broadly defined transaction costs. The two first elements are key technical components of the rice production system and are often indicated as the avenues for improving households' revenues (IRRI 1997 and JICA 2001). Broadly defined transaction costs were also identified as impediments for a development of the rice sector (see IF's sector study on rice). To make an assessment of the impact of a change in these three components, a useful decomposition of the value of the m quality of paddy rice output was presented in Equation 1.A2 above, reproduced here for convenience:

$$\textit{Value of Rice Output} = Q_m^{PaddyRice}(1 - phl_m^{PaddyRice})(1 - t_m^{Rice})(1 - \alpha)\lambda P_m^{Rice} \tag{1.5A}$$

where, again, $phl_m^{PaddyRice}$ denotes the per cent of post-harvested losses due to improper handling, lack of storage facilities, rodents, etc., estimated to be currently around 10 per cent on average; α denotes milling transformation costs, assumed fixed; and λ is the milling yield of paddy-to-rice, assumed to be 0.62 on average with some regional variation, by the MAFF. The term t_m^{Rice} adopts here the form of tax equivalent 'transaction costs', assumed to be 10 per cent.

This simulation assesses the impact of a plausible change in: a) $phl_m^{PaddyRice}$ from its current level of 10 per cent to 5 per cent, due, for instance, to an improvement in handling and packaging; b) in λ from its current level of 0.62 to 0.64, due, for instance, to a plausible and attainable improvement in rice variety; and c) in t_m^{Rice} from its current 10 per cent to 5 per cent, due to, for instance, to an improvement in infrastructure or to a diminishing in other transaction costs.

The impact on total household income would be:

$$\Delta \textit{Value of Rice Output} = Q_m^{PaddyRice}(1 - \alpha)P_m^{Rice}[\lambda_2(1 - phl_{m,2}^{PaddyRice})(1 - t_{m,2}^{Rice})$$
$$- \lambda_1(1 - phl_{m,1}^{PaddyRice})(1 - t_{m,1}^{Rice})] \tag{1.6A}$$

where the subscripts 1 and 2 denote the current value and the simulated new value, respectively.

$$\Delta \textit{Value of Rice Output} = P_0 Q_0 * [0.64 * (1 - 0.05)(1 - .05)$$
$$- 0.62(1 - 0.10)(1 - 010)]$$
$$= P_0 Q_0 * [0.5776 - 0.5022]$$
$$= P_0 Q_0 * 0.0754 \tag{1.7A}$$

NOTES

1. The presentation follows that of Nicita, Olarreaga and Soloaga (2001).
2. Transaction costs are loosely defined here. They can capture the impact of bad roads on net revenues, and also bribes to be allowed to do business, for instance.

2. International Exposure, Unionization and Market Concentration: The Effects on Factor Use and Firm Productivity in Uruguay

Carlos Casacuberta, Gabriela Fachola and Néstor Gandelman

Over the course of three decades, successive Uruguayan governments implemented market-oriented reforms in an economy that had been characterized by strong state intervention and regulation up until the 1970s. However, the small size of the domestic market, increased recourse to inflationary finance through the government budget and the distortions generated by various forms of state interference ended up depleting the possibilities of economic growth via an import-substitution strategy. The Uruguayan economy experienced high inflation, currency devaluation and economic stagnation between the mid-1950s and the mid-1970s, with grave social and political consequences.

When stabilization policies and structural reforms were implemented starting in 1973, inflation decelerated and economic growth resumed, accompanied by an increase in foreign trade and private investment. The reforms included tax structure modernization, trade liberalization and full convertibility of the capital account. Specifically, a value-added tax was introduced, non-tariff barriers to trade were mostly eliminated, import tariffs were gradually reduced, interest rate caps became non-binding, exchange-rate controls were eliminated and access to the market was liberalized for financial intermediaries.

During the 1990s, a second phase of trade liberalization took place. This phase combined a deepened gradual, unilateral tariff reduction with the creation of Mercosur, an imperfect customs union among Argentina, Brazil, Paraguay and Uruguay. The trade liberalization had two distinctive characteristics. First, it took place in a context in which unions still maintained significant power, and in many cases such changes were negotiated with them. Second, the manufacturing industry in Uruguay in the mid-1980s was basically composed of a reduced number of traditional-products exporting firms and by sectors developed under the import-substitution process. Most industries showed high concentration levels. This gave firms considerable market power which allowed them to set prices substantially above marginal costs.

Labor market institutions also were strongly affected in the last decades. During the years of military rule (1973–84), unions were officially banned and their activities ranged from very low to nonexistent. In 1985, with the recovery of democracy and strong government intervention in centralized wage negotiations, unions flourished. In 1991, the government started to step out of the labor bargaining arena, favoring more decentralized negotiations. This and the more competitive environment due to trade liberalization led to lower unionization rates.

Therefore, the Uruguayan experience is an interesting case to study the impact of higher international exposure, unionization and market concentration on the creation and destruction of jobs and capital as well as on productivity dynamics. The following two sections present the expected relationship between variables as suggested by the economic literature, outline the study's methodology and enumerate the main statistics on job and capital reallocation and productivity in the manufacturing sector in Uruguay. Based on descriptive measures and our prior work, the second half of the article is dedicated to each of the three issues in consideration: international exposure, unionization and concentration. Finally, we present the conclusions.

EXPECTED EFFECTS AND RELATED LITERATURE

This section presents a brief review of the relevant literature on the effects of trade liberalization and unionization on productivity and factor flows.

Trade Policy, Factor Flows and Productivity

Working at the plant level, Tybout (2001) reviews the testable implications of trade theories and the related empirical findings. First, Tybout notes that the pricing decisions of firms under imperfect competition are affected by changes in protection. Second, depending on the market structure assumed, changes in prices affect the set of active producers and their output decisions; hence there are different implications for surviving firms and size distributions. Empirically, reduced protection is generally associated with smaller firms in the import-competing sectors. There is also some evidence that foreign liberalization increases the size of the exporting firms. Size adjustments may induce changes in scale efficiency, and market-share reallocations within sectors can affect industry-wide performance as long as firms are heterogeneous in their total factor productivity. Third, changes in the intensity of foreign competition may lead to changes in technical efficiency due to incentives to innovate or due to the elimination of agency problems.[1] Also, openness facilitates firm access to better inputs and capital goods. These effects tend to increase firm productivity.

Using a panel of Brazilian firms, Muendler (2002) analyzes the relationship between trade liberalization and productivity. He identifies three channels by which trade reform may affect productivity. First, the foreign-input push is the process by which firms in more open economies purchase higher quality equipment and intermediate inputs in foreign markets which allow them to adopt new production methods, including substitution of relatively more expensive factors of production. This implies capital creation, job destruction and higher productivity. The second is the competitive push by which increased competition in the product market may lead to innovation and removal of agency problems. Both effects increase firm productivity. This could lead to higher remuneration for the factors of production, to job and capital creation or to a combination of all of the above. There is a third effect observed only at the sector level which is termed 'competitive elimination'; that is, increased foreign competition forces the least efficient firms to close down, destroying jobs and capital, while the more efficient ones gain market share, creating jobs and capital. Average sector productivity is increased. Muendler discounts a significant effect from the foreign-input push channel but points towards increased exposure to foreign competition as a source of significant pressure on firms to raise productivity.

Aw, Chen and Roberts (1997) document the differentials in productivity, turnover and exports in Taiwanese manufacturing firms. They measure total factor productivity differentials among entering, exiting and continuing firms, and they quantify the turnover contribution to productivity growth. They find that cohorts of entering firms have lower average productivity than incumbents. Exiting firms are less productive than survivors. Exporters are also more productive than non-exporters. They conclude that the domestic and the export market both sort out high- from low-productivity firms, and that the turnover contribution accounts for a sizeable proportion of productivity change in manufacturing. This last evidence contradicts other studies (e.g., Baily, Hulten and Campbell 1992) which find that turnover contributes little to productivity change.

Unions, Job Flows and Productivity

Kuhn (1998) and Aidt and Tzannatos (2002) survey the effects of unions on several dimensions. There seems to be agreement in the literature on the wage effects of unions, but the results on other (non-wage) dimensions are less robust. In particular, there are contradictory results with respect to employment growth, investment and productivity.

Freeman and Medoff's 1984 book, *What Do Unions Do?* remains an often-cited reference on how unions affect plant productivity strategies. Their results show that highly unionized plants tend to display higher productivity than those where unions are not present. Although they lack a theoretical model, their argument suggests that manufacturing may respond to reduced turnover and improved management. Therefore, the effects of unions in plant performance may be seen as the net result of two different economic channels of influence: the monopoly effect and the voice-response channel by which workers communicate their preferences to employers.

The monopoly effect translates into higher wage gains which will, in turn, induce capital for labor substitution in firms (capital creation and job destruction), thus having a positive effect on the marginal productivity of labor. While the voice-response channel may have a negative effect on productivity if unions are placing restrictions on managerial discretion, it may also have productivity-enhancing effects if unions cooperate with management, thus inducing less turnover or introducing better personnel policies. These effects depend on the state of industrial relations. Booth (1995) provides a summary of the theoretical underpinnings of the discussion of the effect of unions on productivity and points to some testable implications. First, union presence must be associated with lower turnover rate, since it is precisely through the voice channel that workers can communicate their preferences to management rather than by exiting the firm. If productivity increases and labor demand shifts upward, the union might manage to impose a wage differential with respect to non-union plants; hence the union's effect on employment should be smaller.

Which of these theoretical effects dominates is an empirical matter. Most studies conclude that unionized sectors tend to grow at a lower rate (Boal and Pencavel 1999; Freeman and Kleiner 1990 and Standing 1992). There is no agreement on the empirical effect of unions on productivity. For example, Brunello (1992) finds unions to be associated with lower productivity while Standing (1992) finds the opposite effect. The results by Denny and Nickell (1991) suggest that unionized firms underinvest.

METHODOLOGY AND MAIN FACTS

Our research on these topics is based on annual firm-level observations from the Uruguayan Manufacturing Survey conducted by the Instituto Nacional de Estadística (INE) for the period 1982–95. The survey-sampling timeframe encompasses all Uruguayan manufacturing establishments with five or more employees.

The INE divided the firms in each four-digit International Standard Industrial Classification (ISIC) sector between those with more than and less than 100 employees. Those firms with more than 100 employees were always included in the survey. Those with fewer than 100 employees were subject to a random sampling process.[2] The micro-level data for the whole period were actually obtained from two subsample sets: from 1982 until 1988 and from 1988 until 1995. The Second National Economic Census was conducted in 1988.

In total, we have 1367 different firms present in at least one period. There are 583 starting in 1982, of which just 240 make it to 1995. The 1988 sample is composed of 654 firms included for the first time in that year and 573 from the old sample, not all of which appear in subsequent years.[3]

Job and Capital Flows

The definitions in this section follow Davis and Haltiwanger (1992) and Davis, Haltiwanger and Shuh (1996). The measure of size for firm i at time t is the simple average between employment at period t and t-1: $\phi_{it} = \dfrac{E_{it} + E_{it-1}}{2}$. The rate of growth of employment is defined as in other studies in the literature as:

$Net_{it} = \dfrac{E_{it} - E_{it-1}}{\phi_{it}}$ This growth rate varies from -2 to 2. Calling

$g_{it} = \dfrac{\left[E_{it} - E_{it-1}\right]}{E_{it-1}}$ the traditional growth rate it is possible to show that[4]

$g_{it} = \dfrac{2 Net_{it}}{2 - Net_{it}}$ Job creation is the sum of all job increases in expanding establishments; job destruction is the sum of all the employment reductions in contracting or exiting firms. Formally, they are defined as:

$$Pos_t = \sum_i \phi_{it} \max\left(Net_{it}, 0\right)$$

$$Neg_t = \sum_i \phi_{it} \left|\min\left(Net_{it}, 0\right)\right|$$

The aggregate net job creation is the change in total employment, and job reallocation summarizes the heterogeneity in the outputs of plant-level employment. They are defined as follows:

$$Net_t = \sum_i \phi_{it} Net_{it}$$

$$Sum_t = \sum_i \phi_{it} \left|Net_{it}\right|$$

Note that from these definitions $Net_t = Pos_t - Neg_t$ and $Sum_t = Pos_t + Neg_t$. The rates of capital creation, capital destruction, capital net creation and capital reallocation are computed analogously.

In Casacuberta, Fachola and Gandelman (2006) we present the basic statistics for the whole sample. In that article we showed that over the 14 years covered in this study, there is an average annual net job contraction of 4.5 per cent. Gross job-flow rates vary considerably over time, and there is a sharp contrast between the two subsample periods. In 1982–87 there is a slightly negative net job creation with creation and destruction rates at basically similar magnitudes. In 1988–95 job creation slows down, job destruction almost doubles and there is a higher overall reallocation rate.

Unfortunately we have data on capital stock only after 1988. Over the period 1988–95, capital also experienced negative net creation, but the capital net creation rate is substantially higher than the employment net creation rate. Also, capital destruction rates are smaller than employment destruction rates. As a result of these different rates, the capital-to-labor ratio must have increased due to a switch towards more capital-intensive technologies.

In that same 2006 article we also reported that the rate of net job destruction is slightly higher for blue-collar workers than for white-collar workers. This general result for the entire period obscures a different evolution over time. While in the expansive years of 1985 and 1986, when negotiations were centralized and the state played a very intensive role in union-employer negotiations, the net job creation rate was higher for less skilled jobs than in the more skilled jobs. In the 1990s, when the trade liberalization was stronger and there were more decentralized negotiations for wages and employment (without government participation), blue-collar workers suffered higher job-destruction rates than white-collar workers.

TFP Estimation

We estimate the firm-level total factor productivity using the methodologies proposed by Olley and Pakes (1996) and Levinsohn and Petrin (2003). Both are essentially methods of estimating the parameters of a production function. Loosely speaking, increases in output can be attributed to increases in the quantity and quality of production functions or increases in the total factor productivity. Total factor productivity is obtained by subtracting to output changes the part of the change that can be attributed to increases or decreases in production factors.[5]

The results for the aggregates are rather similar under both methodologies. In Casacuberta, Fachola and Gandelman (2004) we report that between 1988 and 1995 total factor productivity grew at a very high rate: 3.3 per cent according to the Olley and Pakes (1996) methodology and 3.7 per cent according to the Levinsohn and Petrin (2003) methodology. Given the lack of information on capital stocks, we were unable to estimate the total factor productivity before 1988. We report the effects of protection, unionization and market concentration using the Levinsohn and Petrin (2003) estimation because this methodology allows a much larger number of firms to be incorporated in the analysis.

THE IMPACT OF INTERNATIONAL EXPOSURE ON FACTOR FLOWS AND PRODUCTIVITY

Over the period covered in this study there was a process of increased trade liberalization (with simultaneous real exchange-rate appreciation) in the presence of, at least initially, a relatively strong degree of labor-force unionization. Figure 2.1 shows the relative convergence of tariffs and how tariff reductions were a phenomenon common to all sectors of activity (31 food, beverage and tobacco; 32 textile and garment; 34 paper and printing; 35 chemical; 36 non-metal mineral products; 37 basic metal; 38 machinery and equipment; 39 other activities).

Vaillant (2000) describes the trade liberalization process in Uruguay as going through different phases throughout our period of analysis. From 1988 to 1994, he finds that the government pursued a trade policy that would continue and deepen the openness process started in the 1970s, aimed at ending the anti-export bias that characterized previous import-substitution policies. With the recovery of democratic institutions in 1984, the political pressures for modifying trade policy were stronger, but the government did not alter the main policies. There was only a slightly higher protection regime due to

Figure 2.1   Average Tariff by Sector (ISIC, Rev. 2)

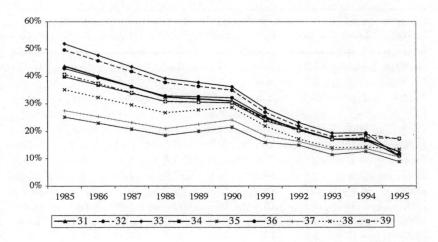

increased use of non-tariff barriers. In 1991 a program of scheduled tariff reductions began according to the Mercosur treaty, an imperfect customs union among Argentina, Brazil, Paraguay and Uruguay.

Vaillant points to a modification in the political-economy conditions of the trade policy-setting process in Uruguay. Before reform, starting from 1958, trade policy was regulated mostly by presidential decrees rather than parliament-approved laws. The main organized lobbying groups were the pro-openness exporters and the pro-protection import-competing sectors. The early stages of the reforms were carried out while organized lobbies sought to maintain the prerogatives of various sectors.

The most important change in the 1990s is that, by signing binding international treaties (Mercosur and the World Trade Organization), the government significantly curtailed its ability to provide discretionary protection to specific sectors.

In 2004 we presented econometric evidence of the effects of trade liberalization on job and capital flows. At the time we found that reduced protection implied a slightly higher job creation level and a large increase in job and capital destruction.

In Table 2.1 we present the average annual rate of job and capital creation

Table 2.1   Creation and Destruction of Jobs and Capital by Protection Level (percentage)

Level	Employment 1985–95				Capital 1989–95			
	Creation		Destruction		Creation		Destruction	
	Low	High	Low	High	Low	High	Low	High
Average	6.3	6.5	10.4	11.3	10.5	8.6	9.4	10.1
1985	5.2	8.5	6.4	3.5	na	na	na	na
1986	6.4	8.5	5.3	3.8	na	na	na	na
1987	8.5	8.0	7.0	5.4	na	na	na	na
1988	10.5	11.4	7.1	11.0	na	na	na	na
1989	8.1	6.6	6.5	8.2	9.3	10.1	6.1	10.7
1990	6.1	6.1	9.4	12.8	5.4	6.4	6.4	9.9
1991	5.3	6.6	14.5	12.9	7.6	8.6	9.9	9.5
1992	4.8	5.2	15.6	18.8	9.0	9.7	14.6	13.9
1993	5.1	3.9	15.4	16.7	15.7	6.9	12.7	9.3
1994	4.5	3.5	13.0	17.3	8.0	11.3	7.1	7.4
1995	4.8	3.0	13.7	14.2	18.7	7.5	8.6	10.1

Source: Authors' own elaboration based on INE.

and destruction for firms with lower and higher tariff protection. We have data on tariff levels only from 1985 onwards. Each year we calculated the average tariff level and divided the firms into two groups: those with tariffs below average and those with tariffs above average. Figure 2.2 reports the rate of net job creation by protection level over time. The results here presented are about the level of protection while those from the 2004 paper are related to the change in tariffs. The initially more protected sectors were those that experienced the higher tariff reductions.

First, in line with the small effect on creation and the larger effects on destruction reported in our previous study, we found that, considering the whole period, the average rate of employment creation does not seem to be significantly affected by the protection level. Second, more protected sectors experienced higher employment and capital destruction rates. Therefore higher international exposure implied negative rates of net creation of jobs and capital. As shown in Figure 2.1, this result is produced mostly by the factor flows of the 1990s when the Mercosur treaty was in effect. Third, on average for the whole period, less-protected sectors have higher rate of capital creation

Table 2.2   Productivity by Protection Level (percentage)

Year	Low	High
1988	100.0	107.8
1989	115.9	121.0
1990	111.6	116.5
1991	114.9	109.1
1992	111.1	117.0
1993	112.1	115.3
1994	130.1	118.0
1995	129.0	123.9
Average TFP level	115.6	116.1
Average growth rate	3.7	2.0

Source: Authors' own elaboration.

and lower rate of capital destruction, implying that the more protected sectors experienced higher capital net destruction rates.

Table 2.2 and Figure 2.2 present the evolution of productivity after 1988. The more protected sectors were initially 8 per cent more productive than those less protected, but the average growth rate of total factor production in the more protected sectors is lower than in the more protected sectors: 2.0 per cent and 3.7 per cent respectively. In the last two years of this study the less protected sectors were already more productive than the more protected ones. In Casacuberta, Fachola and Gandelman (2004) we present econometric evidence on the enhancing effects of trade liberalization on productivity.

THE IMPACT OF UNIONIZATION ON FACTOR FLOWS AND PRODUCTIVITY

Protection and unions are related according to Rama (1994), who assesses two aspects of trade reform. Since unions may imply rigidity in labor reallocation, they may have a negative impact on the effectiveness of trade reform. Also, as rents created by protection are an incentive for union activity, they also may be a barrier to the trade reform itself. Rama points out that unions in Uruguay seemed not to be involved in the decades-long process of establishing trade barriers, although they share the rents created by this process. His work intends to measure the wage and employment effects of trade liberalization. Using a monopolistic competition model, combined with the union monopoly on labor supply, he derives the labor market equilibrium wages and employment

Figure 2.2   Employment Net Creation by Protection Level

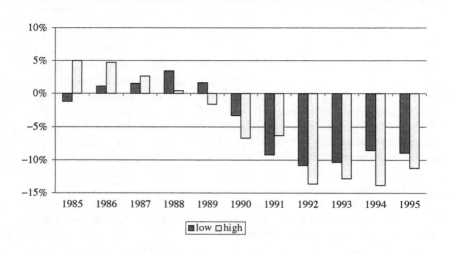

Figure 2.3   Productivity Evolution by Protection Level

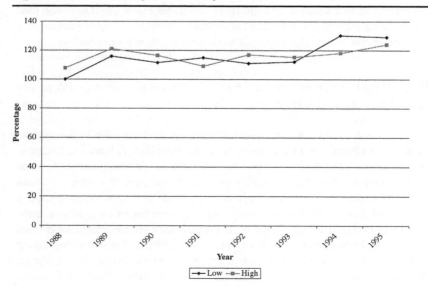

equations as functions of tariffs. The main finding is that tariffs had no significant effect on wage levels from 1978 to 1986, although there was an employment effect.

To describe the main features of the role of unions in manufacturing, it is useful to consider two different periods in our data. During the first period, from 1985 to 1991, coordinated and centralized negotiations took place at the sector level, with active government participation. The government's approval was required to make the agreed wages legally binding on all firms within the sector. The centralization level was mainly identified to be at a four- or five-digit level of the International Standard Industrial Classification (ISIC), although this is not uniform across sectors. Cassoni (1999) points out that the effective centralization level may have been higher, since unions were coordinated by the central union organization (PIT–CNT, *Plenario Intersindical de Trabajadores – Convención Nacional de Trabajadores*).

Forteza (1991) argued that the objective of the government's involvement in these negotiations was to mitigate the inflationary process. In any case, the government's attempts to influence expectations of future inflation were not credible. Wages observed at the firm level tended to follow – or even to exceed – the negotiated wage levels.

From 1991 onward, the government stepped away from negotiations, coincident with the implementation of an exchange-rate-based stabilization program. This radically changed the entrepreneurs' and unions' incentives to participate in sectoral negotiations. After 1992 negotiations conducted at a firm or group-of-firms level comprised an increasing proportion of the total agreements registered at the Ministry of Labor, and in 1996–97 they clearly became the majority (64 per cent, according to Rodríguez et al. 1998).

Over the period in consideration there is also a change in the scope and objectives of negotiations. Cassoni and Labadie (2001) show that wage negotiations dominate in the years prior to 1991. They argue that a plausible model for wage and employment determination was the 'right to manage' model, in which first-stage wages are agreed between unions and employers, and that firms determine subsequent employment along their labor demand curve. They observe that clauses concerning employment start to be added to the wage agreements in 1993. Hence the appropriate framework seems to be an 'efficient contract' model in which firms and unions bargain over both wages and employment.

Union density is defined as the affiliation rate of the industry at the three-digit ISIC level. The time series is built using data on membership reported by the central union in each of its periodic congresses and dividing that figure by total employment. The steady decline in the unionization rate is clear from Table 2.3.

Table 2.3   Unionization Rate

Year	Percentage
1985	57
1986	50
1987	41
1988	40
1989	40
1990	35
1991	37
1992	40
1993	27
1994	29
1995	32

Source: Cassoni, Labadie and Fachola (2002).

Table 2.4 reports the annual creation and destruction rates for employment and capital by unionization level. Figure 2.4 reports the employment net creation rate. The higher and lower unionized sectors are composed of those establishments with unionization rates above and below the annual average unionization rate.

Sectors with higher unionization rates experienced larger employment-creation rates than those less unionized sectors. Higher unionization is also associated with lower employment-destruction rates. In Casacuberta, Fachola and Gandelman (2005) we show that both effects, the higher creation and the lower destruction of the more unionized sectors, are stronger for blue-collar workers than for white-collar workers.

With respect to capital, those sectors with stronger unions experienced a higher creation rate and a lower destruction rate, implying an average annual capital net creation rate of 1.5 per cent. Considering the same period (1989–95), for both more and less unionized sectors, the net creation rates are higher for capital than for employment. This suggests that the switch towards higher capital intensity is a common phenomenon of both groups. Nevertheless, the capital net creation rate of those less unionized sectors was negative, −1.1 per cent, while the net creation rate of those more unionized was positive, 1.5 per cent. This leads us to speculate that in those more unionized sectors, the substitution of employment for capital was stronger, in line with the monopoly costs of union view.

Table 2.5 and Figure 2.5 report the evolution of productivity for those more and less unionized sectors. The evidence presented is in line with the views

Table 2.4   Creation and Destruction of Jobs and Capital by Unionization Level (percentage)

Level	Employment 1985–95				Capital 1989–95			
	Creation		Destruction		Creation		Destruction	
	Low	High	Low	High	Low	High	Low	High
Average	6.1	6.6	11.6	9.4	9.0	10.6	10.1	9.1
1985	6.0	7.0	4.6	6.0	na	na	na	na
1986	5.8	8.6	4.4	4.9	na	na	na	na
1987	10.8	7.5	4.9	6.8	na	na	na	na
1988	11.1	10.8	9.2	8.6	na	na	na	na
1989	5.6	8.0	7.7	7.3	8.1	10.5	7.6	8.5
1990	4.9	7.8	13.3	8.2	5.8	5.9	9.7	5.8
1991	5.9	6.1	15.6	11.1	8.6	7.4	11.6	7.7
1992	5.4	4.6	20.8	12.9	10.4	8.1	14.7	13.8
1993	4.3	4.5	17.9	8.4	12.0	5.6	10.7	10.7
1994	4.3	2.2	15.3	16.7	8.1	15.9	6.8	8.9
1995	3.3	5.9	14.3	12.8	10.2	20.9	9.6	8.8

Source: Authors' own elaboration based on INE.

of Freeman and Medoff (1984) and the Cassoni, Labadie and Fachola (2002) results for Uruguay, which found that higher unionization was associated with higher investment higher productivity but lower firm's profitability growth. They conjectured these results were due to substitution of labor for capital.

According to our data, those sectors with stronger unions in 1988 were, on average, 12 per cent more productive than the less-unionized sectors. The average rate of growth of these more-unionized firms is also higher than those less-unionized firms. Therefore, the gap between both groups is not closing significantly. For the whole period under consideration the sector with the higher unionization rate is 20 per cent more productive that the less unionized sectors.

Table 2.5   Productivity by Unionization Level

	Low	High
1988	100.0	112.0
1989	112.8	129.8
1990	114.2	130.2
1991	109.9	130.3
1992	112.1	134.9
1993	113.4	141.2
1994	120.7	156.4
1995	123.9	158.3
Average TFP level	113.4	136.6
Average growth rate	3.1%	5.1%

Source: Authors' own elaboration.

THE IMPACT OF MARKET CONCENTRATION ON FACTOR FLOWS AND PRODUCTIVITY

Borjas and Ramey (1992) have argued that openness should have greater unemployment effects in more concentrated sectors. Similarly, it can be argued that the incentives for unionization are higher in more concentrated sectors which are more likely to be earning rents due to higher market power.

We measure market concentration as the sum of the market share of the three largest establishments in the industry (defined at four-digit ISIC levels for sector 31– food, beverage and tobacco – and at three-digit levels for the rest). It ranges from a low of 6 per cent to a full 100 per cent concentration, with an average of 34 per cent. Although there is wide variation in concentration levels between sectors, there is not a clear trend over time.

Table 2.6 presents the creation and destruction rates for employment and capital by concentration level. The sample of establishments was also divided between those in more and less concentrated sectors using the average annual concentration rate. Considering the whole period, there does not seem to be significant differences in the creation and destruction of employment and in the creation of capital between those firms benefiting from higher concentration and those in more competitive environments. Those firms in the more concentrated sectors seem to experience lower capital destruction levels than those in less concentrated sectors. In this sense, we infer that market power derived from concentration was translated into higher capital net creation rates. Adding the

Figure 2.4   Employment Net Creation by Unionization Level

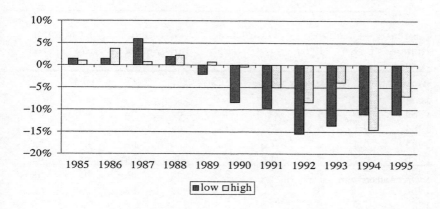

Figure 2.5   Productivity by Unionization Level

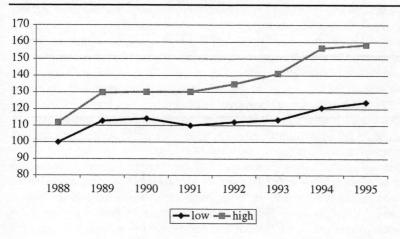

Table 2.6   Creation and Destruction of Jobs and Capital by Concentration Level

Concen-tration	Employment 1983–1995				Capital 1989–1995			
	Creation		Destruction		Creation		Destruction	
	Low	High	Low	High	Low	High	Low	High
Average	6.5	6.2	10.8	10.9	9.5	9.4	10.4	8.7
1983	5.5	4.2	14.0	12.5	na	na	na	na
1984	9.7	6.1	7.7	7.4	na	na	na	na
1985	6.4	6.7	4.6	6.2	na	na	na	na
1986	6.7	8.1	4.8	4.5	na	na	na	na
1987	7.3	9.6	5.2	8.0	na	na	na	na
1988	11.2	10.3	7.6	10.6	na	na	na	na
1989	7.9	6.5	6.8	8.3	12.4	6.4	9.0	7.2
1990	5.1	7.7	10.6	12.1	6.0	5.7	8.3	7.5
1991	6.6	4.9	14.7	11.9	7.7	8.4	8.1	11.7
1992	4.9	5.2	18.2	15.4	10.0	8.5	18.6	8.8
1993	4.8	3.6	16.3	15.9	7.7	13.8	10.2	11.3
1994	4.2	3.3	16.0	14.9	11.0	8.6	7.9	6.5
1995	3.6	4.0	14.1	13.8	11.5	14.1	11.1	8.0

Source: Authors' own calculations.

Table 2.7   Productivity by Concentration Level

Year	Low	High
1988	100.0	128.6
1989	121.4	121.5
1990	113.6	125.0
1991	104.6	136.6
1992	105.0	165.3
1993	103.7	167.7
1994	115.1	164.7
1995	127.2	130.9
Average TFP level	111.3	142.5
Average growth rate	3.5%	0.3%

Source: Authors' own calculations.

Figure 2.6 Employment Net Creation by Concentration Level

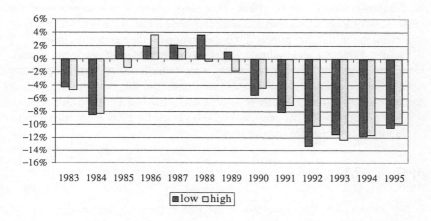

Figure 2.7 Productivity Evolution by Concentration Level

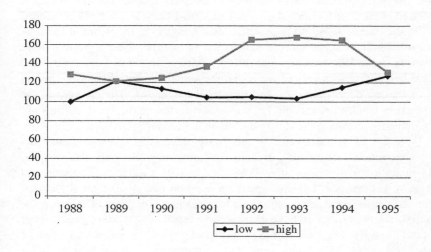

creation and destruction rates, it seems that more concentrated sectors have lower factor reallocation rates.

Figure 2.6 presents the employment net creation rates, and again it is clear that most of the destruction, in both groups, was produced in the 1990s when the Mercosur treaty was in effect. This employment net destruction of the 1990s is somewhat stronger in less concentrated sectors. This is another way of observing the mitigating effects of concentration on the net destruction.

Finally, Table 2.7 and Figure 2.7 present the evolution of productivity after 1988. The highly concentrated sectors were initially more than 25 per cent more productive than the less concentrated ones, but the average TFP growth rate in the concentrated sectors is lower than in the less concentrated sectors, at 0.3 per cent and 3.5 per cent respectively. Thus, by 1995 there seems to be productivity convergence in both sectors.

CONCLUSION

In the last decades, but especially in the 1990s, Uruguay underwent a strong trade liberalization. This economic policy, combined with a deepened, gradual, unilateral tariff reduction through the creation of the Mercosur customs union among Argentina, Brazil, Paraguay and Uruguay. The Uruguayan liberalization exhibited two special characteristics. First, it took place in a context in which unions, at least initially, still maintained significant power. Second, in the mid-1980s the manufacturing industry in Uruguay essentially consisted of a reduced number of traditional products exporting firms and sectors developed under the import-substitution process. Most Uruguayan industries at the time exhibited high concentration levels. At the same time, there were important changes in the labor institutional settings. After a period of very centralized wage bargaining with very active government involvement, there was a period of increasing decentralization and firm-level bargaining. The changes in the protection level, in firms' market power and in the institutional settings are undoubtedly related to the steady decline in the unionization rates.

Over the 14 years covered in this study, there is an average annual net job contraction rate of 4.5 per cent. Unfortunately, we only have capital information for the years after 1988. In 1988–95 capital also experienced negative net creation, but the capital net creation rate is substantially higher than the employment net creation rate for the same timeframe. Therefore, the capital-to-labor ratio must have increased as a result of a switch towards higher capital intensity. The reallocation of factors of production and the adoption of new production technologies generated an important increase in total factor productivity. The average annual growth rate for the 1988–95 period is above 3 per cent.

In the 1985–95 period the average rate of employment creation does not seem to be significantly affected by the protection level, but more protected sectors experienced higher employment and capital destruction rates. Therefore higher international exposure implied negative rates of net jobs and capital creation. The more protected sectors were initially more productive, but the higher international pressure induced a relatively fast productivity convergence.

Those sectors with higher unionization rates experienced larger employment creation rates than the less unionized sectors. Higher unionization is also associated with lower employment destruction rates. With respect to capital, those sectors with stronger unions experienced a higher creation rate and a lower destruction rate, implying an average annual capital net creation rate of 1.5 per cent. Independent of the level of unionization, the net creation rates are higher for capital than for employment, therefore the switch towards more capital-intensive technologies must be a phenomenon common to both groups. According to the estimates, unionized sectors were more productive over the entire period than were the less unionized sectors, and there does not seem to be evidence of productivity convergence.

Market power, as proxied by sector concentration, does not seem to generate significant differences in the creation and destruction of employment and in the creation of capital. Firms in more concentrated sectors seem to experience lower capital destruction levels than those in less concentrated sectors. In this sense, we conjecture that market power derived from concentration translated into higher capital net creation rates. The initial differences in productivity were absorbed by the different productivity growth rates.

NOTES

This paper is based on the main results of three previous papers: Casacuberta, Fachola and Gandelman (2004), Casacuberta, Fachola and Gandelman (2005) and Casacuberta, Fachola and Gandelman (2006). The 2006 paper was a medal finalist presented in the Sixth Annual Global Development Conference in Dakar.

1 An innovation in a firm may face opposition from inside the same firm. Increased competition induces challenges to firms which sometimes can only be addressed by implementing the delayed innovations. In this sense, the higher international exposure aligns the incentives of agents within the firm.
2. For a detailed discussion see INE (1996).
3. For a more detailed description of the database see Casacuberta, Fachola and Gandelman (2004).
4. In order to calculate annual average rates for any period it is necessary to transform the Net-

rates into the g-rates, calculate the average annual g-rate and from there calculate the average annual Net-rate.

5. Both methods provide a remedy for two problems associated with these estimates which are extensively treated in the related literature. They are the selection problem (i.e., in a panel a researcher would only observe the surviving firms, hence those firms which are likely to be the most productive), and the simultaneity problem (the input choices of firms conditional on the fact that they continue to be in activity depending on their productivity).

BIBLIOGRAPHY

Aidt, Toke and Zafiris Tzannatos (2002), *Unions and Collective Bargaining. Economic Effects in a Global Environment*, Washington, DC: World Bank.

Aw, Bee Yan, Xiaomin Chen and Mark J. Roberts (1997), 'Firm Level Evidence on Productivity Differentials, Turnover and Exports in Taiwanese Manufacturing', Cambridge, MA, National Bureau of Economic Research (NBER) Working Paper No. 6325.

Baily, Martin N., Charles Hulten and David Campbell (1992), in Martin N. Baily and Clifford Winston (eds), *Productivity Dynamics in Manufacturing Plants*, Washington, DC: Brookings Papers in Economic Activity, Microeconomics, pp. 187–249.

Boal, William M. and John Pencavel (1994), 'The Effects of Labor Unions on Employment, Wages and Days of Operation: Coal Mining in West Virginia', *Quarterly Journal of Economics*, **109** (1), 267–98.

Borjas, George and Valerie A. Ramey (1995), 'Foreign Competition, Market Power and Wage Inequality', *Quarterly Journal of Economics*, **110** (4), 1075–110.

Booth, Alison L. (1995), *The Economics of the Trade Union*, New York: Cambridge University Press. Brunello, Giorgio (1992), 'The Effect of Unions on Firms in Japanese Manufacturing', *Industrial and Labor Relations Review*, **45** (3), 471–87.

Casacuberta, Carlos, Gabriela Fachola and Néstor Gandelman (2004), 'The Impact of Trade Liberalization on Employment, Capital and Productivity Dynamics: Evidence from the Uruguayan Manufacturing Sector', *Journal of Policy Reform*, **7** (4), 225–48.

——(2005), 'Creación, Destrucción y Reasignación de Empleo y Capital en la Industria Manufacturera', [Creation, Destruction, and Reallocation of Jobs and Capital in Industrial Manufacturing] *Revista de Economía del Banco Central del Uruguay*, **12** (2), 90–124.

——(2006), 'Employment, Capital and Productivity Dynamics: Evidence from the Manufacturing Sector in Uruguay', www.ssrc.com/abstraction=929159.

Cassoni, Adriana (1999), 'Labour Demand in Uruguay Before and After Re–Unionization', Department of Economics, Universidad de la República, Montevideo, Uruguay, Working Paper No. 1/99.

Cassoni, Adriana and Gaston J. Labadie (2001), The Outcome of Different Bargaining Models: The Effects on Wages, Employment and the Employment Mix', Department of Economics, Universidad de la República, Montevideo, Uruguay, Working Paper No. 14/01.

Cassoni, Adriana, Gaston J. Labadie and Gabriela Fachola (2002), 'The Economic Effects of Unions in Latin America: Their Impact on Wages and the Economic

Performance of Firms in Uruguay', Washington, DC, Inter-American Development Bank Research Network Working Paper No. R466.

Davis, Steve J. and John Haltiwanger (1992), 'Gross Job Creation, Gross Job Destruction and Employment Reallocation', *Quarterly Journal of Economics*, **107** (3), 819–63.

Davis, Steve J., John Haltiwanger and Scott Schuh (1996), *Job Creation and Destruction*, Cambridge, MA: MIT Press.

Denny, Kevin and Stephen Nickell (1991), 'Unions and Investment in British Manufacturing Industry', *British Journal of Industrial Relations*, **29** (1), 113–22.

Forteza, Alvaro (1991), 'Los Convenios Salariales y la Inflación', Department of Economics, Universidad de la República, Montevideo, Uruguay, Working Paper.

Freeman, Richard B. and Morris M. Kleiner (1990), 'The Impact of New Unionization on Wages and Working Conditions', *Journal of Labor Economics*, **8** (1), 8–25.

Freeman, Richard B. and James L. Medoff (1984), *What Do Unions Do?*, New York: Basic Books.

Grout, Paul A. (1984), 'Investment and Wages in the Absence of Binding Contracts', *Economica*, **52** (4), 449–60.

Instituto Nacional de Estadística (1996), *Metodología: Encuesta Industrial Base 1988*, Instituto Nacional de Estadística, Montevideo, Uruguay.

Kuhn, Paul A. (1998), 'Unions and the Economy: What We Know; What We Should Know', *Canadian Journal of Economics*, **31** (5),1033–56.

Levinsohn, James and Amil Petrin (2003), 'Estimating Production Functions Using Inputs to Control for Unobservables', *Review of Economic Studies*, **70** (2), 317–41.

Muendler, Marc-Andreas (2002), 'Trade, Technology and Productivity: A Study of Brazilian Manufacturers, 1986–1998', mimeo, Department of Economics, University of California at Berkeley.

Olley, G. Steven and Amil Pakes (1996), 'The Dynamics of Productivity in the Telecommunications Equipment Industry', *Econometrica*, **64** (6), 1263–297.

Pencavel, John (1999), 'The Role of Labor Unions in Fostering Economic Development', Washington, DC, World Bank Policy Research Working Paper No. 1469.

Rama, Martin (1994), 'The Labor Market and Trade Reform in Manufacturing', in Michael B. Connolly and Jaime De Melo (eds), *The Effects of Protectionism on a Small Country: The Case of Uruguay*, Washington, DC: World Bank.

Rama, Martin and Guido Tabellini (1998), 'Lobbying by Capital and Labor over Trade and Labor Market Policies', *European Economic Review*, **42** (7), 1295–316.

Rodríguez, Juan Manuel, Beatriz Cozzano, Graciela Mazzucchi and Maria de Luján Pozzolo (1998), *¿Hacia un Nuevo Modelo de Relaciones Laborales? De la Apertura Política a la Apertura Económica. Uruguay 1985–1998*, [Towards a New Model of Labor Relations? From the Political Liberalization to the Economic Liberalization. Uruguay 1985-1998] Montevideo: Ediciones Trilce.

Standing, Guy (1992), 'Do Unions Impede or Accelerate Structural Adjustment? Industrial versus Company Unions in an Industrializing Labour Market', *Cambridge Journal of Economics*, **16** (3), 327–54.

Tybout, James R. (2001), 'Plant and Firm Level Evidence on "New" Trade Theories', Cambridge, MA, National Bureau of Economic Research Working Paper No. 8418.

Vaillant, Marcel (2000), 'Limits to Trade Liberalization: A Political Economy Approach', Ph.D. dissertation, UFSIA, University of Antwerp, Appendix A.

PART TWO

Aid Strategies and Allocations

3. Trade Capacity Building in Sub-Saharan Africa: Emerging Issues and Challenges

Chantal Dupasquier and Patrick N. Osakwe

Trade negotiations and agreements have become regular features of the world economy and are slowly encompassing aspects of economic and social activities which were previously not considered part of the responsibilities of the multilateral trading system. In the early years of the GATT, market access was considered the prime objective of the multilateral trading system. Today, the scope has been broadened to include issues such as intellectual property rights, development concerns, sanitary and phytosanitary regulations as well as other technical barriers to trade. Clearly, the fact that the negotiations have increased in scope has serious implications for the ability of developing countries to adapt to the trading system. It has also increased the challenges developing countries face in their bid to cope with the enormous resource demands which accompany the negotiations. This issue has emerged as an important concern in the trading system given the unprecedented increase in the number of poor countries involved in the negotiations. Currently, more than two-thirds of World Trade Organization (WTO) members are developing countries. This contrasts with the situation in the early years of the GATT, when there were no developing countries involved in the negotiations.

During the Uruguay Round (1986–94), African countries made several commitments to the multilateral trading system without fully realizing the implications and consequences for their development efforts. These commitments imposed high implementation costs on their economies and diverted resources away from important development projects, with dire consequences for poverty reduction (Stiglitz and Charlton 2004, 9). It is therefore not surprising that these countries have increased their calls for trade-related technical assistance and capacity building with a view toward increasing their understanding of the consequences of trade proposals and agreements before making any binding commitments.

The international community has recognized the fact that poor countries need assistance in trade capacity building if they are to participate effectively in multilateral trade negotiations and derive significant gains from the trading system. As part of efforts to capture this reality, the current round of multilateral trade negotiations was declared to be a Doha Development Round. Under the Doha agenda, developed countries promised to provide more trade-related technical assistance and capacity building programs to developing countries (WTO 2002, 16). Three factors were responsible for this decision. The first is the failure of the 1999 WTO Ministerial Conference in Seattle. The demonstrations and crises witnessed at the conference brought to light the fact that developing countries were disenchanted with the rules and operations of the multilateral trading system and that something had to be done to win their trust as well as to increase confidence in the system. An increase in trade capacity building was seen as a vital step to achieve this objective. Second, developed countries saw the decision to increase support for trade capacity building as essential to persuading developing countries to agree to the launch of a new round of trade negotiations. One of the reasons developing countries objected to the launch of a new trade round was that it would have an ambitious agenda which would impose undue burdens on them in terms of keeping up with the negotiations and implementing potential agreements. An increase in trade capacity building was seen as an effective way to address these concerns. Finally, the terrorist attacks in the United States on 11 September 2001 led developed countries to realize that poverty and alienation from the global economy make weak states vulnerable to terrorist networks. There was, therefore, an urgent need to integrate developing countries into the trading system so as to avoid alienation. Many experts believed that support for trade capacity building would increase the ability of developing countries to participate more effectively in the negotiations and to take advantage of opportunities created in the multilateral trading system.

This chapter focuses on the Doha promise regarding the provision of technical assistance and capacity building programs to poor countries. It is one in a series of recent studies on trade capacity building in developing countries (see for example Solignac-Lecomte 2003; Prowse 2002; Luke 2002; Tandon 2002; Powell 2002; OECD 2001; Land and Ndorukwigira 2001; and Whalley 1999). The present analysis differs from existing studies in three significant respects. First, it examines the links between trade capacity building and domestic macroeconomic variables and assesses the implications for the effectiveness of donor-funded trade capacity building efforts in Sub-Saharan Africa. Second, it identifies the challenges facing Sub-Saharan African countries, donors and executing agencies in the quest for capacity development, and it offers solutions to the region's trade capacity problems which recognize the potential risks posed by political instability, brain drain and the HIV/AIDS epidemic. Third, it presents policy coherence issues which should be addressed by Sub-Saharan African countries to enhance efforts aimed at mainstreaming trade into national development strategies.

The chapter begins by identifying the key trade-related capacity constraints facing Sub-Saharan African countries with a view to providing an understanding of the nature and scope of these constraints. Next, it discusses recent developments in trade capacity building and examines two key trade capacity-building initiatives as well as their shortcomings. The chapter then examines the correlations between trade capacity building and macroeconomic and social variables, which are followed by suggestions on how to build trade capacity in the region. It also discusses the challenges facing recipient countries, donors and executing agencies in trade capacity building. Finally, the focus turns to the link between trade capacity building and national development strategies and identifies pertinent issues which should be addressed by Sub-Saharan African countries if they are to be successful in mainstreaming trade into national development strategies.

IDENTIFYING CAPACITY CONSTRAINTS IN AFRICA

Since the Doha Declaration in November 2001 there has been an enormous increase in discussions as well as writings on trade capacity building for poor countries. Until recently, however, the literature provided very little practical guidance on how to develop trade capacity, reflecting largely the fact that there was no clear understanding among donors and recipients of the objectives or scope of trade capacity building. It also reflects the fact that there has generally been no systematic attempt to distinguish among the various types and causes of capacity problems facing different regions and how to solve them. For a long-lasting solution to the problem, this is quite important because the nature, causes and solutions to trade-related capacity constraints are not necessarily the same across all countries and regions.[1] Addressing the capacity-building constraints of African countries requires a clear understanding of their nature, scope and causes. These constraints fall into six categories.

Negotiate Effectively

Many African states lack a capacity to negotiate effectively on relevant trade issues. Several of the issues discussed in the negotiations are not familiar to African trade officials, making it very difficult for them to be effective participants in the process. Added to this general lack of awareness or understanding of trade negotiations is the lack of timely access to information and resources on trade issues. This lag is compounded by the fact that libraries, research institutes and government departments in these countries are not properly financed and equipped to serve as resources on trade issues. Another factor which makes it difficult for African countries to be active in the negotiations is the general lack of the analytical and research skills necessary to assess the impact of different proposals and agreements on their economies. For negotiating proposals to be effective and maximize the interest of any given country, they must be based on research findings which take into account the structural specificities and interests of the country concerned in relation to its development goals.

Influence Negotiations

African countries are small in both economic size and political power. They often lack the capacity to influence the agenda or pace of negotiations. They account for less than 2 per cent of global trade and output. Consequently, they are typically not in a position to determine which issues should or should not be on the agenda. This is clearly a very important constraint, because trade negotiations are a bargaining game, and countries with political and economic clout are able to determine which issues will be part of the agenda. The fact that developed countries were able to put the four Singapore Issues[2] into the negotiating agenda of the original Doha Work Program despite serious complaints by developing countries, that comprise more than two-thirds of the WTO membership, underscores the importance of economic and political power in trade negotiations.

Fulfill Commitments

African states lack the capacity to fulfill commitments to the multilateral trading system and to exercise the rights of WTO membership without jeopardizing important development goals. The implementation of multilateral and regional trade agreements often requires substantial investments in infrastructure and human resources (Finger and Schuler 2002, 493). It also requires institutional changes and systems of checks and balances. With very limited domestic resources, African countries need external assistance to be able to implement these agreements without creating other development problems. Without external resources, governments will have to divert funds from other pressing domestic projects, thereby putting the key development priorities of African governments at risk. Another related issue is the inability of African countries to fully exercise their WTO membership rights because of limited resources and, more often than not, a lack of understanding of the rights and privileges they have as members of the multilateral trading system.

Formulate Effective Trade Policies

The use of international trade as an effective instrument for development in any economy requires an efficient trade policy process. This requires identifying a country's trade interests and making sure that they are consistent with its key development priorities. The trade policy process in several African countries does not allow the formulation of effective trade policies. Key trade policy decisions are made without proper analysis of the implications for the economy. The lack of trade officials with relevant analytical skills, coupled with the fact that senior government officials do not take economic research seriously, has created a culture in which trade decisions are made without serious economic analysis.

Deal with External Shocks

Trade liberalization exposes countries to trade shocks, thereby increasing their vulnerability to external shocks. This vulnerability stems largely from the fact that several African countries do not have a diversified production-and-export structure. Consequently, they rely on exports of a few commodities for foreign exchange. The problem is exacerbated by market imperfections which make it impossible for agents to insure against risk.

Exploit Trading Opportunities

Taking advantage of the opportunities created by the international trading system requires capacity-enhancing investments in infrastructure, education and health. It also requires changes in trade policies to ensure that they provide an incentive for the private sector to respond to market signals. In several African countries, poor domestic economic and social policies, especially those affecting transaction costs, have reduced the degree of competitiveness of African exports. Supply constraints in several countries have also made it difficult for the region to increase its global-trade share and to reap the benefits from increased trading opportunities. There is therefore a need for technical assistance to help these countries lift supply constraints and position themselves to be able to take advantage of new trading opportunities.

Classifying Africa's capacity-building constraints into six categories does not imply that they are independent of each other. In fact, some are causes or consequences of other constraints. For example, the lack of an ability to

Figure 3.1   Trade Capacity Linkages

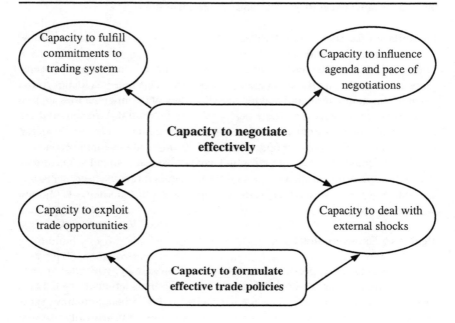

formulate effective trade policies could affect a country's ability to diversify its exports and thus better deal with external shocks. Furthermore, the lack of a capacity to negotiate can affect the ability to influence the agenda and pace of negotiations. Figure 3.1 illustrates some of the possible relationships among the various constraints. These interdependencies suggest that finding a solution to the trade capacity constraints of African countries is not an easy task. That said, it is clear that dealing with some of the constraints requires short-term actions, while others would be better addressed through longer-term measures.

RECENT INITIATIVES AND DEVELOPMENTS IN TRADE CAPACITY BUILDING

In this section, we analyze recent developments in trade capacity building as well as identify countries and types of activities which receive the bulk of trade-related capacity-building assistance in Africa. We also provide an overview of the objectives, scope and features of two key trade-related capacity-building programs: the Joint Integrated Technical Assistance Program (JITAP) and the Integrated Framework (IF).

Although several donors have bilateral initiatives, the bulk of trade-related capacity building is carried out through multilateral agencies and programs. In the literature a distinction is often made between technical assistance and trade capacity building. We do not follow this approach here. Rather we use the phrase trade capacity building to capture both technical assistance and capacity-building programs on trade. Recently, the WTO and the Organization for Economic Cooperation and Development (OECD) developed a database on trade-related technical assistance and capacity building. In the database, activities on trade capacity building are classified under two main categories: Trade Policy and Regulations (TPR) and Trade Development (TD).[3] Available data show that, on an annual average basis, expenditure on trade capacity building between 2001 and 2004 was $2.5 billion. Of this amount, $1.7 billion was for TD while $762 million went to TPR activities. Geographically, Africa is the largest recipient with $786 million (32 per cent) followed by Asia (see Figure 3.2). Between 2001 and 2004, expenditure on trade capacity building in Africa rose by close to 65 per cent compared to an increase of about 50 per cent for the world as a whole. These very large increases are consistent responses to the commitments made to boost long-term funding in the context of the Doha Declaration. Furthermore, African countries have derived benefits from these positive changes in funding for trade capacity building with a majority of them, the Least Developed Countries (LDCs) in particular, reporting significant increases for 2003 and 2004 (OECD 2004, 2005).

Figure 3.3 shows the main beneficiaries of trade capacity building in Africa. About 35 per cent of expenditure on trade capacity building in Africa goes to North Africa, with Egypt as the main beneficiary. Sub-Saharan Africa accounts for 65 per cent of expenditure on trade capacity building on the continent. The main beneficiaries in Sub-Saharan Africa are Uganda, South Africa, Ghana and Tanzania. In general, it is difficult to determine why some countries receive more support for trade capacity building than others at the same level of development. This is due in part to the fact that decisions on country selection are often based on unspecified considerations and even where there are established criteria for selection of beneficiaries, they are often vague and not transparent. For example, under the IF a recipient country must be at a preparatory stage in the development of a poverty-reduction strategy and is required to demonstrate commitment to integrating trade into its national development strategies. It is also required to prove that it has created an environment conducive to mainstreaming trade into its national plans. Clearly these are very difficult criteria to monitor, and there are concerns by LDCs that country selection under the IF is not sufficiently objective and transparent. In

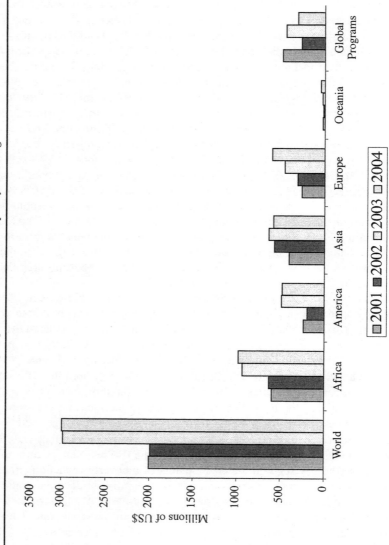

Figure 3.2   Regional Distribution of Expenditure on Trade Capacity Building

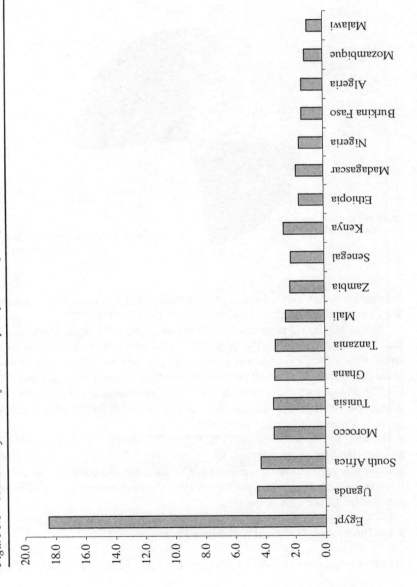

Figure 3.3 Main Beneficiaries of Trade Capacity Building in Africa (%)

Figure 3.4   Trade Development Expenditures in Africa (average for 2001–2004)

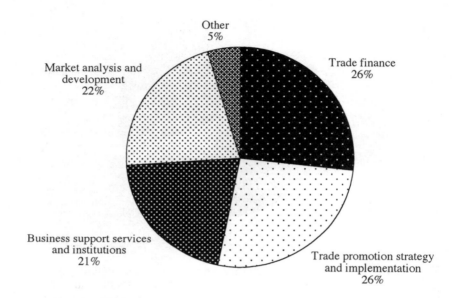

a recent survey of LDCs, seven out of ten respondents indicated that they were not aware of the IF country selection criteria (WTO 2003, 107).

Within Africa, TD accounts for 78 per cent of the total expenditure on trade capacity building while TPR accounts for 22 per cent. This is close to the world shares for TPR of 31 per cent and 69 per cent for TD. The distribution of expenditures on trade development in Africa is presented in Figure 3.4. Clearly, a large part of the expenditure goes to trade finance (26 per cent), trade promotion strategy and implementation (26 per cent) and business support services and institutions (21 per cent).

Turning to expenditures on TPR, Figure 3.5 shows that 31 per cent goes to trade facilitation procedures. Other activities which receive a substantial amount are: regional trade agreements (20 per cent) and trade mainstreaming in Poverty Reduction Strategy Papers (PRSPs) or development plans which account for 14 per cent of the total.

Joint Integrated Technical Assistance Program

JITAP is a response to calls by African countries to strengthen their capacity

Figure 3.5   Trade Policy and Regulation Expenditures in Africa (average for 2001–2004)

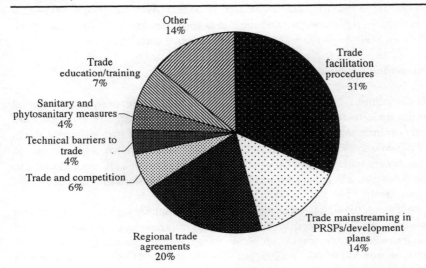

to negotiate and reap the benefits of the multilateral trading system. Consequently, the program was designed primarily to provide trade-related technical assistance and capacity building to these countries. It was launched in 1996 at the Ninth Session of the United Nations Conference on Trade and Development (UNCTAD), held in Midrand, South Africa. The program became operational in 1998. Funding for the program comes from several donors, but its implementation rests with three international organizations: the International Trade Center (ITC), the World Trade Organization (WTO) and UNCTAD.

JITAP has three key objectives: to build national capacity to understand the multilateral trading system; to adapt the domestic trading system of recipient countries to the obligations and disciplines of the multilateral trading system; and to increase the ability of recipient countries to take advantage of new trade opportunities by enhancing the readiness of exporters. The first phase of the program (JITAP I) covered the period 1998–2002 and had eight beneficiaries: Benin, Burkina Faso, Côte d'Ivoire, Ghana, Kenya, Tunisia, Uganda and Tanzania. While it has been widely acknowledged that the program contributed to greater awareness of trade negotiations among the participating countries, there were concerns that eligibility was limited to a few countries and that the program did not make any significant contribution to enhancing export competitiveness and lifting supply constraints (Luke 2002, 512; UNDP 2003,

338). A mid-term evaluation of the program was undertaken in August–September 2000 and led to the launching of a second phase of the program (JITAP II) in February 2003. The second phase covers the period 2003–2006 and includes eight new African countries as beneficiaries: Botswana, Cameroon, Malawi, Mali, Mauritania, Mozambique, Senegal and Zambia.

Integrated Framework

IF is a technical assistance and capacity-building program designed to respond to the trade-related problems of LDCs. It was inaugurated in October 1997 and is jointly managed by the World Bank, the International Monetary Fund, UNCTAD, the WTO, the ITC and the UNDP. It has two main objectives: to mainstream trade into the national development plans of LDCs and to assist in the coordinated delivery of trade-related technical assistance in response to the needs identified by the LDCs.

Although the IF has succeeded in sensitizing donors, agencies and recipient countries about the need to integrate trade into development strategies and programs, there are several problems with the program. First, it had a slow start. It was launched in 1997 but did not really get off the ground until 2000. Consequently, very little was achieved in the first three years of the program. Second, it did not pay attention to issues related to intra-regional trade and regional integration in general, even though there are several African initiatives in these areas aimed at boosting trade in the region. Third, the program failed to achieve its key objective of putting trade issues at the center of national, donor and agency priorities. The key reason why the first phase of IF failed is that there were unrealistic expectations by donors, recipients and the executing agencies. Recipient countries were asked to take on the complex task of identifying their trade capacity-building needs and so were expecting additional resources, but it was difficult to obtain the required funds from donors. Furthermore, executing agencies with diverse mandates and governance structures were expected to coordinate the delivery of technical assistance with no specific plan on how to achieve this objective.

Following a review of the IF process in 2000, a decision was made to revamp the program to enhance its effectiveness. The revamped IF takes more seriously the issue of integrating trade and trade-related activities into the development plans of LDCs, using the PRSPs as the main instrument. The second phase of the IF was initially implemented on a pilot basis in Cambodia, Madagascar and Mauritania. It was extended to eleven new countries in 2003, namely: Burundi, Djibouti, Eritrea, Ethiopia, Guinea, Lesotho, Malawi, Mali, Nepal, Senegal and Yemen. Despite changes made in the second phase of the program and the fact that it is too early to observe its developmental impact in recipient countries, it is becoming clear that the program faces serious challenges in realizing its objective of mainstreaming trade into national development strategies.

STATISTICAL ANALYSES OF TRADE CAPACITY BUILDING PROGRAMS

It is difficult to conduct a rigorous assessment of the impact of trade-related capacity building programs in recipient countries for a variety of reasons. First, the outcomes of some projects are intangible in the short run. For example, the impact of an investment in institutional capacity in a country is likely to be realized in the medium-to-long term, so it is difficult to conduct an assessment in the short run. Second, donor support for trade capacity building is not the only factor that affects capacity development in poor countries. Domestic government policies are also important. But it is often impossible to determine what proportion of a change in capacity development is due to donor-financed capacity building relative to changes in domestic policy. Third, until recently it was very difficult to find aggregate data on trade capacity building by country and by donor. The OECD and the WTO have addressed this issue by providing a database on trade capacity building. However, the data begins in 2001 and the most recent figures available are for 2004. Consequently, the data do not allow for statistical tests of trade capacity building in Africa using time series analysis.

In the light of these methodological and data limitations, this section does not attempt to provide evidence on the impact of trade capacity-building programs. Rather it presents cross-country correlations of trade capacity-building expenditures with domestic macroeconomic and social variables.[4] This gives an idea of the characteristics of the main beneficiaries of trade capacity-building programs and allows us to assess the implications of these characteristics for the effectiveness of capacity-building programs.

Eight variables are used in the analysis: expenditure on trade capacity building; the degree of government effectiveness; the quality of government regulation; the degree of political instability; the number of people with HIV/AIDS; school enrolment ratios; the volume of exports; and the degree of export diversification. The data on trade capacity building used in the analysis here is the sum of expenditures on Trade Policy and Regulations and on Trade Development. As indicated earlier, due to data limitations, the tests are based on cross-country data. Depending on data availability, we used averages of each variable over the period 2001–2004. In general, 46 Sub-Saharan African countries were included in the sample. However, for some of the variables data limitations resulted in a smaller sample size. The sources and definition of the variables can be found in the Appendix.

There are various methods for measuring the degree of association between variables. The most common of these is the correlation coefficient (also known as Pearson correlation). Despite its popularity, the Pearson correlation is very sensitive to outliers and assumes that the statistical distribution of variables is normal. However, for small samples the assumption of a normal distribution may be inappropriate. Because of these deficiencies, we also use nonparametric correlation measures which are distribution-free and not sensitive to outliers. These measures are the Spearman and the Kendall rank correlation tests (Leach 1979; Kruskal 1958).

Table 3.1 presents results of the statistical analysis. For the purpose of comparison we report results based on all three correlation tests, although our analysis will focus on the Spearman and Kendall tests because, as indicated earlier, they are more reliable than the Pearson test. One observation which is evident from the results is that the Spearman and Kendall correlation tests yield similar results for all the variables considered. For example, they show that across countries, there is a positive and statistically significant relationship between expenditure on trade capacity building and domestic regulatory quality. The Spearman and Kendall correlation coefficients are 0.42 and 0.31 and are statistically significant at conventional levels. In other words, countries which are main beneficiaries of trade capacity building tend to have better regulatory policies, in the sense that the burden imposed by domestic regulation in areas such as foreign trade and business development is relatively small.

For the government effectiveness variable, the Spearman and Kendall correlation coefficients are 0.34 and 0.25, respectively, and they are also statistically significant at conventional levels. This means that the main beneficiaries of trade capacity building tend to have more effective governments. In other words, governments of key recipient countries are able to implement good policies and deliver public goods. Interestingly, the results suggest that there is a positive relationship between expenditure on trade capacity building and political instability. Thus, the main beneficiaries of trade capacity building tend to have more political instability. However, the evidence is not strong, because the correlation coefficients are statistically insignificant at conventional levels. Turning to the HIV/AIDS variable, the tests indicate that it has a positive relationship with trade capacity building: countries which are main beneficiaries of trade capacity building tend to have more people living with HIV/AIDS. This result is worrisome, because it suggests that the HIV/AIDS epidemic poses serious risks to the sustainability of trade capacity-building programs in recipient countries. In contrast, the correlation between education (i.e. primary school enrollment ratios) and trade

*Table 3.1   Correlations of Trade Capacity Building with Variables in Sub-Saharan Africa**

		Parametric test**	Non-parametric test**	
Variables		Pearson correlation	Spearman rank correlation	Kendall rank correlation
Governance indicators	Regulatory quality	0.37 (0.01)	0.42 (0.00)	0.31 (0.00)
	Government effectiveness	0.34 (0.02)	0.34 (0.02)	0.25 (0.02)
Political instability		−0.12 (0.55)	0.17 (0.38)	0.09 (0.53)
HIV/AIDS		0.50 (0.00)	0.43 (0.01)	0.31 (0.01)
Education		0.03 (0.86)	−0.12 (0.44)	−0.08 (0.43)
Export volumes		0.41 (0.00)	0.31 (0.04)	0.23 (0.03)
Export diversification		−0.27 (0.14)	0.05 (0.78)	0.04 (0.76)

Notes:

*The number of Sub-Saharan African countries in the sample is 46, except for HIV (37), export diversification (31) and political instability (28).

**P-values are in parenthesis.

capacity building is negative and statistically insignificant. We experimented with other measures of education such as total public expenditure on education and expenditure on primary and secondary education. However, there was no significant difference in the results. We did not use a variable capturing tertiary education because of data limitations.

With respect to exports, the results suggest that there is a positive and statistically significant relationship between trade capacity building and export volumes across countries. This means that the main beneficiaries of trade capacity building tend to export more and thus are more likely to achieve their export promotion objectives. Turning to export diversification, the results suggest that it has a positive relationship with trade capacity building, but the correlation is not statistically significant at conventional levels.

In summary, the results indicate that the main beneficiaries of trade capacity-building programs in the region tend to have more effective government, better regulatory frameworks and more exports. However, they also tend to have a higher number of people living with HIV/AIDS. Consequently, the results suggest that the HIV/AIDS epidemic poses serious risks to the effectiveness of trade capacity development in the region.

A PRAGMATIC APPROACH TO TRADE CAPACITY BUILDING

There is no doubt that some progress, albeit modest, has been made in trade capacity building in developing countries, and Africa in particular. Relative to the situation during the Uruguay Round, the region is more active in negotiations, and several countries are beginning to make informed proposals on some of the issues under negotiation in the Doha Round. That notwithstanding, there is a growing recognition that more needs to be done by both the international community and Sub-Saharan African countries themselves to enhance the effectiveness of existing capacity-building programs. In this section we argue that existing technical assistance and capacity-building programs would be more effective if they pay more attention to the underlying reasons for capacity constraints in Sub-Saharan African countries. There are at least five core reasons for capacity constraints.

Poor Educational Systems

Several countries in the region do not have the required capacity to participate effectively in trade negotiations because the educational systems have not been able to produce the quantity and, sometimes, caliber of economists needed to deal with trade issues in an era of globalization. Furthermore, in several countries, there is a mismatch between domestic needs and the training provided by universities. The curriculum does not adequately reflect the needs of the country on trade issues. For years there was more focus on professional areas such as law, medicine and engineering. Consequently, in several countries the supply of experts in these areas exceeds the demand. Furthermore, although several universities have economics departments, until recently trade negotiation techniques hardly featured in the curriculum of these departments. In countries where curriculum mismatch is not a problem, there is severe pressure on the educational system because the demand for skills on trade issues is growing faster than the supply from universities. Consequently, providing a long-term solution to the problem requires looking at the educational systems in these countries, particularly the tertiary sector.

Poor Information Access

Many of these countries lack access to information on international trade policy and market developments due largely to poor or inadequate infrastructure and facilities. Access to information on trade issues is essential for effective policymaking and exploiting new opportunities arising from the multilateral trading system. Recent advances in information and communication technologies (ICTs) have made it relatively easier to access and exchange information among people. However, exploiting the potential of ICTs requires access to computers and telecommunications equipment which are costly and hence not readily available to Africans. Table 3.2 shows that in 2002 the number of telephone mainlines per 1000 people was 15 in Sub-Saharan Africa compared to 169 in Latin America and the Caribbean, 107 in the Middle East and North Africa and 131 in East Asia and the Pacific. Compounding these problems is the fact that libraries on the continent are often not well financed and as a consequence do not have relevant information which individuals could consult to increase their level of awareness and understanding of trade policies and negotiations.

Brain Drain

Brain drain is a serious problem in several countries in the region. The problem is often caused and exacerbated by dysfunctional social and economic environments which force African intellectuals to migrate to developed countries in search of better living conditions. Available data indicate that one-third of professionals born in Africa live abroad. In addition, the International Organization for Migration (1999) suggests that more than 35 per cent of college graduates in 40 per cent of countries in Africa reside abroad. Political instability has also contributed to the mass exodus of educated Africans to developed countries and there is evidence that this outflow has a direct negative effect on economic growth in Sub-Saharan Africa (Gyimah-Brempong 2003, 275). It also affects economic growth indirectly through a reduction in human and physical capital formation.

HIV/AIDS

HIV/AIDS is the most serious downside risk to long-term capacity building in African countries. It can hinder the development of capacity in trade by

Table 3.2   Infrastructure Indicators by Region

Country Group/Region	Electric power consumption per capita (kilowatt)	Telephone mainline per 1,000 people	Paved roads (% of total roads)	Population with access to safe water (%)	Population with access to sanitation (%)
Lower Middle Income	970	100	31	80	50
East Asia and Pacific	891	131	23	78	49
Europe and Central Asia	2808	228	87	92	82
Latin America and Caribbean	1506	169	27	89	75
South Asia	344	34	43	84	34
Middle East and North Africa	1412	107	64	88	76
Sub-Saharan Africa	457	15	13	59	37

Sources: 2005 World Bank's Africa Database. All data from 2002 except paved roads (1999).

Table 3.3   Estimated and Projected Loss of Labor Force in 2000 and 2020 (%)

Country	2000	2020
Namibia	3.0	26.0
Botswana	6.6	23.2
Zimbabwe	9.6	22.7
Mozambique	2.3	20.0
South Africa	3.9	19.9
Kenya	3.9	16.8
Malawi	5.8	13.8
Uganda	12.8	13.7
Tanzania	5.8	12.7
Central African Republic	6.3	12.6
Côte d'Ivoire	5.6	11.4
Cameroon	2.9	10.7

Source: Food and Agriculture Organization (2001).

threatening the formation of human capital and reducing the growth rate of the labor force. A 2001 publication by the Food and Agricultural Organization (FAO) shows that in the ten most affected African countries the projected decrease in the labor force in 2020 is 10–26 per cent (see Table 3.3). There is no doubt that labor losses of this magnitude have serious implications for economic growth and development. The United Nations (2003) has also shown that in some affected countries, the epidemic could lower GDP growth by 2–4 percentage points.

Expatriate Dependency

The inappropriate use of expatriate technical assistance in some donor-funded programs has created a dependency syndrome and made it more difficult for African countries to develop internal capacity, hence creating the need for more technical assistance. One of the reasons for this outcome is that donor-funded projects often come with restrictions on what recipient countries can or cannot do (Solignac-Lecomte 2003, 21). For example, they often require recipient countries to use consultants from donor countries even though the cost of recruiting foreign consultants is significantly higher than the cost of recruiting an equally qualified local expert (Aryeetey, Osei and Quartey 2003, 17).

A ROAD MAP FOR THE FUTURE

Given these reasons for low capacity in African countries, we believe that five steps are necessary to find a durable, long-term solution to the region's trade-capacity problems. First, African governments must create an enabling environment which would provide the incentives for individuals in both the public and private sectors to pay more attention to the development of human capacity. The emphasis here is for the government to create an environment which encourages individuals to take the initiative to develop their own capacities rather than relying solely on the government.[5] This would require, for example, providing scholarships to individuals who are interested in obtaining degrees in trade policy. It would also require investments in health and education, good governance and policies which engender political and macroeconomic stability.

Second, institutional development requires strengthening educational and research institutions through providing greater, stable financial support; creating better working conditions for teachers and university staff; providing more and better library facilities; and restructuring the educational curriculum to ensure that it reflects the needs of the country on trade issues. Furthermore, to ensure the sustainability of the programs, more emphasis should be placed on institutional capacity building, and efforts should be made to ensure that it complements individual capacity development. An exclusive focus on individual capacity building is risky because some individuals are likely to leave the public sector after they have been trained and therefore cannot assume roles which the government would like them to play in trade negotiations. Furthermore, even in cases where individuals do not leave the public sector, there is a likelihood that they may be transferred to departments where their training in trade may be of limited use to the government.

Third, and most important, decision makers and society must change their attitudes toward policy analysis. They need to be convinced of the need and value of scientific research as an input in decision making. This is necessary to develop a culture which respects knowledge and also to channel efforts toward policy analysis, not administrative processes and procedures. It would also solve the problem of underutilization of professionals in the public sector and encourage government departments to broaden and conserve internal capacity by offering training opportunities to their officials so that they do not lose valued skills on the job.

Fourth, private-sector development is necessary to enable countries to take advantage of trade opportunities which arise from bilateral and multilateral trade liberalization. This change requires creating political and macroeconomic policy environments conducive to economic activities, developing a relationship of trust between the public and private sectors, providing better infrastructure to enhance competitiveness and diversifying exports to reduce vulnerability to external shocks.

Finally, there is the need to address the threats to long-term capacity building in Africa posed by political instability and the HIV/AIDS epidemic. Given the devastating effects of these phenomena on African economies, they can no longer be regarded simply as economic problems but should more appropriately be viewed as severe development crises. When viewed in this light it becomes clear that no capacity-building program can create a sustainable trade capacity in the region without dealing effectively with these issues.

The important lesson which flows from this analysis is the need for a comprehensive approach to trade capacity building in Africa. Obviously, this is not an easy task and will impose enormous challenges on African governments, donors and executing agencies.

Challenges for African Governments

The first challenge for African countries is to balance the degree of attention and priority given to trade and trade capacity building compared to other development concerns. This is particularly important given limited resources and the fact that devoting more resources to trade capacity building would imply spending less on other development priorities. A second challenge is how to reduce the risk of policy reversals arising, for example, from frequent changes of government and ensure the sustainability of trade capacity-building programs. As indicated earlier, complementary domestic policies are needed for trade capacity-building programs to have sustainable impact in recipient countries. Stability and continuity of domestic policies is therefore important. A third challenge facing African countries is how to ensure that all stakeholders participate actively in the process. Sustainable capacity development cannot be achieved without the active involvement of the private sector, civil society, individuals and non-governmental organizations. There is a need to develop a mechanism to foster stakeholder dialogue on trade capacity building. Finally, coordination and timely exchange of information must be encouraged among the various ministries and departments to ensure that there is policy coherence. In several countries policy changes are made in one ministry without consultation with other relevant ministries to ascertain how the proposed changes might affect their programs and objectives.

Challenges for Donors

Donors also face serious challenges in building trade capacity in African countries. First, how can they increase program coordination? The multiplicity of programs increases costs and reduces the effectiveness of the assistance rendered. Second, how can donors reduce the risk of biased aid? This bias is sometimes reflected in the insistence of donors that recipients use consultants from their countries on projects they finance. It is also sometimes reflected in the choice of which trade capacity-building programs donors choose to finance. In the past some donors have financed programs simply because they create more market access for their exporters in the recipient countries (Deere 2004, 14).Third, how can donors ensure that there is local ownership of the programs? Most donor programs emphasize this issue. However, in practice, the process adopted in the implementation of these programs makes it difficult for recipient countries to take full ownership of the programs and outcome. Finally, how can donors generate sufficient funds domestically to support trade capacity-building programs in recipient countries?

Challenges for Executing Agencies

The main challenge facing executing agencies is how to coordinate their trade capacity-building efforts with those of other agencies with diverse mandates and governance structures. Better collaboration among agencies would facilitate agreements on objectives, sequencing of activities and division of labor. Improved coordination would also save resources and enhance the effectiveness of the assistance provided. Another challenge facing executing agencies is how to resist the temptation to focus on outputs rather than outcomes. Finally, there is also the issue of how to ensure the sustainability of project outcomes and create an incentive for recipient countries to develop the ability to help themselves rather than relying on external assistance.

TRADE CAPACITY-BUILDING AND DEVELOPMENT STRATEGIES

There is now widespread recognition and acknowledgement that long-term trade capacity building cannot be done in isolation. It must be integrated into a country's overall development strategy (OECD 2001, 22). This requires mainstreaming trade into national development plans in order to ensure policy coherence. Trade mainstreaming encompasses a host of issues and measures necessary to realize the potential of trade for growth and poverty reduction. These include ensuring that trade reforms have a pro-poor agenda; bringing together ministries of trade, finance, planning and other relevant departments to work together in the design and implementation of a national trade agenda;

ensuring that trade, macroeconomic and regulatory policies complement each other; dealing with market access impediments and strengthening the capacity to trade and exploit trading opportunities.

Despite the widespread recognition of the need for mainstreaming, it is clear that African countries have so far not been successful in effectively integrating trade policies and programs into their national development plans. There are two reasons for this situation. First, mainstreaming is not a costless activity. It requires resources, and African countries have so far not been able to garner the resources necessary to make a significant impact in this area. Donors encourage African countries to embark on programs aimed at mainstreaming but have not really devoted enough resources to it. This means that if African countries want to push this agenda forward, they would have to divert resources from other activities. Second, the approach to mainstreaming adopted in most trade capacity-building programs relies heavily on the Poverty Reduction Strategy Paper as an instrument. However, the coverage of trade in existing PRSPs is limited (Hewitt and Gillson 2003, 11). Furthermore, existing PRSPs do not adequately address the link between trade policy and poverty reduction and so have not been effective vehicles for mainstreaming trade into national development strategies in Sub-Saharan Africa.

One reason why African countries have not been able to use the PRSP to mainstream trade into national development strategies is that it is simply not ideally suited for this sort of exercise (Powell 2002, 10). The PRSP was originally designed to ensure that funds made available through HIPC (Highly Indebted Poor Countries) debt relief are used for poverty reduction programs in recipient countries. Consequently, international financial institutions are heavily involved in the process, making it difficult for recipient countries to have meaningful and complete local ownership of the process and outcomes. Hewitt and Gillson (2003, 17) provide evidence suggesting that in practice international financial institutions have strong influence over the choices made in PRSPs. This lack of complete local ownership of the PRSP process diminishes its effectiveness as an instrument for mainstreaming trade because ownership and participation by local stakeholders are essential ingredients of successful mainstreaming programs. For trade mainstreaming to have a chance to be successful in the region, African countries should enhance policy coherence by addressing the following issues.

Inadequate Statistics

To ensure coherence between trade priorities and national development strategies, it is important for policymakers to understand the structural relationships that exist in an economy. There is also the need for reliable information and timely monitoring of events in the economy, which in turn requires access to reliable data. The fact that African countries do not have easy access to reliable data poses a serious problem. Improvements in data collection and analysis should therefore be incorporated in the trade mainstreaming agenda.

Regional and Multilateral Negotiations

Ensuring consistency between positions taken in the European Union – African, Caribbean and Pacific Countries (EU-ACP) Economic Partnership Arrangements (EPAS) and the WTO negotiation processes is another issue that must be addressed. The fact that African countries tend to have different negotiators dealing with EPAS and WTO creates serious problems. It increases the resource costs of these negotiations. It also reduces the effectiveness of African countries in the negotiations because their representatives in Brussels and Geneva do not have a coherent mechanism to coordinate their activities, exchange information and ensure the consistency of their positions. Clearly, these problems arising from trade negotiations have implications for government budgets and the achievement of trade as well as national development goals.

Loss of Policy Space

WTO membership requires African countries to obey the rules of the multilateral trading system. For example, they are required to lower tariffs on imported goods. But several countries in the region rely on tariffs as an important source of government revenue. The loss of this stable and reliable source of development finance has implications for the provision of health, infrastructure and education services. African countries therefore face the challenge of finding ways to deal with the possible loss of domestic policy space and instruments resulting from binding commitments made under the multilateral trading system. An effective mainstreaming program should incorporate mechanisms for dealing with this challenge.

Compensation of Potential Losers

The trade reforms associated with mainstreaming will create winners and losers in the economy, and governments will have to find ways to compensate the potential losers in order to avoid conflicts. This is a major challenge, given the fact that most African countries do not have social safety nets. To increase the likelihood of grassroots support and participation of key stakeholders in mainstreaming programs, African governments must find ways to cushion the effects of trade reforms on vulnerable groups.

Private Sector Participation

A crucial aspect of mainstreaming trade into the national development strategy is the need to increase the roles of the private sector and civil society in the trade negotiation and development processes. This is a daunting task for African countries because of the fragile relationship between the public and private sector. Why is the private sector important? Trade policies and negotiations are typically done by national governments. But private-sector response is critical in taking advantage of any trading opportunities which result from liberalization. The interests of the two groups sometimes conflict, and it is not always the case that government positions are welfare-enhancing for society at large. The views of African countries on trade facilitation provide a very good example of the possible differences in opinion and interests of the public and private sectors in trade negotiations. While most African countries are hesitant to engage in trade facilitation due in part to valid concerns about implementation costs, exporting firms in the private sector see it as a welcome development which would reduce bottlenecks and enhance their competitiveness in foreign markets. These conflicts and differences of interests underscore the need for the private sector and civil society to have proper representation in the formulation of strategies and positions for trade negotiations.

CONCLUSION

There is no doubt that trade, if well managed, could play a very important role in the economic development of African countries. It provides easy access to foreign exchange, new technology and more consumer choice. It also increases the efficient use of resources through increased competition and allows the exploitation of economies of scale associated with enlarged market size. African countries have recognized the need to be active participants in the international trading system. Since the 1990s, they have shown more interest in trade policy and multilateral negotiations. There has also been a resurgence of interest in regional integration as a means to improve the competitiveness of African economies and integrate them into the multilateral trading system. Notwithstanding this new interest in trade and the multilateral trading system, it is clear that countries in the region have not been able to participate effectively due largely to capacity constraints.

Efforts have been made by the international community to address these problems through an increase in the provision of technical assistance and capacity-building programs. While useful, these programs have had limited success so far, reflecting partly the fact that their scope as well as objectives are often not clear, and partly the fact that they do not really address some of the root causes of poor domestic trade capacity in African countries. It is also a consequence of the fact that donors' actual financial commitments to these programs are quite small relative to what is needed to have substantial impact on capacity building in the region.

We propose a more pragmatic approach to long-term trade capacity building which focuses on the underlying reasons for low capacity building in the region and recognizes three facts, namely trade capacity building cannot be done in isolation; will have maximum impact if it is tackled as part of general capacity building problems of African countries and will have a sustainable impact only if the risks posed by political instability, brain drain and the HIV/AIDS epidemic are quickly and adequately addressed. Furthermore, building trade capacity is not an end in itself. It is useful to the extent that it enables countries to participate more effectively in negotiations, obtain a fair share of the benefits of trade and reduce poverty. If African countries approach it from this perspective they are more likely to make significant progress in reducing the incidence of poverty on the continent through trade.

NOTES

1. For example, relative to other regions of the world, the HIV/AIDS epidemic is a serious constraint to human capital formation in several African countries and so must be given more weight in any framework designed to provide long-term solutions to Africa's trade capacity building problems. To appreciate the magnitude of the problem, note that although Sub-Saharan Africa accounts for 10 per cent of the world's population, it is home to about 70 per cent (25 million) of the people with HIV (UNAIDS 2004, p. 6).

2. The Singapore Issues are trade facilitation, investment, competition policy and transparency in government procurement. In the Doha Round negotiations, these issues generated heated controversies between developed and developing countries and contributed to the collapse of the WTO Ministerial Conference in Cancun. In an attempt to revive the stalled talks and save the Doha Round, WTO members agreed on 31 July 2004, to take investment, competition policy and transparency in government procurement, out of the Doha agenda.

3. There is also expenditure on infrastructure but we do not include this because it is not clear what per centage of this expenditure is trade-related. Trade Policy and Regulations covers support to aid recipients' effective participation in multilateral negotiations, analysis and implementation of multilateral trade agreements, trade-related legislation and regulatory reforms, trade facilitation, support to regional trade agreements, and human resource development in trade. Trade Development covers business development and activities aimed at improving the business climate, access to trade finance, and trade promotion and market development in the productive and service sectors, including at institutional and enterprise level (OECD 2003, p. 3).

4. The macroeconomic and social variables used in the analyses capture whether or not a country

has the complementary domestic policies necessary for trade capacity building to have the desired effect in a recipient country. Clearly, an enabling environment is needed for capacity development to flourish. Whether or not a country has an enabling environment is determined by the degree of political stability, the extent of governance and the nature of domestic economic and social policies on education and epidemics such as HIV/AIDS.

5. The presumption in several African countries is that the responsibility for capacity building rests with the government. While this may be true, it is becoming obvious that the government does not have the resources or the ability to do this alone. The private sector and individuals in particular must be more active in the process.

BIBLIOGRAPHY

Aryeetey, Ernest, Barfour Osei and Peter Quartey (2003), 'Does Tying Aid make it More Costly? A Ghanaian Case Study', manuscript, Institute of Statistical, Social and Economic Research, University of Ghana.

Deere, Carolyn (2004), 'Capacity Building and Policy Coherence: A Role for a Leaders' Level G20?', Paper presented at a meeting on 'Breaking the Deadlock in Agricultural Trade Reform and Development', Oxford, England, 8–9 June.

Dessus, Sébastien, Jean-Dominique Lafay and Christian Morrisson (1998), 'A Politico-economic Model for Stabilisation in Africa', *Journal of African Economies*, **7** (1), 91–119.

Finger, J. Michael and Philip Schuler (2002), 'Implementation of WTO Commitments: The Development Challenge', in Bernard Hoekman, Aditya Mattoo and Philip English (eds), *Development, Trade and the WTO*, Washington DC: World Bank, pp. 493–503.

Food and Agriculture Organization (2001), 'The Impact of HIV/AIDS on Food Security', Report for the 27th Session of the Committee on World Food Security, Rome, 21 May–1 June.

Gyimah-Brempong, Kwabena (2003), 'Political Instability', in Emmanuel Nnadozie (ed.), *African Economic Development*, New York: Academic Press, pp. 259–94.

Hewitt, Adrian and Ian Gillson (2003), 'A Review of the Trade and Poverty Content in PRSPs and Loan-Related Documents', manuscript, Overseas Development Institute, London.

International Organization for Migration (1999), 'Return of Qualified African Nationals Programme', International Organization for Migration Fact Sheet, July.

Kaufmann, Daniel, Aart Kraay and Massimo Mastruzzi (2003), 'Governance Matters III: Governance Indicators 1996-2002', Washington, DC, World Bank Policy Research Working Paper No. 3106.

——(2005), 'Governance Matters IV: Governance Indicators 1996–2004', Washington, DC, World Bank Policy Research Working Paper No. 3630.

Kruskal, William (1958), Ordinal Measures of Association', *Journal of the American Statistical Association*, **53**, 814–61.

Land, Tony and Apollinaire Ndorukwigira (2001), 'Proceedings of the Workshop on Operational Approaches to Institutional and Capacity Development', African Capacity Building Foundation, Harare, Zimbabwe.

Leach, Chris (1979), *Introduction to Statistics: A Nonparametric Approach for the Social Sciences*, New York: Wiley.

Luke, David (2002), 'Trade-related Capacity Building for Enhanced African

Participation in the Global Economy', in Bernard Hoekman, Aditya Mattoo and Philip English (eds), *Development, Trade and the WTO*, Washington DC: World Bank, pp. 509–16.

Organization for Economic Cooperation and Development (2001), *The DAC Guidelines: Strengthening Trade Capacity for Development*, Paris: Organization for Economic Cooperation and Development.

—— (2002), *Regional Integration in Africa*, Paris: Organization for Economic Cooperation and Development.

——(2003), 'Second Joint WTO/OECD Report on Trade-related Technical Assistance and Capacity Building', at http://www.oecd.org/dac/trade.

——(2004), '2004 Joint WTO/OECD Report on Trade-related Technical Assistance and Capacity Building', at http://www.oecd.org/dac/trade.

——(2005), '2005 Joint WTO/OECD Report on Trade-related Technical Assistance and Capacity Building', at http://www.oecd.org/dac/trade.

Powell, Jeff (2002), 'Cornering the Market: The World Bank and Trade Capacity Building', London, Bretton Woods Project Briefing Paper.

Prowse, Susan (2002), 'The Role of National and International Agencies in Trade-Related Capacity Building', *World Economy*, **25** (9), 1235–61.

Solignac-Lecomte, Henri-Bernard (2003), 'Building Capacity to Trade: What are the Priorities?', Paris, OECD Development Center Working Paper No. 223.

Stiglitz, Joseph and Andrew Charlton (2004), 'The Development Round of Trade Negotiations in the Aftermath of Cancun', Report for the Commonwealth Secretariat and the Initiative for Policy Dialogue.

Tandon, Yash (2002), 'Evaluation of WTO and other Forms of Technical Assistance to Developing Countries in the Context of the Uruguay Round of Agreements', Paper presented at the ILEAP Launching Conference, Nairobi, Kenya.

UNAIDS (2004), *2004 Report on the Global AIDS Epidemic*, Geneva: United Nations Joint Programme on AIDS.

UNCTAD (2004), *Handbook of Statistics*, New York: United Nations.

UNDP (2003), *Making Global Trade Work for People*, London: Earthscan Publications.

United Nations (2003), *The Impact of AIDS*, New York: United Nations.

Whalley, John (1999), 'Building Poor Countries' Trade Capacity', University of Warwick, UK, Centre for the Study of Globalization and Regionalization (CSGR) Working Paper No. 25/99.

WTO (2002), *Doha Declarations*, Geneva: World Trade Organization.

WTO (2003), 'Final Report of the Evaluation of the Integrated Framework', WT/IFSC/6/Rev.2, November.

APPENDIX

1. Trade capacity building data is defined as the sum of expenditures on trade development and trade policy and regulations. See OECD/WTO Database at http://tcbdb.wto.org.
2. Export volume data were obtained from UNCTAD *Handbook of Statistics, 2004*.
3. Export diversification index is from the UNCTAD *Handbook of Statistics, 2004*.
4. HIV/AIDS is the estimated number of adults (15–49) living with HIV. The data are from UNAIDS, *2004 Report on the Global AIDS Epidemic*.
5. The education variable is defined as the primary school enrolment ratio obtained from UNESCO Database and African Development Bank Report for 2005.
6. Two governance variables were used: government effectiveness and regulatory framework. Government effectiveness covers the quality of policymaking, bureaucracy and public service delivery. Regulatory quality covers perceptions of market-unfriendly policies and burdens imposed by excessive regulation. For more information on the definition and computation of these variables see Kaufmann, Kraay and Mastruzzi, "Governance Indicators: 1996–2004" (2003 and 2005) at http://www.worldbank.org/wbi/governance/govdata.
7. Political instability data were obtained from the ADB's African Economic Outlook 2004/2005. The data captures political troubles such as strikes, demonstrations, overthrow of governments, and other forms of unrest and violence. For further details on the construction of the index see Dessus, Lafay and Morrisson (1998).

4. Rent-seeking Behaviors and the Perpetuation of Aid Dependence: The Donor-Side Story

Jean-Claude Berthélemy

Transition from aid dependence is a very difficult process in a number of developing countries, particularly in sub-Saharan Africa, where aid dependence has regularly increased over the past decades. Certainly, a number of internal factors prevent this transition process, but it may be also impeded by external factors. In this chapter I concentrate on one peculiar aspect which is related to political economy. In short, aid dependence remains very high because there are economic agents who have vested interests in maintaining the aid system. As far as internal factors are concerned, this argument has been already studied. Svensson (2000) has shown that foreign assistance can trigger rent-seeking in recipient countries. According to this author, 'The mere expectation of aid may suffice to increase rent-dissipation and reduce productive public spending.' This rent-seeking behavior creates forces within the recipient countries which favor the perpetuation of aid dependence, that is in the interest of the rent-seekers.

The donors may also have a role to play in this story. In his study, Svensson concluded that commitments related to foreign aid policy could solve the problem of rent-seeking triggered by aid flows. However, in the donor countries there are also economic agents who have their own vested interest in the aid business, and these agents may have a say, directly or indirectly, in aid allocation decisions. A successful transition from aid dependence will be unlikely if donor policies are themselves influenced by rent-seekers, who gain from the existence of aid dependence. To support this analysis, I will use this chapter to provide some empirical evidence pointing to the influence of such vested interests on aid-allocation decisions taken by donor countries.

A related observation frequently mentioned in the literature describing aid allocation by bilateral donors is that aid is, to some extent, granted by donors to serve their own interests, meaning that aid allocation is influenced by a *bilateralism bias.* There are, however, two possible kinds of bilateralism biases in aid donor policies: political and economic. Political biases are related to the geopolitical interests of the donor countries and may be immune from rent-seeking behaviors, at least in circumstances where they are based on purely political objectives, such as the East–West confrontation during the Cold War. Economic biases are related to economic benefits which some influential economic agents in the donor countries may expect from the supply, by their government, of aid flows to recipients who are potential clients or business partners. They may, more than the political biases, truly reveal rent-seeking behaviors within the donor countries.

The recent literature on aid allocation has been greatly influenced by Alesina and Dollar (2000), who emphasize the colonial and other political biases of donor policies, rather than the economic bias. In this chapter, I attempt to fill this gap. According to Alesina and Dollar,

> The allocation of bilateral aid across recipient countries provides evidence as to why it is not more effective at promoting growth and poverty reduction. Factors such as colonial past and voting patterns in the United Nations explain more of the distribution of aid than the political institutions or economic policy of the recipient.

I fully recognize the role of such political factors, and therefore the existence of a political bilateralism bias in aid allocation decisions, but I submit that the economic component of the bilateralism bias may be at least equally significant. In particular, bilateralism behaviors may be associated with commercial stakes. Aid flows create benefits for the donor's producers who are involved in business with the recipient. In this sense aid allocation decisions may be very much influenced by rent-seeking behaviors in donor countries, and in that case rent-seekers in the North have common interests with rent-seekers in the South in the perpetuation of aid dependence.

To sort out the different factors that may influence aid allocation decisions, I estimate a complete aid-allocation equation, using a yearly panel of bilateral aid commitments granted by 22 OECD/DAC bilateral donors to 137 developing country recipients during the 1980s and 1990s. This extremely rich data source provides a way to estimate an aid allocation equation that incorporates both the generally accepted explanatory variables related to recipient needs and merits and geopolitical and economic variables that may capture the donor-interest motives. The latter set of variables provides a concrete definition of the bilateralism bias in bilateral aid allocation decisions; that is, they measure the extent to which aid allocation is influenced by factors related to donor-recipient bilateral relations rather than merely by the needs and merits of the recipients.

In section two I discuss which variables can be introduced to capture the influence of both the donor self-interest and the recipient needs and merits on bilateral aid allocation patterns. I review in section three some econometric issues to be solved, and I provide a summary of my econometric estimations of the aid allocation equation. Such estimates are used in section four to evaluate the effect of the bilateralism bias, to compare its political and economic components, and to discuss its consequences on overall aid patterns. In section five, I provide some further empirical evidence through a comparison of behaviors of the different donors. I conclude with some considerations on the architecture of the international aid system.

DONOR SELF INTEREST AND RECIPIENT NEEDS/ MERITS VARIABLES

Since the contributions of McKinley and Little (1977, 1978a, 1978b, 1979) and Dudley and Montmarquette (1976), as well as Maizels and Nissanke (1984) and many others, there has been a long debate in the development-finance literature on the question of the true motives behind development assistance: Do bilateral donors grant their assistance to recipient countries in view of improving the development perspectives of those recipients and of reducing poverty or is this assistance driven by self-interested motives?

There is a growing consensus in the most recent literature (see, for example, Berthélemy and Tichit 2004 and Neumayer 2003) that both types of variables help to explain aid allocation decisions. Conversely, multilateral aid is generally viewed as exempt of self-interested behaviors, with the exception of some papers linking IMF/World Bank decisions with U.S. interests.

The self-interest-of-donor argument may be linked to several objectives pursued by the donors. One of them is geopolitical. The usual assumption in the previous literature is that providing aid to a recipient may influence this recipient's attitude in favor of the donor. In this context, it is usually assumed that a donor will provide assistance to recipients who are like-minded or, at any rate, potential political allies. Alesina and Dollar (2000) use data on votes at the UN to measure such a political-alliance effect. However, political alliance may be a result as well as a determinant of aid allocation. Another possibility is to link this political-alliance factor to the colonial past of the donors. A related argument suggests a link to internal politics: Lahiri and Raimondos-Møller (2000) propose a theoretical model in which lobbying by ethnic groups may influence aid patterns. They illustrate this analysis with data showing the significant amounts of aid given by the United Kingdom to India, the United States to Israel, Germany to Turkey and France to Cameroon. They conclude that, assuming that there is a positive correlation between ethnic composition and the colonial experience of a donor country, this may explain why former colonies are usually major recipients of official development assistance from their former colonial rulers.

In this chapter I use a combination of dummy variables for former colonial ties and for other broad geopolitical interests of the donors to capture these effects:

- Dummy variables for former colonies of Belgium, France, Portugal, Spain and the United Kingdom.
- A dummy variable for the pair USA–Egypt, because Egypt has received large amounts of assistance from the United States since its peace accords with Israel. If Israel were in my database, I would need obviously to introduce a similar dummy variable for its link with the United States, but Israel is no longer a developing country, and I consider here only developing country recipients.
- A dummy variable capturing the close ties that exist between the USA and Latin American countries.
- A dummy variable capturing the geopolitical interest of Japan in assisting Asian developing countries.

I also tested whether European Union countries were giving more assistance across the board to ACP countries (associated states from Africa, the Caribbean and the Pacific Ocean), to whom the EU/European Community has granted preferential treatment since 1963, but this variable is never significant in my regressions. As shown by Grilli and Riess (1992), there is possibly a bias in the aid budget managed by the European Commission towards ACPs, but, according to my estimations, this bias is not revealed by bilateral aid data when all other factors are controlled.

Aid may be used also to deepen commercial linkages with a recipient. Not all donors have strong geopolitical interests, but all of them have exporters and importers which have trade interests. A donor's foreign assistance policy based on his business sector interests will typically be biased toward countries which tend naturally to have more trade with him. This is, after all, the clear motive of tied aid, that persists despite continuous OECD/DAC efforts to keep it under control. Therefore, following Berthélemy and Tichit (2004), I have also introduced commercial interest motives, as measured by the flow of bilateral trade (imports + exports) with the recipient country, expressed as a percentage of the donor GDP. There might be a simultaneity bias when aid is tied, since more tied aid will imply more imports from the donor. However, the risk is limited because I am working on aid commitment flows, and aid disbursements usually lag behind commitments, particularly for project loans or grants which require building new equipment. In order to be on the safe side, I have lagged this variable.

The combination of the geopolitical dummies and the trade-intensity variable will define what I call the bilateralism effect in my aid allocation equations.

As a complement, it is useful to consider financial motives, particularly for the period under observation, during which a large number of recipients has been affected by a debt crisis. This is known as the 'defensive lending' argument in the debt-crisis literature (see, for example, Birdsall, Claessens and Diwan 2003). Donors could be locked in a 'debt game', in which they have to provide new resources to highly indebted countries simply to prevent these debtors from falling into arrears, whatever the quality of economic management among these debtors and their responsibilities in the debt crisis. However, it is not possible to include this argument in the bilateralism effect for two reasons. First, theoretically speaking, a donor cannot protect its own financial interest alone through defensive lending, because refinancing and other financial relief mechanisms are usually subjected to a burden-sharing rule, for instance under the auspices of the Paris Club. Second, bilateral debt data are hardly accessible – when they even exist. Nevertheless, I will introduce a debt-burden variable, defined as the ratio of net present value of debt over export, as an explanatory variable in my aid allocation equations. Although this variable cannot be taken into account in the 'bilateralism effect', it may be interpreted to some extent as a self-interest variable. There is, however, some irreducible ambiguity in this interpretation, because one could also argue that a heavy debt burden increases the needs of the debtor, which could motivate donor assistance.

Let me turn now to the development motives behind aid. These development motives are, according to most donor statements, the actual motives for their assistance programs. Such motives can be captured by the introduction of two different categories of variables. The first category is based on the argument that aid is granted to the neediest countries for the sake of poverty alleviation. The second category takes into account the issue of aid efficiency: if the objective is poverty alleviation, then aid should be given to recipients where it can have an impact on poverty and that may depend on the quality of economic policies in recipient countries and on the governance of these countries.

The most straightforward indicator of beneficiary needs is income per capita, measured at international prices (in purchasing power parity terms). If aid is to be allocated on the basis of recipient needs, the poorest countries should receive more and the richest countries less.

The quality of economic policies is more difficult to measure. I have tried several policy variables similar to those introduced by Burnside and Dollar (2000), such as openness, government deficit and inflation. None of these variables was significant. However, the outcome of these policies, measured by real GDP growth rates, is positively linked to aid allocation. In order to avoid simultaneity bias, I have introduced this variable with a lag, so that the estimation can clearly be interpreted as showing the impact of past growth on new aid allocation. I have also tried social outcome variables, such as life expectancy at birth, child mortality, literacy rate and school enrolment rates, but none of these variables showed any robust correlation with aid allocation, possibly because their introduction reduces drastically the number of available observations due to the lack of complete data.

Concerning governance, I have used the civil liberty and political freedom evaluation provided by Freedom House. This variable is a multinomial qualitative variable which takes values from 1 (highest quality of democracy) to 7 (lowest quality of democracy). Introducing this variable directly into the regression would introduce possible bias, since there is no reason, for instance, to assume that the marginal impact of a shift of this variable from 1 to 2 would be the same as the impact of a shift from 2 to 3, or half the impact of a shift from 1 to 3. The only proper treatment of this variable is to decompose it into as many dichotomous dummy variables as it has occurrences, and to introduce each and every of these dummy variables in the regression. In principle, since I use the average of two indices (civil liberty and political freedom), each with seven occurrences, I would have to deal with 13 occurrences. However, the differences of parameter estimates on these 13 dummy variables are not all significant. Tests of differences of such parameters suggest actually that countries can be regrouped into only two categories: those who have an index equal or below 4 and those which do not. This amounts to simply defining a democracy/non-democracy dummy variable, based on this threshold.

I have also attempted to introduce some other variables linked to governance. The first one concerns the occurrence of conflicts, be they internal or interstate. For this measure I used the database built by PRIO (International Peace Research Institute of Oslo), that defines four categories of conflicts: extrastate (colonial conflicts – not relevant in our case), interstate, internal and internationalized internal. For each category, PRIO defines three levels of intensity, from minor conflict to war. I have used a methodology similar to the one used for the Freedom House index. The end result is the introduction of two dummy variables: one corresponding to non-minor internal conflicts and the other corresponding to non-minor interstate conflicts. In the final results, these two variables will be merged into a single conflict dummy variable.

Another variable that may be used to check whether aid is granted to supposedly well-governed recipients is the per capita amount of assistance that they receive from multilateral donors, given that multilateral assistance acts very often as a catalyst for bilateral assistance. Such multilateral assistance is usually conditional on the implementation of structural adjustment or reform programs, and the bilateral donors therefore use the aid package as a signal that the recipient is committed to use the external resources wisely.

Similarly, I have also entered the total aid commitments (per capita) provided by other bilateral donors. This variable, utilized for instance by Tarp et al. (1999), is introduced to test whether a donor reacts on average positively to aid allocations decided by other donors. This may happen if a particular donor believes that other donors tend to give more aid to countries that deserve assistance. In such a case, the aid flows by other donors can be considered as complementary to one's assistance. This variable must be considered with caution for at least two reasons. First, the aid granted by other donors may be considered as a substitute for, rather than a complement of, one's assistance, in which case the correlation between a donor's aid commitment and the other donors' aid would be negative, instead of positive. Second, this variable may create a simultaneity bias.

Finally, I have introduced data on military expenditures, as a share of GDP, available since 1988 from SIPRI (Stockholm International Peace Research Institute). One could argue that 'excessive' military expenditures should trigger a reduction of foreign assistance because it would imply a high risk that this assistance might be used for non-developmental purposes. However, this variable is never significant.

ECONOMETRIC ESTIMATION

I have introduced all the previously mentioned variables in the estimation of an aid allocation equation. One original feature of this exercise is that the estimation is performed on a very large three-dimensional panel dataset, covering yearly data for the 1980s and the 1990s, 22 donors and 137 recipients. The dependent variable is the amount of aid commitment per capita received yearly by each recipient from each donor, converted in constant U.S. dollars at 1985 prices, using the OECD GDP deflator. The explanatory variables are those introduced in the previous section, augmented by two auxiliary variables, as discussed below.

Following the previous literature, I have included in the list of explanatory variables the population of the recipient. The size of the recipient is not neutral, as initially shown by Dudley and Montmarquette, because there are aid administrative costs which are not proportional to the amount of aid granted. As a consequence of the presence of this type of fixed costs in aid administration, per capita aid granted to a recipient may depend positively or negatively on its population, depending on the elasticity of administrative costs with respect to the amount of aid granted, and on the elasticity of the expected aid impact with respect to the recipient's population. Empirically, one usually observes that small countries receive more assistance per capita than large countries.

I have also entered the total amount of aid granted by the donor during the year of observation. This provides a way to take into account the fact that some donors have larger aid budgets than others, and that such aid budgets fluctuate over time. I do not attempt here to explain the size of donors' aid budgets, which is usually a decision made prior to aid allocation *per se*.

The definition of all variables and their sources is provided in Appendix 1.

Another important step is to choose an appropriate specification and method of estimation. In the previous literature, the specification and estimation method of aid allocation equations has been debated at length. Different issues are at stake.

The principal issue is that we deal with a censored variable, given that aid commitment cannot be negative. This implies that there is possibly a selection bias if this feature is not taken into account. There are several ways of correcting the selection bias (see Berthélemy 2006 for technical discussion). I started here with a standard Heckman maximum likelihood method, in which the probability of selection of a recipient and the amount that it receives are jointly determined. However, an inconvenience of this procedure is that it does not permit the introduction of fixed effects, because standard maximum likelihood estimates are not consistent when one introduces fixed effect in a Probit selection model. This may be a major limitation for estimations performed on a very large database with considerable heterogeneity among donors and recipients; in such a situation, it is necessary to take account of donor and recipient specificities that would not be taken into account by the explanatory variables, which usually implies introducing fixed effects. There is, therefore, no perfectly satisfying parametric method available. I do not need here to introduce fixed effects for the donors, given that I have already introduced the explanatory variables affecting the donors' total aid budget. I have, however, to take account of the unobservable recipient specificities. To solve this issue, I used the following procedure.

First, I checked that the allocation equation in the Heckman procedure is qualitatively not very different from the one obtained in the second step of a so-called two-part method, that consists simply of a linear estimation based on observations for which aid commitment is strictly positive. Therefore, in this case, the properties of the selection equation do not matter much for the estimation of the determinants of the size of aid allocation.[1] This result is similar to the one obtained with a smaller dataset by Alesina and Dollar (2000), who concluded that a linear estimation on strictly positive observations was as good as a Heckman estimation.

Second, I introduced fixed effects in the single equation for aid allocation. Introducing such fixed effects does change a few results significantly, in particular concerning aid commitment from other donors, suggesting that taking account of fixed effects matters for the end result.

For double-checking, I introduced recipient dummy variables in the Heckman procedure. Unsurprisingly, this has a major impact on parameters estimated in the selection (Probit) equation. However, the aid allocation equation provides results that are very similar to those obtained in step two, confirming the initial conclusion that, in our case, correcting the potential selection bias does not matter very much. I have therefore kept estimates obtained in step two.

The results, and the comparison of different methods, are reported in Appendix 4.2. Most estimates are very significant and robust to changes in method of estimation. They are also very robust to changes in the list of explanatory variables. To summarize, I find that the per capita aid commitment a pattern which is influenced by the different explanatory variables as reported in Table 4.1.

Using these estimates, I can now study the pattern of the bilateralism effects and discuss the respective roles of geopolitical influence and business interests in the aid allocation decisions. I report results of this exercise in the next section.

ASSESSING THE IMPACT OF BILATERALISM ON AID ALLOCATION

A simple examination of estimated parameters suggests that bilateralism has a very large influence. Given that our specification is log-linear, our parameters define multipliers on aid commitment. As shown in Table 4.2, all these multipliers are very large in magnitude. In this table the multipliers associated with geopolitical dummy variables indicate by how much a bilateral aid flow is multiplied when the observed recipient and donor belong to the specified category. For the trade-intensity variable, which is not a dummy variable, I consider by how much aid is multiplied when the explanatory variable increases by one standard deviation.

Table 4.2 may also underestimate the actual impact of the bilateral variables, because most (but not all) of them have an impact on the probability of being selected as an aid recipient by a donor. For example, being a former French colony also implies a higher probability of receiving development assistance, from France. Some recipients might not receive any aid at all from France if they were not former French colonies; conversely, countries that are not selected as recipients by France perhaps could have been selected if they were

Table 4.1   Summary of Estimation Results (final equation)

Explanatory variable	Sign	Comments for interpretation
Self interest of donor variables		
Bilateral trade/donor GDP[a]	>0	Commercial interest
Post-colonial dummies	>0	Geopolitical ties
USA – Egypt dummy	>0	Geopolitical ties
USA – Latin America dummy	>0	Geopolitical ties
Japan – Asia dummy	>0	Geopolitical ties
Net present value of debt to export ratio (non-bilateral variable)	>0	Defensive lending
Recipients' needs and merits		
Real GDP per capita[a]	<0	Recipients' need
Real growth rate of the recipient[a]	>0	Recipients' performance
Civil liberty & political freedom dummy[a]	>0	Recipients' governance
Dummy for non-minor internal conflict[a]	<0	Recipients' governance
Dummy for non-minor interstate conflict[a]	<0	Recipients' governance
Per capita multilateral aid commitment	>0	Catalyst of bilateral aid
Per capita aid commitment granted by the other bilateral donors	<0	Substitute to one's aid
Auxiliary variables		
Donor total aid commitment budget	>0	Parameter close to 1
Population of recipient	<0	Fixed effects also depend on population[b]

Notes:

a. Lagged one year.

b. The parameter for recipient population cannot be directly interpreted for two reasons. First, at least one explanatory variable depends on the size of the recipient (the trade intensity variable). Second, fixed effects are also correlated with population. All in all, however, our estimations confirm the usual finding that larger countries receive less assistance per capita than smaller countries.

Source: Appendix 2.

Table 4.2   Multiplier Effect of Bilateral Variables on Aid Commitments Received by Recipients

Explanatory variable	Multiplier of aid commitment
Former Spanish colony	17.2
Former Belgium colony	8.0
Former French colony	6.7
Former Portuguese colony	5.7
Former British colony	3.7
Egypt – USA ties	25.2
Asia – Japan ties	3.6
Latin America – USA ties	2.0
Trade: + 1 standard deviation of explanatory variable	2.4

Source: Computed from estimation results reported in Appendix 2.

former colonies. However, appraising the magnitude of the influence of the bilateralism on the selection of aid recipients is impossible here, for technical reasons: for several dummy variables (concerning former French and Belgium colonies and the specific ties between the United States and Egypt and between Japan and Asian recipients), it is impossible to estimate the corresponding parameters, because such variables predict success (i.e. selection as recipient) perfectly.

It is nevertheless possible to estimate the marginal impact of the trade variable on the probability of being selected as recipient through a Probit estimation (equation not shown). This marginal impact is relatively small (0.04) and implies that increasing the trade variable by one standard deviation boosts the probability of being selected by only 10 per cent. Therefore, neglecting this aspect should not affect too much our assessment of the effect of bilateralism on aid distribution. This merely leads to underestimating it by a small margin.

The next step is to compute the total impact of bilateral variables on the bilateral aid pattern, which I call the bilateralism effect. To define this variable, I first compute the notional amount of aid that recipients would receive, assuming that the trade-intensity variable is equal to its average and that the bilateral dummy variables are equal to zero for all recipients. However, the sum of these notional aid flows is not equal to the sum of actual aid flows. This is essentially due to the log-linearity of my equation, that implies that the impacts of bilateral variables on aid flows are multiplicative, not additive. Moreover,

Table 4.3   Implicit Shift of Aid Resources Due to Bilateralism: The 'Bilateralism Effect'

Negative bilateralism effect	Number of countries	Aid actually received by such countries	Aid that would be received without bilateralism
Asia	13	0.5	1.3
Latin America	18	1.0	1.5
Middle East & North Africa	8	0.5	1.0
Sub-Saharan Africa	39	5.6	10.6
Others	16	0.4	1.3
Total	94	8.1	15.6

Positive bilateralism effect	Number of countries	Aid actually received by such countries	Aid that would be received without bilateralism
Asia	12	8.5	3.7
Latin America	12	1.6	1.2
Middle East & North Africa	7	3.6	1.6
Sub-Saharan Africa	9	1.2	0.8
Others	0	0.0	0.0
Total	40	14.8	7.3

Note: All aid flows considered here are yearly averages over the 1980–99 period.

Source: Author's estimates based on Appendix 2 and aid data.

there are indirect effects, given that neutralizing the effect of bilateral variables also modifies the total aid assistance received from other donors. To correct all this, I make the neutral assumption that total aid flows should not be affected by the neutralization of bilateral variables. This simply amounts to multiplying all notional aid flows by a given scalar, determined so as to ensure that the total flow of aid – net of the bilateralism effect – is equal to the total flow of actual aid. The result is what I call the aid commitments which would be received in the absence of bilateralism. The final step consists of computing the bilateralism effect as the difference between actual aid commitments and the commitments which would be received in the absence of bilateralism.

Table 4.4   Implicit Shift of Aid Resources Due to Trade Intensity

Negative Trade–Intensity Effect	number of countries	aid actually received by such countries	aid without trade–intensity factor
Asia	14	0.7	1.5
Latin America	18	1.2	1.6
Middle East & North Africa	8	0.5	0.8
Sub-Saharan Africa	38	5.4	9.2
Others	16	0.4	1.0
Total	94	8.1	14.1

Positive Trade–Intensity Effect	number of countries	aid actually received by such countries	aid without trade–intensity factor
Asia	11	8.3	4.4
Latin America	12	1.4	1.0
Middle East & North Africa	7	3.6	2.3
Sub-Saharan Africa	10	1.5	1.1
Others	0	0.0	0.0
Total	40	14.8	8.8

Note: All aid flows considered here are yearly averages over the 1980–99 period.
Source: Author's estimates based on Appendix 2 and aid data.

The results suggest that very large amounts of aid are linked to decisions based on purely bilateral criteria. Some countries would receive much more assistance in the absence of bilateralism, other would receive much less.

The conventional wisdom is that former colonies would receive less assistance in the absence of bilateralism. However, as shown in Table 4.3, this is not necessarily the case. Actually, the main result of this exercise is that it shows that aid allocation based on bilateralism is biased against sub-Saharan Africa, instead of in favor of this region. A vast majority of African countries (39 out of a sample of 48) would have higher aid flows in the absence of the bilateralism effect (column 2). Such countries actually receive about half of what they would receive in the absence of bilateralism (they receive a total of $5.6 per year compared to the $10.6 billion which they would receive in the

Table 4.5   Correlation between the Two Components of Bilateral Aid and Multilateral Aid

Region	Correlation between bilateralism effect & multilateral aid		Correlation between bilateral aid net of the bilateralism effect & multilateral aid	
Asia	0.48	**	0.82	***
Latin America	−0.36	*	0.82	***
Middle East & North Africa	0.78	***	0.85	***
Sub-Saharan Africa	−0.35	**	0.66	***
Others	−0.72	***	0.78	***
All countries	0.35	***	0.60	***

Note: All aid flows considered here are yearly averages over the 1980–99 period.

Source: Author's estimates based on Appendix 2 and aid data.

absence of bilateralism, as indicated in column 3). Conversely, it is favorable to Asia and the MENA (Middle East and North Africa) region. This comes from the fact that geopolitical ties such as post-colonial relations are quantitatively a much smaller component of the bilateralism effect than trade intensity: sub-Saharan African countries enjoy favorable treatment from the former colonial powers, but the fact that they are very small trading partners has in the end a much more significant impact than post-colonial ties. More generally, even though the multipliers attached to geopolitical dummy variables are very large, most of them (particularly concerning former colonies) apply to relatively small aid flows, and this significantly reduces their impact on the end result. As a consequence, the trade component of the bilateralism effect has a much higher influence on aid allocation patterns than its geopolitical component.

This analysis is confirmed in Table 4.4, where I have replicated the previous exercise taking into account only the trade-intensity variable. The results are very similar to those in Table 4.3, suggesting that most of the bilateralism bias is related to commercial interests. This result gives support to the view that rent-seeking behaviors within donor countries, related to trade interests, may have a strong influence on aid allocation decisions. Symmetrically (result not shown), the same exercise using only the geopolitical dummy variables shows that a very small component of the bilateralism effect is attributable to such geopolitical variables.

An indirect way of controlling the relevance of the proposed measure of the effect of bilateralism is to check that aid that would be allocated to countries even without the presence of bilateralism is correlated with multilateral aid received by the same countries. This is the case, as reported in Table 4.5 (column 3), both for the whole sample and for regional sub-samples. Conversely it appears in Table 4.5 (column 2) that the bilateralism effect is not systematically positively correlated with multilateral flows – with even a negative correlation in Latin America, Sub-Saharan Africa and Others. The only region where it seems that bilateral interests and multilateral behaviors are mutually consistent is the Middle East and North Africa.

COMPARISON AMONG DONORS

Not all bilateral donors behave the same. In this section, I compare the different bilateral donor behaviours. This is easily done, in my framework, by interacting all explanatory variables with donor-related dummy variables. This provides a direct test of differences of parameters. Based on this test, I compare donor behaviors with respect to the variable that best describes the influence of rent-seeking in donor behaviors: the trade-intensity variable. This comparison (fully reported in Appendix 3), leads to the following results:

First, among bilateral donors for which donor specific parameters can be estimated,[2] only one, Switzerland, has a non-significant parameter for the trade-intensity variable. This is probably the only case where one may conclude, with some degree of confidence, the absence of rent-seeking behavior in the aid allocation decisions.

Second, most Nordic donors (Denmark, Ireland, the Netherlands and Norway) together with Austria may be considered, according to my results, as less influenced by rent-seeking behaviors than the average donor, in the sense that their parameter associated with the trade-intensity variable is significantly lower than for other donors. Sweden is not part of this group, but this is due to missing information for the 1990s, where many Swedish aid flows are not reported with geographic allocations, which very much reduces the precision of estimation for this country.

Third, Belgium, Canada, Finland, Germany, New Zealand, Sweden and United States behave, in terms of rent-seeking, like the average donor.

Fourth, Japan is in-between this category and the next one, of countries where the business interest motive is particularly present in aid allocation decisions. This is because Japan displays a significant correlation between the trade-intensity variable and the Asian-recipient dummy variable. The latter may be considered as purely geopolitical, but it could also be considered as a proxy of Japanese trade interests. When this dummy variable is dropped, the Japanese aid allocation decisions appear particularly influenced by the trade-intensity variable; when it is kept, Japan is comparable, in this dimension, to the average donor.

Finally, Australia, France, Italy and United Kingdom are significantly more influenced by commercial interests in their aid allocation decisions than the average donor.[3]

Such results fit reasonably well with the usual perception of the various donor policies, with the Nordic countries and Switzerland considered as reasonably altruistic donors. The altruistic stance of the aid policy implemented by such countries is confirmed by other information. On average over the period of observation, Denmark, the Netherlands and Norway had the highest aid performances, with a total aid-to-GDP ratio close to 0.9 per cent. Ireland, which was initially a much poorer country than the others, had on average in the 1980s and the 1990s a relatively small aid budget, but channeled more than 50 per cent of its assistance through multilateral aid instead of through bilateral aid. Switzerland is yet a different case, with also relatively modest levels of aid budget (0.33 per cent of GDP) and not much assistance channeled through multilaterals. However, in the case of Switzerland, such data should be interpreted cautiously, given that this country became a member of the World Bank only in 1992 and of the United Nations only in 2002. Moreover, Switzerland has consistently offered untied aid to developing countries, unlike most other donors. Conversely, Australia, France, Italy and the United Kingdom, are known (together with Canada and the United States) for frequently tying their assistance.

CONCLUSION

A successful transition from aid dependence may be impeded by political economy factors – that is, by the fact that some rent-seeking economic agents with vested interests in perpetuating aid dependence have a say in aid allocation decisions. I considered here the donor side of the story. I provided empirical evidence consistent with the rent-seeking hypothesis by showing that aid allocation policies implemented by donors, or at least by a vast majority of them, are significantly correlated with their business interests, as measured by trade linkages.

In order to do so, I examined in detail the motives of bilateral aid allocation decisions, as they are revealed by data on bilateral aid commitments. I identified both self-interest motives and recipient needs and merit motives of aid allocation. Bilateral variables which describe self-interest motives are related to economic and political ties between donors and recipients. I then used such variables to define what I call the bilateralism effect in aid allocation decisions, that appears to be a significant factor influencing bilateral aid patterns. By far the largest part of this bilateralism effect is related to commercial, rather than to geopolitical, factors.

I then used these estimates to compute what would have been, on average over the past two decades, the amount of aid commitments granted to each recipient without this bilateralism effect. Unsurprisingly, this aid allocation net of the bilateralism effect is highly correlated with multilateral aid commitments received by the different recipients. Perhaps more surprisingly, given the conventional wisdom, it appears that the bilateralism effect is adverse to the Sub-Saharan African region, despite its strong post-colonial ties with European donors, and is favorable to Asia and the Middle East. This result comes from the fact that trade linkages play by far the largest role in self-interest aid allocation motives.

A paradox coming out of these computations is that in the absence of rent-seeking behaviors the aid allocation policies implemented in the North would lead to more assistance to Sub-Saharan Africa, which is also the region where aid dependence is the most pervasive. However, these are only average results. Within Sub-Saharan Africa, the largest trade partners of donor countries receive more assistance than the smallest partners. Moreover, saying that more – but also better allocated – aid to Africa would be necessary to eventually reduce its aid dependence is consistent with the current proposals for a sort of Marshall plan for poor countries. These proposals advocate doubling aid flows to poor but well-governed countries to help them escape their current poverty trap.[4] My analysis suggests that a critical aspect for the success of such a strategy would lie, from a microeconomic standpoint, in the elimination of incentives given to economic agents in the North (as in the South) to perpetuate aid dependence. This would imply, in particular, reducing aid giving based on trade ties. However, further research would be needed to study how, from a macroeconomic standpoint, such big push policies, that would initially increase aid dependence, could reduce it in the long run.

My results also suggest some interesting conclusions regarding a possible new architecture for the international aid system, in which the bilateral donors and the multilateral donors would play different roles: the bilateral donors would take care of the most promising economic partners – which they do relatively well by focusing their assistance on main trading partners – and the multilaterals would concentrate their assistance on the neediest countries. This approach would help find incentives for non-altruistic bilateral donors to increase their aid budgets. Achieving significant increases in aid flows from developed countries – particularly the largest ones – based only on altruistic behaviors, seems unlikely; but the self-interest motive of bilateral donors may be, after all, a good second-best solution to stimulate bilateral official development assistance in favor of relatively good performers. This is, of course, only a second best, because bilateralism in aid allocation is unavoidably blended by motives which have nothing to do with economic development. In any case, such self-interested motives cannot be prevented if one relies on a bilateral aid system, because they are part and parcel of the reasons why most bilateral donors provide assistance to developing countries when they are not the main motive itself.

In such a system, the multilaterals should concentrate their efforts on assistance to the neediest recipients, instead of targeting the good performers, to correct the bias of bilateral aid in favor of their major trading partners and their geopolitical allies. If the multilateral agencies focus too much on aid efficiency, the needy countries which are not significant political allies of the bilateral donors will be inevitably almost excluded from all aid sources, because almost by definition their poor economic performances reduce their attractiveness as business partners.

This sharing of responsibilities between bilateral and multilateral donors would also avoid a too heavy concentration of aid on a few good performers, that would be inevitable if all donors adopted the same pattern of aid allocation as the multilateral agencies. According to my econometric estimates, this diversification of overall aid allocation would also be reinforced by the fact that there is a negative correlation between the bilateral aid commitments of a donor and aid provided by other donors.

In this framework, one difficult aspect would be the refinancing of the grant element of multilateral agency operations. Their actions are clearly of a global public good nature, with all the classical difficulties arising in global public-good financing. But this problem already exists in the current setting, and the framework that I propose would merely make it more explicit. In fact, making it explicit that the role of multilateral institutions is fully to take care of pure global-public goods might possibly facilitate discussions on their financing. The recent success encountered by global public good schemes such as the Global Fund to Fight AIDS, Tuberculosis and Malaria, and the Global Alliance for Vaccines and Immunization, suggests that this approach has some value.

NOTES

I thank Befekadu Degefe, Patrick Guillaumont, Bill Lyakurwa and other participants at the sixth annual GDN meeting for their helpful comments. All errors and shortcomings remain mine.

1. In technical words, the two-part estimation is acceptable because the correlation of residuals of the selection and allocation equations is small.

2. There are no results for Greece, Luxembourg, Portugal and Spain, for lack of sufficient data.
3. This result may be somewhat surprising for the UK, but it should be remembered that our estimations are based on the 1980–99 period, and not on the most recent years, when the British aid policy has be reshuffled.
4. See, for example, recent proposals by the United Nation's Millenium project and by Tony Blair's Commission for Africa.

REFERENCES

Alesina, Alberto and David Dollar (2000), 'Who Gives Foreign Aid to Whom and Why?', *Journal of Economic Growth*, **5** (1), 33–63.

Burnside, Craig and David Dollar (2000), 'Aid, policies, and growth', *American Economic Review* **90** (4), 847–68.

Berthélemy, Jean-Claude (2006), 'Bilateral Donors' Interest vs. Recipients' Development Motives in Aid Allocation: Do All Donors Behave the Same?', *Review of Development Economics*, **10** (2), 179–94.

Berthélemy, Jean-Claude, and Ariane Tichit (2004), 'Bilateral Donors' Aid Allocation Decisions – A Three-dimensional Panel Analysis', *International Review of Economics and Finance*, **13** (3), 253–74.

Birdsall, Nancy, Stijn Claessens and Ishac Diwan (2003), 'Policy Selectivity Forgone: Debt and Donor Behavior in Africa', World Bank Economic Review, **17** (3), 409–36.

Dudley, Leonard and Claude Montmarquette (1976), 'A Model of the Supply of Bilateral Foreign Aid', *American Economic Review*, **66** (1), 132–42.

Easterly, William (2001), 'Growth Implosions, Debt Explosions and My Aunt Marilyn: Do Growth Slowdowns Cause Public Debt Crises?', Washington, DC, World Bank, World Bank Policy Research Working Paper No. 2531.

Grilli, Enzo and Markus Riess (1992), 'EC Aid to Associated Countries: Distribution and Determinants', *Weltwirtschaftliches Archiv*, **128** (2), 202–20.

Lahiri, Sajal and Pascalis Raimondos-Møller (2000), 'Lobbying by Ethnic Groups and Aid Allocation', *Economic Journal*, **110** (462), 62–79.

Maizels, Alfred and Machiko K. Nissanke (1984), 'Motivations for Aid to Developing Countries', *World Development*, **12** (9), 879–900.

McKinley, Robert D. and Richard Little (1977), 'A Foreign Policy Model of U.S. Bilateral Aid Allocation', *World Politics*, **30** (1), 58–86.

——(1978a), 'The French Aid Relationship: A Foreign Policy Model of Distribution of French Bilateral Aid, 1964–1970', *Development and Change*, **9** (3), 459–78.

——(1978b), 'A Foreign Policy Model of the Distribution of British Bilateral Aid, 1960–70', *British Journal of Political Science*, **8** (3), 313–31.

——(1979), 'The U.S. Aid Relationship: A Test of the Recipient Need and the Donor Interest Model', *Political Studies*, **27** (2) 236–50.

Neumayer, Eric (2003), *The Pattern of Aid Giving: The Impact of Good Governance on Developmental Assistance*, New York: Routledge.

Svensson, Jakob (2000), 'Foreign Aid and Rent-Seeking', *Journal of International Economics*, **51** (2), 437–61.

Tarp, Finn, Christian F. Bach, Henrik Hansen and Søren Baunsgaard (1999), 'Danish Aid Policy: Theory and Empirical Evidence', in Kanhaya L. Gupta (ed.), *Foreign Aid: New Perspectives*, Boston: Kluwer Academic Publishers, pp. 149–69.

APPENDIX 4.1

Table 4.A1   List and Sources of Variables

Variable	Definition	Source
ODA	Real ODA (OA) commitments divided by the population of the recipient country, using the OECD GDP deflator	OECD DAC[a] database and OECD national account statistics
Total ODA of donor	Total real ODA of the donor (totalled over the 137 recipients)	Author's own calculation
Other Donors ODA	Total ODA given by other donors to the recipient country	Author's own calculation
Multilateral ODA per cap	Real ODA (OA) commitments of multilateral donors divided by the population of the recipient country, using the OECD GDP deflator	OECD DAC database and national account statistics
GDP per cap	Real GDP per capita in constant dollars (international prices, base year 1985) of the recipient countries	Penn World Tables
Population	Population, total	World Bank WDI[b]
Trade	Sum of bilateral imports and exports (corrected for the OECD inflation) in % of donor's GDP	OECD trade database
Growth	GDP growth (annual %) of the recipient lagged one period	World Bank's WDI
Global freedom	Mean of civil liberties and political rights indexes, ranging from 1 (most free) to 7 (less free)	Freedom House website

Table 4.A1 continued

Variable	Definition	Source
Interstate conflict	Dummy variable for non-minor interstate conflict	PRIO[c]
Internal conflict	Dummy variable, for non-minor interstate conflict	PRIO
NPV of debt/ export	Ratio of net present value of debt over export	Easterly (2001)
Global freedom	Mean of civil liberties and political rights indexes, ranging from 1 (most free) to 7 (less free)	Freedom House website

Notes:
a. OECD Development Aid Committee.
b. World Bank World Development Indicators.
c. International Peace Research Institute, Oslo.

APPENDIX 4.2   DETERMINANTS OF BILATERAL ODA PER CAPITA COMMITMENT (in logarithm)

Column (1) in Table 4.A2 reports the estimates of the aid allocation equation using the standard Heckman maximum likelihood method. It fits parameters of the joint system:

$$Y = bX + u$$

$$Y \text{ observed if } cZ + v > 0$$

where u and v are normally distributed error terms, with $cov(u,v) = \rho$, and
   Y= the dependent variable, i.e. the log of aid commitment per capita (ODA)
   X= explanatory variables
   Z= explanatory variables for the selection equation. Here Z=X.

   In this equation, the pseudo-student statistics are computed using correction for cluster autocorrelation of residuals (cluster being defined by recipients).
   Column (2) provides similar estimates with Z defined as level instead of logarithm variables for all variables which may have null values. This saves some 6400 censored observations for the selection equation. With this improvement of the selection equation, the correlation between u and v becomes non-significant, suggesting that the aid allocation equation can be estimated independently of the selection equation. Pseudo-student statistics are estimated using the correction for cluster auto-correlation.
   Column (3) reports ordinary least square estimates of the same aid allocation equation, and, consistently with the previous finding, exhibits parameter estimates very close to those obtained in column (2). Student statistics are

estimated using the correction for cluster auto-correlation.
   Column (4) provides estimates of the same equation, augmented with a random effect for recipient, i.e.:

$$Y_{ijt} = bX_{ijt} + e_i + u_{ijt}$$

where i stands for the recipient, j the donor ant t the year of observation, and e_i and u_{ijt} are normally distributed random variables.
   Column (5) reports estimates obtained with the fixed-effect method, i.e. the same as above, but where e_i is not a random variable but a deterministic parameter, which is estimated together with the b parameters (estimates not reported). The Hausman specification test suggests that this fixed-effect method

is preferable to the random-effect method.

Column (6) is the same as column (5), but where the parameters for internal and interstate conflicts have been constrained to be equal (they were not significantly different in the previous estimation).

I have also estimated the Heckman model augmented with recipient dummy variables, in order to estimate the equivalent of a fixed-effect model. However, it is known in the econometric literature that such estimates are not consistent in a selection equation. The aid allocation equation obtained with this method is very similar to equations (5) and (6) (not shown).

Results for the selection equations corresponding to models (1) and (2) are not shown, but are available upon request. In summary, parameters are also very significant, and of the same sign as parameters reported for the allocation equation.

APPENDIX 4.3   TESTING DIFFERENCES AMONG DONORS

The objective here is to test whether the parameters for a given donor α differ from parameters for other donors. Let us define a dummy variable D_α associated with this donor. This dummy variable is interacted with all explanatory variables entered in the equation previously reported in Appendix A.2. This defines the following model:

$$Y = bX + b'_\alpha D_\alpha X + u$$

where both b and b_α vectors of parameters are estimated. A sample of the obtained results, regarding the parameter associated with for the trade intensity variable, is reported below.

Table 4.A2 Determinants of Bilateral ODA Per Capita Commitment (in logarithm)

	(1) Heckman		(2) Heckman		(3) OLS		(4) Random effect		(5) Fixed effects		(6) Fixed effects	
ln(GDP per cap) (lagged)	-0.626 (5.65)	***	-0.573 (5.38)	***	-0.588 (5.49)	***	-0.749 (14.12)	***	-0.772 (7.81)	***	-0.769 (7.78)	***
ln(population)	-0.467 (7.35)	***	-0.486 (7.85)	***	-0.478 (7.74)	***	-0.662 (23.87)	***	-1.250 (11.04)	***	-1.252 (11.05)	***
ln(trade) (lagged)	0.281 (5.82)	***	0.265 (5.74)	***	0.265 (5.75)	***	0.328 (35.01)	***	0.328 (34.06)	***	0.328 (34.05)	***
Global freedom<=4 (lagged)	0.192 (2.38)	**	0.153 (2.03)	**	0.169 (2.17)	**	0.141 (3.97)	***	0.167 (4.36)	***	0.169 (4.40)	***
Growth (lagged)	0.016 (3.64)	***	0.015 (3.33)	***	0.015 (3.47)	***	0.011 (4.77)	***	0.012 (4.98)	***	0.012 (5.04)	***
ln(total ODA of donor)	0.990 (28.16)	***	0.928 (23.63)	***	0.946 (26.60)	***	0.967 (109.52)	***	0.964 (108.96)	***	0.964 (108.95)	***
ln(oth. donors ODA per cap)	0.281 (4.51)	***	0.274 (4.50)	***	0.273 (4.48)	***	-0.041 (1.90)	*	-0.153 (6.49)	***	-0.153 (6.50)	***
ln(multilateral ODA per cap)	0.234 (5.97)	***	0.227 (6.01)	***	0.228 (6.02)	***	0.204 (11.13)	***	0.185 (9.82)	***	0.184 (9.80)	***
Former French colony	1.996 (8.16)	***	1.946 (7.98)	***	1.980 (8.19)	***	1.944 (20.40)	***	1.904 (20.00)	***	1.904 (20.00)	***

Table 4.A2   continued

	(1) Heckman		(2) Heckman		(3) OLS		(4) Random effect		(5) Fixed effects		(6) Fixed effects	
Former British colony	1.471 (8.77)	***	1.373 (8.41)	***	1.418 (8.78)	***	1.302 (16.08)	***	1.289 (15.97)	***	1.289 (15.97)	***
Former Portuguese colony	2.349 (4.18)	***	2.400 (4.59)	***	2.376 (4.48)	***	1.752 (5.42)	***	1.733 (5.38)	***	1.735 (5.39)	***
Former Spanish colony	2.801 (16.82)	***	2.916 (16.93)	***	2.858 (18.04)	***	2.793 (12.95)	***	2.842 (13.24)	***	2.845 (13.25)	***
Former Belgium colony	2.714 (10.23)	***	2.550 (9.85)	***	2.621 (10.17)	***	2.119 (6.87)	***	2.079 (6.75)	***	2.080 (6.76)	***
USA–Egypt tie	3.590 (35.03)	***	3.603 (35.67)	***	3.615 (34.89)	***	3.363 (8.46)	***	3.226 (8.14)	***	3.225 (8.14)	***
USA–Latin America tie	0.787 (2.46)	**	0.819 (2.64)	***	0.813 (2.59)	**	0.693 (7.17)	***	0.675 (7.00)	***	0.675 (7.00)	***
Japan–Asia tie	1.720 (7.55)	***	1.732 (7.68)	***	1.738 (7.66)	***	1.388 (12.52)	***	1.285 (11.61)	***	1.285 (11.61)	***
interstate conflict (lagged)	-0.346 (2.33)	**	-0.303 (1.95)	**	-0.317 (2.10)	**	-0.126 (1.47)		-0.103 (1.19)		-0.207 (4.95)	***
internal conflict (lagged)	0.226 (2.22)	**	0.218 (2.21)	**	0.218 (2.20)	**	-0.141 (2.98)	***	-0.243 (4.91)	***	-0.207 (4.95)	***
ln(NPV of debt/export)	0.131 (1.91)	*	0.116 (1.78)	*	0.121 (1.82)	*	0.182 (6.43)	***	0.225 (7.03)	***	0.222 (6.96)	***

Table 4.A2   continued

	(1) Heckman		(2) Heckman		(3) OLS		(4) Random effect		(5) Fixed effects		(6) Fixed effects	
intercept	-8.737	***	-7.495	***	-7.964	***	-2.828	***	7.245	***	7.248	***
	(3.94)		(3.39)		(3.66)		(4.00)		(3.63)		(3.63)	
Number of observation	27416		33844		19773		19773		19773		19773	
Uncensored observations	19773		19773									
Rho (Heckman model)	0.145	***	-0.053									
R²					0.547							
Hausman test (RE model)							251.18	***				
Fisher test (FE model)									27.56	***	28.04	***

Notes:
1. Standard Heckman maximum–likelihood model
2. Heckman maximum–likelihood model without logarithm for trade, other donors' aid and multilateral aid in the selection equation
3. OLS without sample selection correction
4. Random–effect model
5. Fixed–effect model
6. Fixed–effect model with same parameter for interstate and internal t–or z–statistics between brackets (estimated with robust recipient cluster method whenever relevant) significant at 1% (***), 5% (**) and 10% (*) levels.

134

Table 4.A3   Testing Differences among Donors

Donor country	Elasticity of aid to trade intensity		Difference with average other donor	
Australia	0.725	***	0.42	***
	−24.74		−5.79	
Austria	0.193	***	−0.127	***
	−4.83		−2.86	
Belgium	0.309	***	−0.032	
	−9.02		−0.82	
Canada	0.309	***	−0.027	
	−9.73		−0.75	
Denmark	0.144	**	−0.187	***
	−2.39		−2.81	
Finland	0.272	***	−0.059	
	−7.88		−1.52	
France	0.505	***	0.202	***
	−14.84		−5.4	
Germany	0.254	***	−0.058	
	−6.54		−1.37	
Ireland	0.122	***	−0.213	***
	−2.95		−4.62	
Italy	0.498		0.189	
	−12.85	***	−4.41	***
Japan	0.318			
	−9.75	***	0	
Japan[a]	0.401		0.069	
	−12.66	***	−1.95	*
Netherlands	0.184		−0.143	
	−4.88	***	−3.44	***
New Zealand	0.279		−0.071	
	−6.93	***	−1.57	

Table 4.A3   continued

Donor country	Elasticity of aid to trade intensity		Difference with average other donor	
Norway	0.183	***	-0.152	***
	-5.8		-4.25	
Switzerland	-0.055		-0.39	***
	-1.34		-8.68	
United Kingdom	0.465	***	0.158	***
	-10.25		-3.2	
United States	0.277	***	-0.061	
	-6.76		-1.34	
United States[b]	0.389		0.066	
	-10.4		-1.59	

Notes:

The estimation specification corresponds to column (5) in Appendix 2.

a. Models estimated without the Japan–Asia dummy variable.

b. Models estimated without the United States– Latin America dummy variable.

5. Impact of Revamped Australian Assistance to the Pacific Islands

Satish Chand

Australian assistance to the Pacific islands has increased significantly in recent years. Australian aid to the Solomon Islands in 2003, for example, increased to $101 million, almost five times the approximately $20 million average for each of the previous four years.[1] Australian aid to Nauru more than doubled between 2001 and 2003, while assistance to Papua New Guinea increased by 44 per cent over the same period. These trends are likely to continue, given Australian Prime Minister John Howard's announcement that the government would be doubling the total foreign aid budget, and that the 2005–2006 budget would include an aid package of A$1 billion to Indonesia for reconstruction following the December 2004 tsunami and A$841 million to the Solomon Islands to 'restore law and order and sound public finances'.[2]

Security has been the principal factor motivating revamped Australian development assistance to the small island nations located within the Pacific Ocean. According to the *Pacific Regional Aid Strategy 2004–2009*, launched by the minister of foreign affairs on 9 December 2004 at Parliament House:

> Australia has sharpened its focus on the region following the deterioration of security in Solomon Islands and in the context of global security increasing trans-boundary challenges and the understanding that a porous and undeveloped region is not in the interests of the Pacific or Australia (AusAID 2004, 11).

The revised aid strategy, moreover, involves an interventionist approach to delivering assistance. Since July 2003, Australian public servants have been posted at civil service positions in three Pacific nations. Australian police and military personnel were deployed to the Solomon Islands on 19 April 2006 to quell the breakdown of law and order in the capital, Honiara, immediately following their national elections. This assertive Australian stance has been justified as being necessary 'to pre-empt economic collapse, improve security, reduce corruption and promote strong economic growth' (AusAID 2004, 11).

The success of the interventions remains to be gauged, however.

The shift in aid policy is due to a confluence of several factors. First, analysts have become pessimistic about regional prospects. According to several Australian think tank reports: 'Aid has failed the Pacific' (Hughes 2003); 'Solomon Islands, one of Australia's nearest neighbors, is a failing state' with potentially serious consequences for Australia (Wainwright 2003, 3); 'It is no longer possible ... to separate international security from domestic, intra-state issues such as internal conflict, governance and state capacity' (Reilly 2002, 21); and, the challenge in Papua New Guinea, a former colony and a close neighbor, is that of strengthening the nation state, including assistance with 'nation-building' (White and Wainwright 2004, 6). These pronouncements received widespread local media attention, particularly ahead of a second factor: the Australian federal elections of October 2004. The interventionist policies for the Pacific region were launched in a heightened international security environment, where the incumbent administration, led by Prime Minister John Howard, was keen to consolidate its credentials on border security and regional leadership.

Poverty reduction, however, has been the longer-term goal of Australian assistance (see Commonwealth of Australia 1984 and 1997). The overarching objective of Australian aid is 'to advance Australia's national interest by assisting developing countries reduce poverty and achieve sustainable development' (Commonwealth of Australia 2006, ii). The poor, and in a few cases deteriorating, developmental record in many of the Pacific island states has supported a rethink of the strategies for overseas development assistance (ODA). While social indicators of development within the Pacific region remain favorable relative to countries with a similar level of per capita income (see Table 5.1), the rates of growth of per capita income have been low, while incidences of poverty, social conflicts and life-style diseases such as diabetes have risen in some of the countries over the past three decades. The Asian Development Bank, using data for 1996, for example, notes that progress by Pacific island states on the Millennium Development Goals has been mixed. For example, half of the population of Kiribati ranks below the national poverty line; poverty in Papua New Guinea is increasing; and 'signs of emerging pockets of poverty challenge countries and donors to focus policies and action programs' (2003, 19, 24, 9). Donors, led by Australia, are converging on a consensus to support good governance, including effective and accountable democratic governments, and law and order to foster growth in both output and poverty reduction.

The deterioration of law and order in the Solomon Islands following a five-year civil conflict prompted Australia to lead a regional assistance mission into the country in July 2003. This was followed some five months later with the

Table 5.1 Basic Indicators for Pacific Island Countries, Australia and New Zealand

Country/ Group	Land area (km²)	Pop. (1000s) (2004)	Pop. density (people/ km²)	GDP per capita (PPP, 2004$)	Aid per capita (2003 US$)	Life expectancy at birth (2003)
Cook Isl.ᵃ						
Fiji	18270	848	46	6092	61	70
Kiribati	730	98	134		191	63
Marshall Isl.	181	60	331	1600ᵉ	991	70ᵉ
Micronesia	702	127	181	2000ᶠ	923	69
Nauruᵃ	21	13	619	5000ᵇ	na	63
Niueᵃ	260	2	8	3600ᶜ	na	na
Palau	460	20	43		1295	
Papua New Guinea	452860	5625	12	2564	40	57
Samoa	2830	179	63	5694	186	70
Solomon Isl.	27990	471	17	1773		70
Tonga	720	102	141	7236	270	71
Tuvaluᵃ	26	11	423	1100ᵈ	na	68
Vanuatu	12190	215	18	2893	154	69
Australia	7682300	20120	3	30116		80
New Zealand	267990	4061	15	22912		79

Notes: The most recent data available has been used; na indicates data not available.

a. These countries are not members of the World Bank, thus their data has been sourced from the *CIA World Fact Book*; data accessed online on 16 March 2006.

b. Per capita GDP for Nauru is for 2001.

c. Data on per capita GDP for Niue is for 2000.

d. Per capita GDP data for Tuvalu is for the year 2000.

e. Data on per capita GDP (data for 2001) and life expectancy for Marshall Islands are taken from the *CIA World Fact Book*.

f. Data for per capita GDP for Micronesia is for the year 2002 and taken from the *CIA World Fact Book*. Data from *World Fact Book* is only used when this is not available from *World Development Indicators*.

Source: Unless otherwise stated, the source for all data is World Bank *World Development Indicators* online. Data accessed on 15 March 2006.

announcement of an Enhanced Cooperation Program (ECP) with Papua New Guinea (PNG) which was to have deployed Australian police and civilians into civil service and advisory positions in key PNG agencies by the end of 2005. The police deployment program, however, was brought to a premature halt following a 13 May 2005 ruling by the PNG Supreme Court that elements of the ECP-implementing legislation were inconsistent with the PNG Constitution. Australia posted three public servants to Nauru by July 2004 to assist the island nation climb out of its fiscal crisis. Australia also deployed some 300 military and police personnel to the Solomon Islands in April 2006 to restore law and order following riots in the capital following their national elections. Policymakers within Canberra, in the interim, had been working on a new paradigm for ODA to the region which was published as the *Pacific Regional Aid Strategy 2004–2009* and the *White Paper on Australian Aid*.

The Australian government rationalized the interventions into the Solomon Islands, Papua New Guinea and Nauru as being necessary for regional security. Moreover, they closely followed the U.S.-led interventions into Afghanistan (2001) and Iraq (2003) and, according to Greg Fry, amount to 'a robust and serious attempt at social engineering for the Pacific on a massive scale' (2004, 6). These interventions are in sharp contrast with the post-colonial attitude which Australia, and the West more generally, took regarding ODA. The recent security focus of ODA, moreover, is in sharp contrast with the focus on poverty reduction which had emerged in the post-Cold War and pre-security eras. The Millennium Development Goals established by the membership of the United Nations in 2000, for example, enunciate a commitment to poverty reduction as the goal of ODA.

This chapter uses Australia's revamped security efforts in the Pacific island region to assess their impact on development. There are three principal findings: first, the large efforts at improving security will draw resources away from funding basic services, thus compromising the ability to achieve the Millennium Development Goals by the target date of 2015. Second, the aid effort in Australia will rise while its focus could narrow to the immediate neighborhood. Third, if well-managed, Canberra's focus on regional security could lead to improved developmental outcomes over the long term. The rest of the chapter outlines the international ODA scene, discusses the recent Australian interventions into the Pacific island region and presents evidence on the effectiveness of Australian ODA.

THE HISTORICAL CONTEXT OF ODA

International aid in the form of transferring resources from Western governments with the aim of promoting economic development in recipient countries predates the nineteenth century (see Kanbur 2003 for a succinct survey). Such transfers increased rapidly in the reconstruction stage of war-ravaged Europe in the immediate aftermath of World War II. The Marshall Plan, for example, involved significant transfers of bilateral assistance from the United States to Europe. The United Nations and the two Bretton Woods institutions, namely the World Bank and the International Monetary Fund, were created to provide multilateral channels for ODA.[3]

The U.S. shift towards assisting the non-industrialized world began in the early 1950s with the Act for International Development. Poverty was the motivating factor for this legislation, as President Harry S. Truman explained in his inaugural address of 20 January 1949. He said this Act represented:

A new bold program for ... the improvement and growth of underdeveloped areas. More than half the people of the world are living in conditions approaching misery ... For the first time in history, humanity possesses the knowledge and the skill to relieve the suffering of these people (quoted from Easterly 2002, 226).

Security concerns remained in the background, however. The United States, then the major Western donor and the one donor which was largely spared the damage of World War II, wanted to rebuild Europe to protect and consolidate its capitalist allies from communism. The ensuing 40 years of Cold War took center stage on the geopolitical scene: the West in this period used ODA to keep several developing economies on their side of the Iron Curtain. The Soviet Union was equally successful in holding onto its communist members, although this was achieved with a combination of aid and military force. The collapse of the Soviet Union in 1991 tipped the balance in favor of capitalism. Development assistance in the 1990s was thus expanded to formerly communist economies which were now in transition to market-based systems. More importantly, the end of the Cold War brought a consensus on poverty reduction as the primary goal of ODA.

Development strategies in the 50 years since World War II underwent significant change. The 1950s and the 1960s were characterized by central planning and import-substituting industrialization policies with domestic savings supplemented by ODA on the belief that the lack of savings was the primary cause of underdevelopment. From the 1970s to the 1990s ODA emphasized the role of markets and international trade in the growth of income. The more recent emphasis is on the 'primacy of institutions' in growth (Rodrik et al. 2004). The search for recipes for economic growth and the role of aid – and donors – in this process has produced a large literature on the theory of economic growth and the preconditions for economic development. The recent Australian forays into the Pacific island region are a continuation of this exploration with potential lessons for development policy.

The motivations for providing aid based on humanitarian considerations remain, but in the bilateral context they are tempered by strategic, commercial and political considerations. Longer-term aid, such as that committed to meeting the Millennium Development Goals, is motivated by the global community's desire to see deprivation and suffering by the billion-plus poor be reduced measurably by 2015.[4] The goal of poverty reduction, however, is not orthogonal to the other objectives: sustained poverty reduction, for example, enhances political stability and thus contributes to economic prosperity over the long run. Any trade-off between poverty reduction on the one hand and strategic and economic interests of the donor on the other, therefore, is limited to the short term only. The time path of poverty reduction and improvements in security, however, will differ depending on which of the two is given priority.[5]

The ODA scene has increased in complexity over time. The end of the Cold War and the tightening of government expenditure in rich countries led to a sharp decline in the total volume of ODA. Assistance from Development Assistance Committee members of the Organization for Economic Cooperation and Development, for example, fell from around $58 billion or 0.33 per cent of gross national income (GNI) in 1991 to $52 billion or 0.23 per cent of GNI by 2001 (see Table 5.2).[6] This fall was contrary to the earlier commitments to increase ODA to 0.7 per cent of GNI.[7] While the total volume of aid has fallen, the number of donors and recipients has risen over time. The increasing fragmentation of ODA has been the result of the graduation of some former recipients (such as Germany, Japan, South Korea, Taiwan, etc.); the offer of aid by large developing nations such as China and India; and the arrival of new recipients, mostly East European states from the former Soviet bloc. The mode of aid delivery has also undergone several changes: it started as a transfer of budgetary resources, sometimes as goods and services procured from the donor and sometimes at inflated prices; moving toward arm's-length delivery following demands for untying aid; and a more recent trend towards active engagement of donor governments in delivering ODA in countries deemed to be lacking the institutional infrastructure for proper distribution.

Widespread dissatisfaction with aid effectiveness in a number of poor recipients led to aid conditionality, including the use of ODA to induce reforms. Experimentation with aid conditioned on policy reforms has been a disappointment, however. There is overwhelming evidence to show that aid conditionality has not worked (Svensson 2003). Several empirically based studies (not without disagreement, however) show that aid is effective in enhancing development only when policies are conducive to growth (see

Table 5.2   Net Official Development Assistance from DAC Countries to Developing Countries

			Per cent of GNI				
	1986–87 avg	1991–92 avg[a]	1998	1999	2000	2001	2002
Australia	0.40	0.37	0.27	0.26	0.27	0.25	0.26
Austria	0.19	0.14	0.22	0.24	0.23	0.29	0.26
Belgium	0.48	0.40	0.35	0.30	0.36	0.37	0.43
Canada	0.48	0.46	0.30	0.28	0.25	0.22	0.28
Denmark	0.88	0.99	0.99	1.01	1.06	1.03	0.96
Finland	0.48	0.72	0.31	0.33	0.31	0.32	0.35
France	0.58	0.62	0.40	0.39	0.32	0.32	0.38
Germany	0.41	0.38	0.26	0.26	0.27	0.27	0.27
Greece	na	na	0.15	0.15	0.20	0.17	0.21
Ireland	0.23	0.18	0.30	0.31	0.29	0.33	0.40
Italy	0.37	0.32	0.20	0.15	0.13	0.15	0.20
Japan	0.30	0.31	0.27	0.27	0.28	0.23	0.23
Luxembourg	0.17	0.29	0.65	0.66	0.71	0.76	0.77
Netherlands	0.99	0.87	0.80	0.79	0.84	0.82	0.81
New Zealand	0.28	0.25	0.27	0.27	0.25	0.25	0.22
Norway	1.13	1.15	0.89	0.88	0.76	0.80	0.89
Portugal	0.10	0.32	0.24	0.26	0.26	0.25	0.27
Spain	0.08	0.26	0.24	0.23	0.22	0.30	0.26
Sweden	0.87	0.96	0.72	0.70	0.80	0.77	0.83
Switzerland	0.30	0.41	0.32	0.35	0.34	0.34	0.32
United Kingdom	0.29	0.32	0.27	0.24	0.32	0.32	0.31
United States	0.21	0.20	0.10	0.10	0.10	0.11	0.13
Total DAC	0.33	0.33	0.23	0.22	0.22	0.22	0.23

Note:

a. Including debt forgiveness of non-ODA claims in 1991 and 1992, except for total DAC.

Source: Development Assistance Committee, OECD 2004.

World Bank 1998; Burnside and Dollar 2000).[8] This observation leads to the policy implication that aid should *only* flow to countries with 'good policies'. Such a policy, according to the Low Income Countries Under Stress (LICUS) initiative of the World Bank, would lock out around one-third of the world's poorest individuals from accessing aid, as their countries lack the necessary preconditions.[9] Doubts about the value of aid disbursed into poor policy environments and the fact that 'aid-selectivity' for the poorest economies is not practical provides a 'development-based' rationale for direct intervention by donors.

The new institutional economics literature, stressing the need for good governance and basic institutions to be available in order for investments to be effective in accelerating growth, provides further support for outside intervention to instill the preconditions for development when and where they are perceived to be lacking. This provides a rationale for the import of 'jurisdictional authority' in failed or failing nation-states. Donors have been willing to insert their own institutions (and personnel) into countries deemed to be lacking the above characteristics. However, success in terms of imbedding these within the recipients has been limited (Fukuyama 2004).

AUSTRALIAN AID POLICY

Australian experimentation with ODA follows the broader global trends identified above. Within the span of the past two decades, Australia conducted two broad-ranging reviews of its development assistance where the objectives, volume and effectiveness of ODA were considered at length. The first of these reviews, commonly referred to as the Jackson Committee, noted:

> Australians generally agree that the overall aims of foreign aid are to achieve humanitarian, strategic and commercial goals, and [they] are prepared to support an aid program which achieves these objectives. Australian aid policy has, therefore, not one but several mandates, and these need to be balanced against each other through the political process (Commonwealth of Australia 1984, 19).

The subsequent Simons Review in 1997 was highly critical of the triple mandate contained in the Jackson Review, claiming that it had eroded the developmental impact of ODA. It stated:

> The objective of the Australian aid program is to assist developing countries to reduce poverty through sustainable economic and social development (Commonwealth of Australia 1997, 69).

The Simons Review not only saw poverty reduction as the primary objective of ODA, it also stipulated that economic and social development were the only route to this goal.

The debate between the single versus multiple goals of ODA is an old one (see Easterly 2002 and Kanbur 2003). However, the tension over the primacy of poverty reduction displayed in the Jackson and Simons Reviews precedes much of the recent debate within the broader donor community. As an example, the poverty focus of the Simons Review is echoed in the Millennium Declaration of the United Nations, particularly those goals enumerated under Section III, 'Development and Poverty Eradication' (United Nations 2000).[10] The more recent debate on supplying global public goods and interventions to contain the widening impact of conflicts abroad echoes the sentiments expressed in the earlier Jackson Report.

On first taking office in March 1996, the Howard government, in conformity with contemporary thinking, announced that the primary objective of aid would be 'poverty reduction and the promotion of economic development'. One of the major initiatives at the time was the abolishment of the Development Import Finance Facility (DIFF), a mixed credit scheme created in 1982 to 'assist [local] industry in the face of aid-supported foreign competition' (Commonwealth of Australia 1997, 200). Simons argued that DIFF was flawed, as it was an attempt to achieve two frequently competing objectives with one instrument – ODA.

Surprisingly, the multiple ODA goals reflected in the earlier Jackson Report once again gained currency, both within Australia and abroad. The multifaceted humanitarian, strategic, economic and political demands placed on bilateral aid are being increasingly acknowledged, and an emphasis placed on the individual components seems indeed to be balanced via the political process. The Regional Assistance Mission to the Solomon Islands (RAMSI) provides an excellent case in point. In his address to parliament regarding the government's decision to deploy troops to the Solomon Islands, Prime Minister Howard stated that Australia was 'willing, in a cooperative and collegiate way, to play a supportive, stabilizing, and if it is required, more interventionist role in the region' (Howard 2003).[11]

Services funded with Australian aid, prior to RAMSI, were delivered at arm's length but this is changing rapidly. Australian contractors together with in-country service providers and non-governmental organizations have been engaged via a competitive tendering process managed by Australia's Overseas Aid Program (AusAID). There has, however, been a recent shift towards engaging Australian public servants in delivering services funded with the aid budget. RAMSI, for example, involved the placement of Australian police together with officials from the Commonwealth Treasury, the Department of

Finance and the Office of Financial Management into civil service positions in the Solomon Islands bureaucracy. The recent assistance to Nauru (2004) and Papua New Guinea (2003) also entail placement of Australian public servants within the recipient country's bureaucracies.

Security has been a major consideration in this shift to a more interventionist mode of delivering aid. In justifying the need for RAMSI to the Australian public, the prime minister warned:

> A failed state would not only devastate the lives of the peoples of the Solomons but could also pose a significant security risk for the whole region. Failed states can all too easily become safe-havens for transnational criminals and even terrorists. Poor governance and endemic corruption provide the conditions that support criminal activities (Howard 2003).

Two further, albeit less ambitious, interventions were announced in the aftermath of RAMSI. In December 2003 Canberra announced the Enhanced Cooperation Program (ECP) with the government of Papua New Guinea; the program seeks to revamp law and order, border control and budgetary management. Some six months later the government also announced plans to post three senior Australian bureaucrats to Nauru to assist the financially troubled country to sort out its financial crisis. These interventions reflect a recent global trend toward a greater willingness on the part of several Western governments to intervene in jurisdictions that are perceived as posing a security threat to them. The recent Australian intervention into the Pacific Island region thus provides an excellent case study in the evolution of aid policy more broadly.

Australia is a relatively small donor on the world stage, but it has a large presence in its immediate neighborhood. As of 2002, the most recent year for which data is available from the OECD, Australia accounted for approximately 2 per cent (around to $989 million) of the total $58 billion provided in overseas development assistance from DAC members. Most of the Australian funds were channeled to the Pacific islands. Papua New Guinea received approximately 19 per cent of total Australian ODA, another 10 per cent went to the small island states of the Southwest Pacific, 27 per cent went to East Asia and the remaining 44 per cent was distributed to aid recipients in the rest of the world. Australia is by far the largest donor to Papua New Guinea: it accounted for all of PNG's ODA receipts until independence in 1975, well over 90 per cent up until 1986, and approximately 80 per cent since then (see Table 5.3).[12] The major beneficiaries of Australian ODA were as follows: Nauru (97 per cent of total receipts), PNG (89 per cent), Solomon Islands (75 per cent), Vanuatu

Table 5.3   Per Capita Aid, Per Capita GDP, and Australian Share in Aid for PNG, 1960–2001

	Aid per capita (1995 US$)	Per capita GDP (1995 US$)	Australian share in aid (%)
1960		565	
1961		588	
1962		611	
1963		622	
1964		660	
1965	171	711	100
1966	161	735	100
1967	166	746	100
1968	173	760	100
1969	173	804	100
1970	199	870	100
1971	182	902	100
1972	211	931	100
1973	146	968	100
1974	173	970	99
1975	211	939	99
1976	141	886	96
1977	136	872	99
1978	140	923	99
1979	114	917	97
1980	112	874	96
1981	114	849	94
1982	109	830	95
1983	108	835	96
1984	101	811	93
1985	87	821	94
1986	82	838	92
1987	85	839	85
1988	86	842	78
1989	79	811	81
1990	98	768	82
1991	87	821	82
1992	93	911	70
1993	65	1050	83

Table 5.3   continued

	Aid per capita (1995 US$)	Per capita GDP (1995 US$)	Australian share in aid (%)
1994	66	1084	85
1995	82	1021	79
1996	78	1071	70
1997	71	993	78
1998	90	941	80
1999	62	988	73
2000	75	952	74
2001	62	897	80

Notes: PNG achieved independence in 1975; data for per capita GDP and aid sourced from World Bank Development Indicators via the International Economic Database, The Australian National University; share of Australian aid calculated using data extracted online from DAC database.

(36 per cent), Kiribati (34 per cent), Tonga (34 per cent), Fiji (25 per cent) and Timor-Leste (20 per cent). As of 2002, Australia accounted for 21 per cent of the total ODA to Oceania and Timor-Leste as a whole; this share rises to 53 per cent once Timor-Leste and the two French territories of French Polynesia and New Caledonia are excluded from the group of aid recipients in the South Pacific (see Table 5.4).[13] While approximately 20 per cent of total Australian ODA is disbursed via multilateral channels, the bulk of aid to PNG and the Pacific island states is delivered bilaterally. All of Australian aid to Nauru and more than 99 per cent to PNG and the Solomon Islands, for example, is delivered bilaterally. Australia, consequently, has the largest presence of all donors within Papua New Guinea and among the island states of the Southwest Pacific.[14]

The next section summarizes recent interventions into the Pacific island region and is followed by an assessment of the effectiveness of these interventions.

RECENT AUSTRALIAN INTERVENTIONS IN THE PACIFIC

Australian interventions into the Solomon Islands, Papua New Guinea and Nauru were at the invitation of the host governments. The arrival of the

Table 5.4   Total Net ODA Flows for 2002

Recipient	Total net ODA (US$m)	Recipients share in total (%)
Timor-Leste	219.77	0.15
Cook Islands	3.77	0.00
Fiji	31.27	0.02
French Polynesia	417.37	0.29
Kiribati	20.87	0.01
Marshall Islands	62.42	0.04
Micronesia	111.68	0.08
Nauru	11.72	0.01
New Caledonia	323.83	0.23
Niue	4.41	0.00
Palau	31.25	0.02
Papua New Guinea	203.28	0.14
Samoa	37.76	0.03
Solomon Islands	26.31	0.02
Tokelau	4.78	0.00
Tonga	22.27	0.02
Tuvalu	11.16	0.01
Vanuatu	19.6	0.01
Wallis & Futuna	52.73	0.04
Oceania Unspecified	42.61	0.03
Total	1439.09	

Australian-led 2225-person contingent of regional peacekeepers from Australia, Fiji, New Zealand, Tonga and Samoa into the Solomon Islands on 29 July 2003 heralded a new beginning for the Pacific in terms of foreign assistance to restore peace in a troubled neighbor. The entire force was on the ground within a matter of months and was complemented with another 17 Australian public servants posted into the Ministry of Finance and tasked to restore fiscal discipline. The achievements as of December 2004 are impressive, including: the arrest of some 3800 people including militia leaders, suspected murderers and extortionists; the seizure of some 4000 firearms and 300 000 rounds of ammunition and the restoration of law and order in the capital city (Dusevic 2004). Budgetary processes have also been restored. Officials within the Ministry of Finance are now able to perform their duties without being subjected to threats by the militia. A sense of security has returned, enabling

Table 5.4   continued

Recipient	Major donor	Share of major donor (% of receipt)	Australian share (% of receipt)
Timor-Leste	Australia	20	20
Cook Islands	New Zealand	71	19
Fiji	Japan	55	25
French Polynesia	France	100	0
Kiribati	Japan	45	34
Marshall Islands	USA	79	1
Micronesia	USA	89	1
Nauru	Australia	97	97
New Caledonia	France	100	0
Niue	New Zealand	84	9
Palau	Japan	53	<1
Papua New Guinea	Australia	89	89
Samoa	Japan	41	24
Solomon Islands	Australia	75	75
Tokelau	New Zealand	95	<1
Tonga	Australia	34	34
Tuvalu	Japan	69	18
Vanuatu	Australia	36	36
Wallis & Futuna	France	100	0
Oceania Unspecified	New Zealand	26	24

Notes:

a.   New Zealand provided a small amount of aid to French Polynesia and New Caledonia, and
    Wallis and Futuna as does the EC for the last.   Data sourced from DAC online database.

children to return to schools and their parents to resume their daily activities.[15] These milestones were achieved at a cost of approximately A$202 million, that is a significant jump from the pre-intervention aid allocation of A$38 million.

Negotiations commenced between Canberra and the government of Papua New Guinea, and in December 2003 the two foreign ministers jointly announced an Enhanced Cooperation Program (ECP). The ECP envisaged the placement of some 230 Australian police within the Royal Papua New Guinea Constabulary and approximately 70 Australian public servants into civil service positions in the PNG bureaucracy. The latter included placing 18 legal specialists into the Solicitor General's Office, Prosecutor's Office, National and Supreme Courts, the Department of Justice and correctional institutions; 36 economic and public administration specialists in key economic (such as Treasury) and sectoral (such as the National Department of Health) agencies and up to ten officials into transport and security agencies (including Immigration, Customs and Civil Aviation). The insertion of Australian public servants into the PNG bureaucracy was intended to strengthen the capacity of the PNG state to provide law and order and to ensure stronger economic management.

Australia has also assisted Nauru with its financial problems, providing approximately A$7 million in emergency aid in May 2002 and another A$22.5 in March 2004. Continuing problems with creditors led the Australian government to post three officials, one of them as secretary of finance, to Nauru in July 2004. These officials have been tasked with assisting the island nation to work through its fiscal problems, including sorting out Nauru's outstanding debt of some A$230 million.

Security concerns within Australia over the recent past played a significant role in its willingness to intervene within Nauru, the Solomon Islands and Papua New Guinea. Australia, for example, turned down a 2000 invitation by the prime minister of the Solomon Islands for military assistance to quell the violence which led to his removal from office by militants, but then Canberra embarked on RAMSI three years later.[16] Australia was quick to respond to the riots with troops and redeployed police to Honiara within 24 hours of riots in the capital which followed the announcement of a new prime minister. The Australian government has signaled its readiness to respond to a breakdown in law in the region, but will this improve the prospects for development within the recipient states?

EFFECTIVENESS OF AUSTRALIAN ODA

Australia's experiment with interventionist aid to the Pacific island region provides an excellent case study on the success or failure of such a strategy in inducing development. Peter Bauer, an ardent critic of ODA, conceded:

> In the very exceptional circumstances, foreign aid from a politically powerful country may both supply necessary capital and restore confidence. But in these conditions aid will restore confidence only in so far as it is interpreted as guaranteeing political security; a military presence in the recipient country, supplied by the donor country, would restore confidence perhaps more effectively even without aid (Bauer 1971, 98).

Bauer, thus, would have supported Australia's military intervention in the Solomon Islands and perhaps the police deployment to PNG for restoring confidence, but he warned: 'Foreign aid is ... not generally necessary or sufficient for advance from poverty' (98). The Australian interventions into the Pacific island have risks, including underwriting bad policies and/or bad governments which contributed to the crisis in the first place. The recipient governments face risks too. The intervention could be seen as patronizing, and the recipient could be viewed as being a puppet of the intervening force, thus undermining the credibility of the local leadership in the eyes of their electorate. These caveats do not negate the case for intervention, but rather call for the risks to be managed.

Intervention does not guarantee success. The experience of the United States with its assistance under the Compact of Free Association to the Federated States of Micronesia and the Republic of Marshall Islands has lessons for Australian interventions into the Pacific island region. The U.S. General Accounting Office (GAO), in testimony to the Committee on International Relations of the U.S. House of Representatives, for example, notes in relation to transfers of $1.8 billion (in 1999 prices) over the 1987–99 period that they had 'led to little improvement in economic development' and 'investments of Compact funds in business ventures had been a failure' (2000, 3). The GAO, however, notes that the national security objectives of the three partners were achieved. This raises the interesting question of whether Australia would be content with achieving the security objective without the anticipated developmental outcomes from its revamped aid effort into the Pacific island region. How effective is aid when it is delivered under an interventionist mode?

Australian Prime Minister Howard, in announcing the scaling up of aid, had made it clear that this was subject to 'the effectiveness of the application of additional resources' and 'conditional on strengthened governance and reduced corruption in recipient countries' (quoted in AusAID 2005, xii). The Australian government will, in increasing its assistance to the Pacific island region, pay greater attention to the effectiveness of this support. The past is not much of a guide on this matter. The effectiveness of Australian ODA, particularly in PNG, which is by far the largest recipient, is less than enviable. While the debate on the effectiveness of Australian aid is far from over (see Hughes, 2003 and AusAID, 2003a for opposing views), the simple correlation between the (per capita) levels of ODA and GDP for PNG is −0.31 at best (see Figure 5.1), suggesting an insignificant relationship between the two variables.[17]

RAMSI was motivated by concerns within Australia about the deteriorating law and order situation in the Solomon Islands and the threat this posed to security within Australia. The Mission was highly successful in restoring peace and law and order in the nation within a short presence, but the riots of April 2006 suggest that the task of imbedding this presence for the long term is far from over. The peacekeepers were successful in disarming the militia and in bringing to justice the locals implicated in the four years of violence preceding RAMSI. Many have been prosecuted and are serving prison terms. There have been concerns within the broader community that the instigators of the violence (the so-called 'big fish') remain free; some of these 'big fish' are alleged to be among the senior government leadership. RAMSI, given its success in restoring state institutions, is seen as propping up a leadership which is perceived to be less than completely clean. The riots that followed the April 2006 national elections were the worst seen in the country's history and specifically protest the reappointment of the 'old guard'. Ironically, this followed what was considered by the international media to be 'free and fair' elections held under the watchful presence of RAMSI. An intervening force such as RAMSI walks a tightrope in terms of creating legitimacy for the nation-state while working with a government which is its host and which may have attained office under questionable circumstances. The fragility of peace in the Solomon Islands, as demonstrated by the April 2006 riots, suggests that state-building could be a very slow process. The final verdict on RAMSI may not be known for years.

The PNG Enhanced Cooperation Program was initiated with a view to addressing deficiencies within the areas of law and order, justice, economic management, public-sector reform, border control and transportation security and safety. The police component of the program is on hold, but the Australian public servants placed in other government agencies remain. The fiscal position of the state has improved over the past two years, but extracting the impact of ECP on improved macroeconomic management from other exogenous factors such as improvements in the nation's terms of trade and improved weather leading to bumper harvests remain to be assessed. Furthermore, the capacity of the government to protect its budget surplus from being raided as the 2007 elections approach will be a litmus test on improved economic management. Thus, judging the effectiveness of ECP may also be premature, even though there is some evidence of success.

Time will reveal the success of the Australian ODA interventions into the Pacific island region. The success of the interventions will entail a transition over the medium term in PNG and the Solomon Islands to economic growth, fiscal sustainability and consolidation of law and order and democracy such that the need for continued intervention expires. The record of interventions

Figure 5.1   Per Capita ODA and GDP in Papua New Guinea, 1960–2001

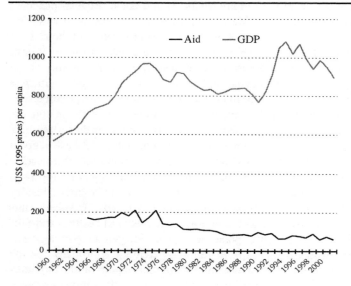

Source: Data sourced from World Development Indicators; nominal per-capita aid deflated by the GDP deflator.

in achieving these goals is less than promising, but the experiments within the Pacific island region may have several lessons for the donor community.

CONCLUSION

Australian assistance to the Pacific island region has increased in volume and has become more interventionist since 2003. These trends conform with development assistance to fragile states more broadly, thus the Australian 'experiment' may have lessons for the broader development community. While it may be a bit too early to judge the effectiveness of the Australian interventions discussed in this chapter, there are good reasons to track progress. The Australian interventions into the Pacific island region were motivated by security concerns. The interventions were targeted at restoring law and order where it was perceived to be failing, and Australian personnel posted into inline positions in target countries were tasked with creating functioning states. The interventions into Nauru, the Solomon Islands and Papua New Guinea have had some success in restoring peace, improving law and order and balancing the budget. The April 2006 riots in the Solomon Islands suggest that these achievements remain fragile, thus the commitment may need to remain for much longer if state-building is to take place. The promptness of the Australian response in terms of redeploying troops and police to the Solomon Islands following the riots signals that Australia remains committed to ensuring that law and order prevails in the Pacific region. Donor countries providing support through interventions on behalf of the incumbent governments risk being seen as propping up 'neopatrimonial' regimes; that is, regimes which use political power to service their own clientelist network of supporters. Such a perception is likely to erode the credibility of the intervening force. The process of state-building is both time consuming and is prone to failure, thus history will judge the success of the current interventions.

The path that the intervention takes will be keenly followed, given its relevance for the broader development community. Overseas development assistance has a relatively short history, having gained center stage in policymaking within the United States in the early 1950s and in Australia approximately a decade later. The end of the Cold War in 1991 witnessed a convergence on poverty reduction as the primary goal of development assistance. The UN Millennium Development Goals reflect this consensus. The heightened security agenda following the 9/11 terrorist attacks on the United States has provided added impetus to the role of aid in development, but this security agenda is not necessarily in conflict with the goals of poverty reduction. The Australian government argues that poverty reduction is in its national interest as it improves security. Overseas development assistance can thus constitute 'enlighted self-interest'.

NOTES

This research has benefited from funding from the Australian Research Council and the Australian Agency for International Development.

1. Data is the most recent as made available by DAC online database, accessed on 23 November 2005.
2. Commonwealth of Australia, 'Budget at a Glance', http://www.budget.gov.au/2005-06/at_a_glance/download/at_a_glance.pdf.
3. The IMF was created to stabilse international finance and not as an aid agency, but has over time 'delivered concessional loans on a sustained basis, part of which were later forgiven, which is observationally equivalent to delivering aid' (Easterly 2003, 37).
4. Estimates of the number of poor – that is, people with income less than $1 a day – differs between 800 million and 1.3 billion.
5. The overlap between the goals of poverty reduction to those of internal security has been used to rationalize ODA as being 'enlightened self-interest'.
6. ODA since 2001 has been on a bounce-back with total disbursements from DAC as of 2004

exceeding \$90 billion.

7. Pearson Report of 1969 set the 0.7 per cent of GNI target for industrial country donors. The United States and Switzerland are the only two countries that have not endorsed this target.
8. Easterly, Levine and Roodman (2003) show that the alleged impact of aid on growth in favorable policy environment as per Burnside and Dollar (2000) is fragile.
9. See World Bank, http://www1.worldbank.org/operations/licus/.
10. The Millennium Development Goals (MDGs) constitute paragraph 19 of this Declaration.
11. The announcement took many commentators by surprise as the Foreign Affairs Minister had announced six months earlier that military intervention in the Solomon Islands would be 'folly in the extreme' (*Australian*, 8 January 2004).
12. The figures in Tables 5.3 and 5.4 differ due to the different sources. The figures reported in Table 5.3 are for ODA from all sources while the figures in Table 5.4 are from DAC members alone.
13. DAC includes French Territories of French Polynesia and New Caledonia as Oceania.
14. The country focus of other donors include: France on its trust territories of French Polynesia and New Caledonia as well as Wallis and Futuna; New Zealand on Cook Islands, Niue and Tokelau; the United States on Marshall Islands and the Federated States of Micronesia; and Japan on Fiji, Palau, and Samoa.
15. The first fatality, of an Australian Protective Service Officer by a sniper attack took place on 22 December, 2004. Australia, in response to this attack, sent in 100 soldiers the very next day.
16. Such assistance, if provided then, could have averted the need for RAMSI subsequently.
17. Multivariate analysis of this relationship is being explored as part of ongoing work.

BIBLIOGRAPHY

Asian Development Bank (2003), *Millennium Development Goals in the Pacific: Relevance and Progress*, Manila: Asian Development Bank.

Australia's Overseas Aid Program [AusAID] (2003a), 'The Contribution of Australian Aid to Papua New Guinea's Development 1975–2000: Provisional Conclusions from a Rapid Assessment', *Evaluation and Review Series*, No. 34.

——(2003b), *Statistical Summary: Australian Government Overseas Aid Program*, Canberra: AusAID.

——(2004), *Pacific Regional Aid Strategy 2004–2009*, Canberra: AusAID.

——(2005), *Core Group Recommendations Report for a White Paper on Australia's Aid Program*, Canberra: AusAID.

Bauer, P.T. (1971), *Dissent on Development: Studies and Debates in Development Economics*, London: Weidenfeld and Nicolson.

Burnside, Craig and David Dollar (2000), 'Aid, Policies, and Growth', *American Economic Review*, **90** (4), 847–68.

Collier, Paul (1997), 'The Failure of Conditionality', in Catherine Gwin and Joan M. Nelson (eds), *Perspectives on Aid and Development*, Washington, DC: Overseas Development Council, pp. 51–78.

Commonwealth of Australia, (1984). *Report of the Committee to Review the Australian Overseas Aid Program*, AGPS, Canberra (Jackson Report).

Commonwealth of Australia (1997), *One Clear Objective: Poverty Reduction Through Sustainable Development*, Report of the Committee of Review, AusAID, Canberra (Simons Report)

Commonwealth of Australia (2004), *Pacific Regional Aid Strategy 2004–2009*,

Canberra.

Commonwealth of Australia (2006), *Core Group Recommendations Report for a White Paper on Australia's Aid Program*, Australian Agency for International Development, Canberra, Australia.

Development Assistance Committee (2004), 'Improving the Aid Effectiveness of Europe's Largest Donor Country', Organization for Cooperation and Development, 27 May, http://www.oecd.org.

Dollar, David and Jakob Svensson (1998), 'What Explains the Success or Failure of Structural Adjustment Programs?', Washington, DC: World Bank, Policy Research Working Paper No. 1938.

Dusevic, Tom (2004), 'The Storm: An Australian-led Rescue Mission Has Stopped the Bloodshed – But the Job of Rebuilding Solomon Islands Has Only Just Begun', *Time* (6 December), 17–23.

Easterly, William (2002), 'The Cartel of Good Intentions: The Problem of Bureaucracy in Foreign Aid', *Journal of Policy Reform*, **5** (4), 223–50.

Easterly, William (2003), 'Can Foreign Aid Buy Growth?', *Journal of Economic Perspectives*, **17** (3), 23–48.

Easterly, William, Ross Levine and David Roodman (2003), 'New Data, New Doubts: A Comment on Burnside and Dollar's "Aid Policies and Growth",' Cambridge, MA, National Bureau of Economic Research (NBER) Working Paper No. 9846.

Fry, Greg (2004), 'The "War Against Terror" and Australia's New Interventionism in the Pacific'. Paper presented at the Australian National University conference 'Foreign Policy, Governance and Development: Challenges for Papua New Guinea and Pacific Islands', Madang, PNG 22–23 March.

Fukuyama, Francis (2004), 'The Imperative of State-Building', *Journal of Democracy* **15** (2), 17–31.

Howard, John (2003), 'Ministerial Statement to Parliament on the Regional Assistance Mission To The Solomon Islands (RAMSI)', Office of the Prime Minister. 12 August.

Hughes, Helen (2003), 'Aid Has Failed the Pacific', Sydney, Center for Independent Studies, Issue Analysis No. 33.

Kanbur, Ravi 2003. "The economics of international aid", http://www.arts.cornell.edu/poverty/kanbur/HandbookAid.pdf.

Reilly, Ben (2002), 'Internal Conflict and Regional Security in Asia and the Pacific', *Pacifica Review* **14** (1), 7–22.

Rodrik, Dani, Arvind Subramaniam and Francesco Trebbi (2004), 'Institutions Rule: The Primacy of Institutions Over Geography and Integration in Economic Development', *Journal of Economic Growth* **9** (2), 131–65.

Sen, Amartya (1999), *Development as Freedom*, New York: Oxford University Press.

Svensson, Jakob (2003), 'Why Conditional Aid Does Not Work and What Can Be Done About It', *Journal of Development Economics* **70** (2), 381–402.

United Nations (2000), *United Nations Millennium Declaration*, Resolution A/RES/55/2 18 September 2000.

United States General Accounting Office (2000), *Foreign Assistance: U.S. Funds to Two Micronesian Nations Had Little Impact on Economic Development and Accountability Over Funds Was Limited.* Testimony before the U.S. House of Representatives, Committee on International Relations, Subcommittee on Asia and the Pacific, 28 June.

Wainwright, Elsina (2003), 'Our Failing Neighbour: Australia and the Future of Solomon Islands', Canberra, Australian Strategic Policy Institute.

White, Hugh and Elsina Wainwright (2004), 'Strengthening Our Neighbour: Australia and the Future of Papua New Guinea', Canberra, Australian Strategic Policy Institute.

World Bank, (1998), *Assessing Aid: What Works, What Doesn't, and Why*, New York: Oxford University Press.

PART THREE

Interdependence and Migration

6. Migration and Development: Managing Mutual Effects

Dhananjayan Sriskandarajah

The nexus between migration and development has been high on the research and policy agendas in recent years, with numerous initiatives aimed at understanding the relationship better. This work has been motivated by – and further contributed to – the belief that migration can have significant effects on development outcomes, especially in developing countries experiencing significant outflows of migrants. Consequently, these impacts need to be managed more effectively.

Interest in the effects of emigration on the development potential of sending countries is by no means new. Indeed, the very term 'brain drain' is thought to have been first used soon after World War II to refer to the apparently large numbers of scientists leaving the United Kingdom and going to the United States. Since then, the term has come to refer to the out-migration flows of highly skilled people, largely from developing countries, and has been a key feature of debates since the 1960s over whether large-scale emigration was bad for developing countries (see, e.g., Adams 1968). More recently, as the scale and complexity of migratory flows have grown, contemporary discussions have moved beyond focusing only on the ill-effects of brain drain and instead have taken a broader focus which looks at the mutual development impacts of the flows of people, skills, knowledge and remittances.

The renewed interest in the nexus is welcome, because researchers have hitherto tended to focus more on the economic, political and social effects of migration on individual immigrants and the societies they enter than on how emigration affects the societies they leave behind. Similarly, policymakers have tended, especially in developed countries, to focus on the politically salient issues of immigrant integration rather than on the impacts felt in their erstwhile homelands, perhaps reflecting the overwhelming public concern about the situation in the 'new' country and relative ignorance of the home country.

This chapter reviews some of the burgeoning literature on the nexus between migration and development in order to explore ways in which migration and its effects can be managed to optimize development outcomes. While the study is certainly concerned with empirical and theoretical issues arising from this literature, its primary focus is on policy options which may lead to fairer flows of people, skills and remittances which will enhance economic development and poverty reduction in developing countries. Adopting what some have called a 'nationalist' position (see Ellerman 2003), this chapter recognizes that it is important to take into account the adverse impacts of migration on particular countries, even if that migration has led to global welfare gains.

The study identifies both general measures which apply to all migrants in all countries (e.g., the cost of transferring money) and also specific contexts in which the relationship between migration and development is particularly relevant (e.g., low-income, high-emigration countries; countries experiencing 'brain strain'; post-conflict situations). Before turning to these policies, however, the following section outlines some of the main challenges which migration poses for development outcomes.

MIGRATION AND DEVELOPMENT: A WHIRLWIND TOUR

The global scale of migration has been growing considerably: from an estimated 82 million international migrants in 1970 to 175 million in 2000 (see Table 6.1). The latest estimates suggest that some 200 million people, or around 3 per cent of the global population, live outside their country of birth (GCIM 2005, 83). Almost all regions are experiencing rising stocks of migrants, with substantial rises in migrant numbers in Europe and North America.

Theoretical and empirical analysis tells us that economic disparities between countries account for much of the dynamics of international migration – people often move to seek economic opportunities in more prosperous countries. Not only does this account for the relatively large rise in migrant stocks in developed countries shown in Table 6.1, but it also fits with evidence which suggests that about one-quarter of all international migrants have moved from non-OECD (Organization for Economic Cooperation and Development) countries to OECD countries (Table 6.2). Moreover, even among the more substantial movements between non-OECD countries, many people move from poorer to richer countries, for example from many parts of Sub-Saharan Africa to South Africa and from many parts of Asia to the Gulf states.

Economic theory also suggests that migration can have significant benefits for global economic welfare. When migrant workers move between differently endowed countries (e.g., from a country where there are large labor surpluses in one sector to another country where there are labor shortages in that sector), that movement can enhance economic conditions in both sending and receiving

Table 6.1   International Migrants by Region of Destination, 1960–2000 (in millions)

Region	1960	1970	1980	1990	2000
World	75.9	81.5	99.8	154.0	174.9
Developed countries	32.1	38.3	47.7	89.7	110.3
Developed countries (excl. USSR)	29.1	35.2	44.5	59.3	80.8
Developing countries	43.8	43.2	52.1	64.3	64.6
Africa	9.0	9.9	14.1	16.2	16.3
Asia[a]	29.3	28.1	32.3	41.8	43.8
Latin America & Caribbean	6.0	5.8	6.1	7.0	5.9
North America	12.5	13.0	18.1	27.6	40.8
Oceania	2.1	3.0	3.8	4.8	5.8
Europe[b]	14.0	18.7	22.2	26.3	32.8
USSR (former)	2.9	3.1	3.3	30.3	29.5

Notes:

a. Excluding Armenia, Azerbaijan, Georgia, Kazakhstan, Kyrgyzstan, Tajikistan, Turkmenistan and Uzbekistan.

b. Excluding Belarus, Estonia, Latvia, Lithuania, Moldova, the Russian Federation and Ukraine.

Source: UN/DESA 2004, viii.

countries. Indeed, one estimate suggests that if developed countries were to increase the proportion of migrant workers in the labor force to 3 per cent, world output would increase by over $150 billion per year (Winters 2002).

Evidence suggests that migration can have significant economic benefits for developed countries. For example, given the preferences of the resident workforce in developed countries, migrant workers are more likely to fill vacancies in the so-called dirty, dangerous and difficult jobs. In the medium term, industries in developed countries which face critical vacancies can benefit from tapping into the excess labor supply of developing countries (in recent years the health or information technology sectors, in particular). Over the long term, as dependency ratios in developed countries rise, there will be a need to attract migrant workers to keep an economy dynamic. This would suggest that migration from areas of relative labor surplus to areas of relative shortage will

Table 6.2   Migrants Moving between OECD and the Rest of the World, 2000

	From OECD countries	From rest of the world	Total
To OECD countries	22.2 million (16.2 %)	34.1 million (24.9%)	56.3 million (41.1%)
To rest of the world	2.5 million (1.8%)	77.9 million (57.0%)	80.4 million (58.8%)
Total	24.7 million (18.0%)	112.0 million (81.9%)	136.7 million (100.0%)

Source: Harrison et al. (2004, 4).

continue as long as there is a political willingness to permit such movement. In many parts of the developed world, this willingness is in evidence, accounting for some of the rises in migrant stock.

However, movements from poorer to richer countries can have adverse economic effects on sending countries. If these flows lead to a drain of highly skilled people from developing countries, the ability of those countries to develop may be compromised. The absence of these key workers hampers the ability of these countries to come up with home-grown solutions to their problems; that is, it creates a 'brain strain'. Where those migrants move and contribute to economic dynamism in destination countries, there is a risk that migration can widen the gap between richer and poorer countries.

Yet, migration can also have positive effects on countries of origin. The money which migrants send home (remittances) can contribute significantly to both the recipients' welfare as well as the receiving country's economic well-being. If migrants return home, either permanently or for short periods, with new skills which they put to good use, they and their communities can benefit. Even when they do not return in person, members of a diaspora can contribute to the development of their erstwhile homelands through trade, investment, networking and skills transfer. A rough 'balance sheet' of the economic effects of migration is presented in Table 6.3.

The negative impacts of emigration are often worst in the poorest countries. For some low-income countries which have high rates of permanent emigration, especially of highly skilled people, migration can pose a significant threat. Where these countries have a poor economic and financial infrastructure, the

Table 6.3   The Economic Effects of Migration on Countries of Origin

Positive effects	Negative effects
Provides opportunities to workers not available in the home country.	Loss of highly skilled workers and reduced quality of essential services.
May ease the effect on the domestic market of the supply of excess labor.	Reduced growth and productivity because of the lower stock of highly skilled workers and its externalities.
Inflow of remittances and foreign exchange.	Lower return from public investments in public education.
Technology transfer, investments and venture capital contributed by diasporas.	Selective migration may cause increasing disparities in incomes in the home country.
Can contribute to increased trade flows between sending and receiving countries.	Loss of fiscal revenue from taxation of workers.
Stimulus to investment in domestic education and individual human capital investments.	Remittances may diminish over time.
Return of skilled workers may increase local human capital, transfer of skills and links to foreign networks.	

Source: UN/DESA (2004, 97).

potential which emigrants can contribute to development through remittances, investment and return or circulation migration is not fully exploited.

Whether the effects of migration are adverse or beneficial will depend to a great deal on the balance between temporary and permanent migration and between high-skilled and low-skilled migration. While it is important to recognize that all four combinations of these streams (temporary high-skill, permanent high-skill, temporary low-skill and permanent low-skill) are likely to remain important into the future (albeit to different degrees for different countries), policymakers face a choice of shaping the flows themselves or shaping the impacts of these flows. The choices for managing these processes for high-emigration developing countries are often complex and difficult to achieve unilaterally.

Adding to that difficulty is the fact that migration is an extremely complex phenomenon. For example, migrants move within their own country and between countries; some move for short periods, others permanently; some are forced to move, others do so willingly; some people move with high levels of financial and human capital, others are not so well endowed and so on. Making conclusive generalized observations (based on good quality, comparable data) about these migratory flows is not easy – let alone making them about their effect on economic development. Framing appropriate policy interventions given this empirical complexity is a considerable challenge. Nevertheless, there are three broad areas in which policy interventions may prove fruitful: people flows, financial flows and diaspora potential. Each of these is dealt with in turn below.

PEOPLE FLOWS

Evidence of the movement of highly skilled people (brain drain) is not hard to find. Lowell et al. (2004, 9) report that nearly one in ten tertiary-educated adults born in the developing world now reside in North America, Australia or Western Europe. Jamaica, for example, loses about 20 per cent of its specialist nurses annually, mainly to the United States or the United Kingdom (Wyss 2004). Africa Recruit (2003), an organization which aims to replenish skills in Africa, noted that about 40 per cent of all African professionals have left the continent's shores in the post-colonial period. Other studies have found that between one-third and one-half of the developing world's science and technology personnel live in the developed world. By the end of the 1990s, Indians working in the United States on temporary working visas accounted for 30 per cent of the entire Indian software labor force (Commander et al. 2003).

Figure 6.1 shows workers with a tertiary education as a percentage of the migrant population from the source country and as a percentage of the total population, respectively. These data confirm the general impression that highly skilled workers have a higher propensity to migrate than other workers. Skilled workers are attracted to developed countries not only because of higher wages, but also because of better working conditions offering higher productivity. On the demand side, developed countries are keen to attract skilled workers who can fill gaps in the labor force. The flight of skilled workers will further lower productivity and wages in developing countries, hence increasing the problems that cause emigration in the first place. This vicious cycle is compounded by the fact that countries with a lack of skilled workers will face difficulties attracting foreign direct investment.

However, the movement of highly skilled workers itself is not necessarily a bad thing. Instead, it is the potential of these movements to have adverse

Figure 6.1   The High Propensity to Migrate for Skilled Workers

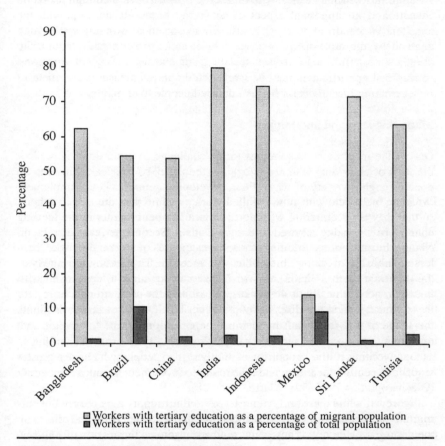

□ Workers with tertiary education as a percentage of migrant population
■ Workers with tertiary education as a percentage of total population

Source: CPS, OECD, UNESCO, cited in Kapur 2004.

consequences on the development of a sending country which needs attention. Brain drain does not necessarily lead to brain strain. For example, highly skilled migrant workers do not necessarily represent a loss to the economy when they migrate, especially if they would not have been employed effectively in the domestic labor market due to an oversupply of workers with those same skills. The sector they left (e.g. India's IT sector) may be able to develop and thrive despite this leakage of workers, and the sending country's economy may actually benefit from remittances which migrant workers send home. In other words, the out-migration of skilled workers must be seen in the context of the requirements of the country in question.

Countries which face clearly adverse effects face a difficult dilemma. While education is an important aspect of achieving economic development, the excellent education of workers is also the reason those workers are in high demand by the developed countries. Also, as Carrington and Detragiache (1999) note, 'Efforts to reduce specific skill shortages through improved educational opportunities may be largely futile unless measures are taken to offset existing incentives for highly educated people to emigrate.'

Managing Demand and Supply

One of the most obvious solutions to the challenge of brain drain is to slow the flow of emigrants who are 'clogging' the drain, so to speak. This can be done through a variety of ways. First, developing countries could implement 'bonding' contracts with future skilled workers while they are still in school, so that they are required to work for a certain number of years in the sending country before being allowed to emigrate again. Second, governments could change the education curriculum for some categories of workers to make them less suitable for working abroad but still adequate for meeting the needs of the domestic sector. Ghana, Malawi, Tanzania and Zambia have toyed with this approach for health professionals. Obviously the standard of training for these workers must not drop below a certain level, and this threshold limits the scope of this method. A more fruitful approach might be to devote more resources to primary and secondary education rather than tertiary schooling so as to reduce the relative proportion of highly skilled people (who have a greater tendency to emigrate) and increase the return to investment in education overall (Psacharopoulos 1985, 591; Martin 2003, 28).

However, while these sorts of measures to limit supply may reduce the out-migration of highly skilled workers, they may have other detrimental effects on the domestic economy of any country which institutes these sorts of policies. A more prudent strategy might be initiatives to limit demand, especially in key sectors. This could be done several ways.

First, establishing codes of practice, such as the Commonwealth Code of Practice for International Recruitment of Health Workers, that encourages countries and agencies to recruit responsibly and make sure that migrant-sending countries benefit in the form of overseas assistance and/or return migration. One of the most important principles of such a code should be to avoid recruiting workers from particular sectors in particular countries known to have a shortage of skilled workers in that sector. Employers should be strongly encouraged – if not required – to embrace this code, and there needs to be cooperation within and between countries. If only some employers adopt a code or practice, it will have a very limited effect. Similarly, if only some countries address the problem of brain drain while others continue to recruit indiscriminately, the desired effect will not be achieved. Hence, one of the strongest recommendations must be for the establishment of multilateral agreements on this issue.

Second, international recruitment agencies should be regulated to ensure that companies adhere to the code of practice. Not only would employers be provided with the certainty that they are in compliance with ethical guidelines in their recruitment policies, but in addition migrant workers would be offered added safety against exploitation.

Compensate Sending Countries

Another option which is often suggested is compensating sending (developing) countries for their loss of human capital through emigration. Though attractive to many political leaders, at least three key questions must be addressed if any compensation scheme is to become operational. First, who pays – migrants themselves, their employers in host countries, the host government or some combination of these three? Second, who benefits – the migrant's country of origin or at-risk developing countries in general, sending country governments, non-governmental organizations or particular sectors of the sending country's economy, such as education? Third, what channels are used – direct transfers to sending countries or indirect administration of funds collected by host country or intermediary institutions?

One way of funding compensation schemes, most famously articulated by Jagdish Bhagwati (1976), involves an extra tax on migrant workers which is then repatriated to the country of origin. More recently, Kapur and McHale (2005) have suggested that destination countries should set high visa fees for highly skilled migrants and then share the proceeds with the source country. At first, these seem to be attractive propositions. However, requiring migrants themselves to pay extra (over and above any private remittances they send) may create disincentives to migrate or to work legally after migration. They also may be difficult to implement, and taxing some groups of workers higher than others could conflict with constitutional law.

Alternatively, migrants could be taxed at the same rate as nationals of the host country, but part of that revenue could be repatriated. The Netherlands, Denmark and Sweden use another approach, whereby temporary workers pay a lower tax rate than residents, partly in order to attract foreign workers, but also partly because the government recognizes that they are less of a drain on public expenditure in areas such as child care and pensions.

Another option which may or may not be linked to taxation schemes for migrant workers is having developed countries sponsor training schemes in high-emigration countries and regions. Lowell et al. (2004, 28) propose having the U.K. government spend some of its overseas assistance on paying to train staff which are in short supply due to recruitment from the U.K. and other developed countries. However, it would be unwise to spend a large proportion of the aid budget on a problem which is essentially created by developed countries, and – unless the size of the budget was increased – would inevitably 'crowd out' spending on the very poor.

Promoting Circular and Return Migration

Migration is often viewed as a process in which migrants settle permanently in a new country with their family. However, there is evidence of more circular patterns emerging in which migrants return to their country of birth, once or many times over a period of time. Encouraging such circularity can make sense for several reasons. First, return migration means that the sending country can benefit from skills learned by the migrant and that human capital is not lost. Second, migrants are more likely to remit if they still have close links with their sending country. This is particularly the case if temporary migration results in family separation. Third, circular migration is likely to be more acceptable to voters in developed countries (HCIDC 2004, 41). Thus effective temporary migration programs may lead to more workers in the developing world being able to make use of migration.

Both the sending and hosting countries can benefit from circular migration by implementing a range of policies. For example, they could make it easy for workers to obtain temporary work visas; evidence shows that this actually promotes return migration. Countries could operate a centralized temporary visa-program in which work cycles last a few years. They could provide financial incentives for return such as reimbursing part of income tax paid upon return to the home country. Finally, governments could promote assimilation back into the migrant-sending country by providing loans for housing and cars and ensuring a reintroduction into the local labor market at a level which corresponds to the skills and experience acquired by the migrant.

In addition to these steps, in order to encourage return migration in the long term, it is vital that many migrant-sending countries focus on implementing good governance, anti-corruption measures and sound policies which foster economic growth (HCIDC 2004, 47). Countries racked by civil war or oppressive political regimes will not be attractive to highly skilled workers, despite strong family ties and other social links.

While promoting circular migration, it is also important to keep in mind that temporary workers are often vulnerable, and that they are frequently unaware of their rights. Bilateral agreements of temporary migration between countries could be effective in protecting labor rights, as embassies and consulates are already in place to provide representation of the country's citizens and because national administrations have more bargaining power in ensuring that workers are treated properly. The agreement between Mexico and Canada on agricultural workers presents a good example of how temporary migration can benefit both countries.

FINANCIAL FLOWS

The importance of migrant remittances is clear. They are a large and still rising source of income. Formal remittances to developing countries reached $167 billion in 2005, up 73 per cent from 2001 (World Bank 2005). In fact, remittances now approximately double the size of net official finance and are rising relative to foreign direct investment (World Bank 2004, 169). Usually they are less volatile than private capital flows, that tend to move cyclically and may even rise during recessions (Ratha 2003, 157), thus helping to stimulate vulnerable economies during recessions.

They constitute an important source of both income and foreign exchange earnings for many migrant-exporting countries, especially for countries with foreign-exchange constraints which can use them as a means to pay for imported goods and to service foreign debt. Remittances are more likely to reach areas of economies and societies which are left relatively untouched by overseas development assistance (ODA) and private capital from foreign investors.

Remittances benefit certain types of countries and regions more than others. Latin American countries and South Asia take the lion's share of global remittances between them (while Sub-Saharan Africa only receives 4.1 per cent); and Mexico,[1] China, India and the Philippines are the largest recipients of remittances in absolute terms. Remittances are extremely important for some small countries with large diasporas: as a percentage of national income, they constitute some 37 per cent of GDP for Tonga and 27 per cent of Lesotho's GDP (see Figure 6.2). They are likely to be acutely important in situations of conflict and post-war reconstruction (HCIDC 2004, 56). South–South flows are also believed to be substantial, comprising 30–45 per cent of total remittances received by developing countries (World Bank 2005).

Not much is known about remittance behavior, although we can assume that remittances are motivated by altruism (Lucas 2005, 6), usually sent in small amounts and mostly sent to close relatives. They also appear to be likely to reduce over time for permanent migrants and likely to have effects at both the individual and aggregate levels (see Table 6.4).

Figure 6.2 Top 20 Receiving Countries of Remittances as Percentage of GDP

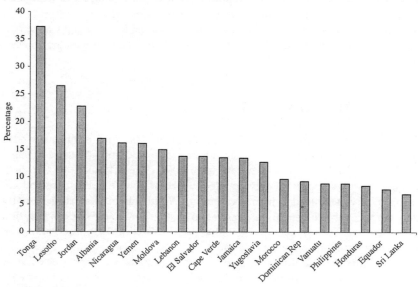

Source: Ratha 2003.

Any set of policies which seeks to shape remittance flows must recognize at least four principles about remittances. First, remittances are almost always legitimate private transfers of post-tax income and therefore should not be subject to undue governmental regulation. Regulators cannot and should not seek to control the size, nature or use of remittances. Second, formal transfers are preferable to informal flows to avoid clandestine laundering networks, minimize the risk of exploitation and improve analysts' ability to account properly for flows. Third, it is better to use carrots rather than sticks to make sure that remittances are declared, because sanctions may reduce flows or increase the likelihood of informal transfers. Finally, the goal of remittance policies should not be to maximize remittances *per se* (there is no clear economic argument to justify this) but rather to facilitate their transfer and optimize their impact.

Promote formal remittances

The $167 billion of annual remittances noted above excludes unrecorded or informal remittances. Goods which are carried or sent, also known as

Table 6.4   A Typology of Potential Impacts of Remittances

	Individual	Country
Sending	Strengthens ties with former home	Relatively small leakage from developed countries
	May repay financial and other debts at home	May serve as indirect compensation for brain drain
	Risks being an excessive drain on often meager disposable incomes	
Receiving	Increases incomes	Important source of foreign exchange
	May lead to human capital investment	May help to alleviate poverty, especially in particular regions or during emergencies
	Steady source of windfall income may act as an economic disincentive to participate in the domestic labor force	May boost financial sector and investment

remittances-in-kind, are not recorded. More important however, are remittances which are sent through unofficial channels, such as the Hawala system used by South Asian migrants. According to the World Bank (2005) the informal remittance sector is likely to be at least 50 per cent of the official sector.

Several factors influence migrants' decisions regarding how to remit, including the existence of parallel exchange rate markets and financial infrastructure in the migrant-sending country. In particular, an undeveloped banking sector and the inability of official transfers to reach some parts of the country will encourage migrant workers to use informal channels. It has been widely suggested that countries which would like to attract formal remittances should ensure that their exchange rate is not overvalued and that imported goods which can be carried are not subject to high tariffs.

Transfer fees for formal remittances are very high, in come cases as much as 20 per cent of the money sent (World Bank 2004, 171). This means that it is easier for the informal sector to compete with formal remittance channels. High costs are a concern not only because they provide an incentive to remit informally but also because they shave off a substantial amount of income for relatively poor families. Suro (2003) estimates that for remittances from the United States to Latin American countries alone, lowering those fees to about 5 per cent of total remittances would free up an extra $1 billion, which would benefit many poor households. The high cost of transfers is usually ascribed to a lack of competition, lack of information and high fixed costs for the banking sector (Suro 2003; HCIDC 2004). In addition, without access to the formal banking system, migrants have fewer choices and there is likely to be less competition between money-transfer services.

As long as the magnitude of unrecorded remittances is so great, it is difficult to get meaningful results from data analysis, and an effort should be made to encourage remittances through formal channels. A greater use of the banking sector for transfers also opens up sources of finance for the migrant-recipient, and it allows remittances kept as savings to be used as funds for investment. From the discussion above, it is clear that policies designed to encourage a switch away from informal transfer methods must focus on providing the means and incentives for migrants to remit formally. Hence, these policies would, first, make it easier for migrants to access the formal banking system (HCIDC 2004, 59). A greater number of transfers would lower the average fixed costs faced by banks, give migrants greater choice and also increase competition. Second, encouraging greater transparency would allow migrants to compare various costs of transferring money. Increasing the amount of information available to migrants is important, especially since there is evidence that their knowledge of the banking sector and the actual cost of transferring is very limited. This role could be filled by NGOs which are better positioned than government institutions to collect, analyze and distribute information on specific remittance service providers (Carling 2004, 5). Third, facilitating cooperation between major international banks and smaller banks in developing countries would better connect networks of branches in migrant-hosting and migrant-sending countries. One way of achieving this is to ensure that such cooperation is legal (World Bank 2004, 172).

Optimize the Use of Remittances

Remittances usually constitute small payments sent by individual migrants to their relatives. Since remittances are person-to-person flows, they are well targeted to meet the needs of the recipient (World Bank 2004) and they have the ability to lift people out of poverty. Based on a study of panel data, Adams and Page (2003, 20) conclude that 'on average, a 10 per cent increase in the share of international migrants in a country's population will lead to a 1.9 per cent decline in the share of people living on less than $1.00 per person per day'.

At the same time, remittances have been thought to increase inequality, since wealthier workers are better able to pay the costs of migrating (Ratha 2003). However, studies show that a large proportion of international migrants (certainly those who move between developing countries) are unskilled or low-skilled individuals from lower income groups. Remittances may actually help these groups to catch up. Further, educated migrants are less likely to remit, as they tend to settle permanently and bring their families with them.[2] Finally, even if the poor themselves do not receive remittances, they can still benefit indirectly through increased demand for their labor, and this benefit can explain the positive correlation between remittances and the alleviation of poverty described above. Hence, a number of different factors are at play and the empirical evidence on this issue is very mixed (Lucas 2005).

Although remittances may have a positive effect on poverty within a country, the impact of remittances on inequality between countries is problematic. As already noted, there are initial costs of migrating, and the very poor countries tend to have a low number of migrants for this reason. Indeed, since lower-middle-income countries often have relatively high rates of emigration compared to the poorest countries (sometimes called the 'migration hump'), these countries stand to gain the most from remittances, while very poor, low-emigration countries stand to miss out on the potential economic benefits of migration. This can partly explain why the share of global remittances received by Sub-Saharan Africa is so low. Although low-income countries can arguably be said to need migrant remittances the most, they do not receive nearly as much as middle-income countries. Therefore, remittances cannot be viewed as an adequate substitute for ODA.

The majority of remittances are spent on consumption goods such as food, clothing and health care, with some funds also spent on improving housing and buying durable consumer goods, but generally only a small portion is invested. One survey suggests that only 6 per cent of remittances sent home by the African diaspora are reinvested (Banjoko 2004). However, investment spending tends to have large 'multiplier effects', since money spent on productive uses will increase the number of jobs and the output of the economy; hence, this has been a matter of concern to many policymakers. Although multiplier effects are also present in consumption spending, it is generally thought to be smaller, and this is particularly the case if remittances are spent on imported goods or if the increased demand for consumption leads to inflation because it is not matched by an increase in supply. Thus, if migrant remittances can somehow be geared toward productive investment, the economic gains are likely to be greater (van Doorn 2002).

Given these parameters, several policy options emerge. One would be to correct for the information gap between remitter and recipient. This disparity often means that remitters cannot control whether or not their money is being spent in the most productive manner (Chami et al. 2003, 4). Indeed, the lack of transparency and information were identified as the two major obstacles to diaspòra return investment in a recent survey of members of the African diaspora (Banyoko 2004). The remitter may be led to believe that remittances are actually saved, when they are actually being spent on consumer products and handouts to needy relatives.[3] By harnessing new opportunities offered by technologies such as the Internet, policymakers may be able to correct some of these asymmetries. More control by the remitter may be a worthy goal in itself, but may also be a better way of ensuring that remittances are used effectively. There may also be options for offering remitters opportunities to purchase goods or services directly, such as health insurance (Carling 2004, 6). African Investment Advisory's initiatives to set up an African diaspora venture capital fund for African small- and middle-sized enterprises is a good example of trying to channel diaspora funds toward productive uses.[4]

Matching the funds invested by migrants may be another productive channel. Although migrants will spend remittances in ways which most benefit their families, their preferences could coincide with government policies which seek to invest in education, health care and improved housing. One option would be for governments in remittance-receiving countries (or even the governments of the countries where migrants work) to promise 'matching funds' to induce migrants to spend some of their remittances on productive or worthwhile endeavors. For example, a government could promise to match any remittance spent on school fees in the country of origin, with extra investment in that particular school. This would provide an incentive to the migrant, since government funding would hopefully improve the quality of education (not just for their sponsored school but for all pupils in the country) and perhaps even raise the migrant's esteem within his community. It would also mean that the local area could benefit from migration regardless of whether multiplier effects are present to distribute income.

Finally, a good financial infrastructure is essential for ensuring economic development. In the financial sectors of developed countries, savings are used as investment funds. However, in the case of remittances to developing countries, the relationship is not so clear-cut, especially where money is sent through non-banking channels. At the same time, micro-entrepreneurs in the developing countries cannot obtain credit at a reasonable interest rate due to an underdeveloped banking network, and lack of bank accounts and assets which can be offered as collateral. This lack of access to credit can hamper economic growth and create the dependency on remittances described above. Hence, there is a role to be filled by micro-finance schemes which supply the type of credit required by small-scale entrepreneurs while providing a link between remittances and investment (Puri and Ritzema 1999).

DIASPORA POTENTIAL

The involvement of migrant communities, or 'diasporas' more generally, in the life of their erstwhile homelands goes well beyond financial flows. Diasporas can be the source of 'social remittances'– the ideas, behaviors, identities and social capital which flows between countries (Levitt 1996, 3). Similarly, migrants can transfer knowledge and skills – 'technological remittances' – or even political identities and practices – 'political remittances' (Goldring 2004, 805).

Despite the potential significance of diaspora involvement, many mainstream development institutions such as NGOs and governmental organizations have hitherto been reluctant to engage diaspora communities. The House of Commons International Development Committee (2004, 68) encourages increased cooperation between the diaspora and other players and writes, 'Diaspora organizations must not be seen as marginal players in international development; rather, the Government, DFID,[5] the private sector and mainstream NGOs should work harder to involve them more fully.'

In recent years, there has been great optimism in the potential for what diaspora organizations can do but, unfortunately, there seems to be very little systematic evidence of what role diasporas do play. Below are three options for optimizing diaspora involvement.

Encourage Collective Remittances

Although the majority of remittances are sent by individuals, a small part is sent by diaspora organizations, that can be linked by place of origin or religious or political beliefs. A common type of diaspora organization is a Hometown Association (HTA), that is organized around links to a specific area, such as a village. Despite the modest economic base of these organizations, there is evidence that villages connected to HTAs tend to have better roads, electricity and employment opportunities (Soerensen 2004, 17). Hence, these associations should be encouraged, and one way of doing so is to provide 'matching funds', which provide an additional incentive to save and invest by adding to the funds already being spent by HTAs. J. Van Doorn found these arrangements to be useful: 'One example is a project in the Mexican state of Zacatecas, where each dollar contributed in remittances is matched by three dollars (one from

the municipality, one from the state and one from the federal government)'
(Van Doorn 2002). As an indication of the success of this program, it will
be extended to cover the whole of Mexico (quoted in Goldring 2004, 802).
Matched-funding programs could also be carried out by NGOs or governmental
organizations such as DFID or the U.S. Agency for International Development.
This would also strengthen the links between these players, as recommended
in the section above.

Communication between the diaspora organizations and the government in
the country of origin should also be promoted. As an example, the government
could help to identify specific small-scale projects which could be sponsored by
the diaspora. However, as Van Hear et al. (2004, 22) write, diaspora members
'are primarily interested in the advancement of their own particular group or
sectional interest'. As a consequence, policymakers must not loose sight of the
impact on equity and equality in the country supported by the diaspora. As an
example, if most migrants have come from a particular region of the country,
relying heavily on the diaspora for both organization and contacts can lead
to aid assistance exacerbating inequality in infrastructure, services and other
sectors.

Promote Trade and Investment

Lucas argues that migrants can promote both trade and investment in their
country of origin (2005, 3). First, they are better informed about trading
and investment opportunities, and, second, they are able to enforce contracts
through a network of contacts at home. This can be important in countries
which lack a legal framework for conducting business. Some migrant-sending
countries do indeed offer very good opportunities for migrants to become
investors. For example, a case study of foreign-born professionals in Silicon
Valley showed that 76 per cent of Indian and 73 per cent of Chinese immigrants
would consider starting a business in their country of birth, and a majority of
them cited the availability of skilled labor as one of the most important reasons
for doing so (Saxenian 2002).

This finding highlights the fact that social ties are not enough to ensure that
migrants choose their country of birth as a target for investment. Rather, a
healthy business environment is important for attracting investment (Soerensen
2004, 24). This includes adequate physical and financial infrastructure and a
sound legal framework. A skilled labor force with low labor costs is also an
important asset. This means that low-income countries with many obstacles
to investment, such as poor infrastructure and the lack of an adequate legal
framework and skilled workers, will struggle to make migrant workers in the
developed world invest in their home country. As highlighted before, low-

income countries which are already severely disadvantaged will be in a poor position to make use of migration and the resulting linkages as a strategy for development.

Even for countries which can offer an attractive business environment, other obstacles remain. Despite the information and contacts possessed by migrants, many of them lack the experience of entrepreneurship and knowledge of business methods. Training programs and business counseling could be useful additions to help better utilize the potential of migrants.

A better approach might be to encourage migrants to invest indirectly, through savings. Many migrants keep their savings in bank accounts outside their home country, especially if overseas banks can offer higher interest rates on savings or a lower risk of inflation and exchange-rate devaluations. If saved in the migrant-sending country, their assets could provide foreign currency and funds for investment. At least two policies have already been developed to try to encourage migrants to save in their home country: mandatory remittances and foreign-currency accounts. Under the first approach, migrants are required to send a certain percentage of their savings to their country of origin. Yet this has only been successful in the case of Korean workers, who are mainly employed overseas by Korean companies for a limited period of time.

Another approach is to offer foreign-currency accounts and foreign-currency-denominated bonds. These options pose no risks of exchange rate devaluations and can be offered in combination with an attractive premium over world interest rates, that could attract migrant savings. However, as Puri and Ritzema (1999) note, 'A major limitation of foreign currency accounts as a tool for stimulating remittances is that they, by their very nature, are attractive only to migrants belonging to professional and higher-skilled categories who earn relatively higher incomes.' It is also important to consider whether the premium which has to be paid to attract savings in this way is worth paying.

The case for providing micro-credit as a tool for economic development has already been presented in relation to remittances. However, another approach involving this type of finance would be to encourage permanent migrants, who do not remit but who have both savings and the intention to contribute to economic development in the home country, to invest in micro-finance institutions. Such a scheme would make use of the desire to help the country while generating a return on investment.

Consolidate Knowledge Networks

Networks of highly skilled workers may be one way of addressing brain strain. Meyer and Brown (1999) call this the 'diaspora option' and examine several networks among nationals working mainly in science or engineering. The

Table 6.5   Managing Threats and Opportunities for Developing Sending Countries

	Permanent Emigration		Temporary Emigration	
	High-skill/ wage	Low-skill/ wage	High-skill/ wage	Low-skill/ wage
Brain strain	Ensure depleted skills are replaced	na	Ensure key sectors are not depleted through limits;	Need to maximize skills-acquisition while abroad
Remittances	High potential for remitting but may fall off after some time	Low and falling potential for remittances	Highest potential for remittances	High total remittance potential but at lower amounts
Diaspora/ Circulation	High potential, especially through circulation	Can lead to brain gain of emigrants, gain skills while abroad and circulate	Ensure return migrants use skills and experience gained abroad	Potential for skills and information transfer

Internet is the main communications tool for these networks and, perhaps due to difficulties of organizing a network before the Internet became widespread, many of these networks are very recent. This also means that there is very little empirical evidence on the effect of these networks on the economic development of the country of origin. Nevertheless, there have been projects which attempt to promote cooperation between expatriates and the national community. These include research projects, technology transfers and expert consulting. The UN Development Programme has set up the Transfer of Knowledge Through Expatriate Nationals (TOKTEN) program, that aims to send qualified professional migrants back to their home country for a short period of time. This program is currently running successfully in 35 developing countries (Van Hear et al. 2004, 28).

CONCLUSION

The relationship between migration and development is at once incredibly significant and yet marginal in many ways. When considering all the various aspects of managing migration, the development impacts on countries of origin are rarely going to be as prominent a research or policy issue as issues such as immigrant integration, migrant rights and the economic impacts of immigration.

That said, it is clear that migration has the potential to significantly shape the economic development of some sending countries. It is clear from the growing evidence in this area that whether the impacts of migration are positive or negative will depend very much on the context and how the situation is managed. Much will depend on the rate and nature of emigration. The complexity of migratory flows, as noted at the very beginning of the chapter, mean that no one set of policies will be universally applicable. Table 6.5 shows a tentative sketch of what sort of policies might be appropriate for particular contexts.

Some countries have recognized the potential held by migration, while others risk losing out or – worse still – being adversely affected. One of the most striking observations from the study of the relationship between migration and development is that very poor countries stand to lose the most and gain the least from migration (brain strain, low return migration potential, poor environments for the productive use of what remittances flow in etc.). This differential impact of migration may compromise the ability to pursue poverty reduction and achieve the UN Millennium Development Goals (MDGs). Importantly, where migration leads to the depletion of key health and education workers in developing countries, their ability to make progress on critical MDGs may be compromised.

However, cooperation between states to manage migration may be an exemplar of the sort of partnership which will be required to achieve the MDGs and other global policy challenges. Individual states often see migration in terms of local impacts and national interests. However, the global nature of flows means that managing the mutual impacts of migration will need a robust, supranational framework. Moreover, managing the process for the mutual benefit of developed and developing countries will require partnerships between states.

It is important to note that efforts to manage migration need to sit alongside efforts to promote development, democracy and human rights around the world. Improved living conditions in sending countries will increase the incentive for the highly skilled to stay and encourage those who migrate to return.

This study has focused on three fruitful avenues of exchange which need to be pursued further. First, in research there needs to be more intellectual exchange between the growing field of 'migration studies', to which the issue of development in countries of origin is somewhat marginal, and development economics, to which the impact of migration is, at best, marginal. There is much to be done in order to present a comprehensive empirical picture of the nexus between migration and development. Global organizations such as the Global Development Network may have a unique and important role to play in generating good quality, comparable data and analysis which can inform policymaking.

Second, in policymaking, there needs to be more effective dialogue among branches of governments which do not traditionally work together very often. In the developed world, this means departments responsible for home or immigrant affairs and those responsible for international development.

Finally, in terms of international cooperation, there is also a need for more productive partnerships between developed and developing countries to address areas of mutual interest in the management of migration. This is likely to require a considerable overhaul of the normative and institutional infrastructure of multilateral migration management. This may be some way off, but action on shared development objectives may be one relatively easy step forward. Given the global and interdependent scope of the challenges, it would seem wise to have global and interdependent approaches to tackling them.

NOTES

The author is indebted to Bente Nielsen for providing invaluable research assistance.

1. Remittances from the United States to Mexico reached record levels in 2004, totalling approximately $15 billion at $327 per transaction on average. See http://www.el-universal. com.
2. Faini (2003, 7) shows that remittances decline as the proportion of migrants with a tertiary education increases.
3. According to a study cited in Wehrfritz and Vitug (2004), the typical domestic worker in Saudi Arabia will remit most of her salary. Her husband then uses the money to buy consumer products and to support the extended family, and often the overseas worker only discovers that nothing has been saved on her return.
4. See www.aiaprojects.com; www.africadiaspora.com.
5. The U.K. Department for International Development.

BIBLIOGRAPHY

Adams, Walter (ed.) (1968), *The Brain Drain*, New York: Macmillan.

Adams, Richard and John Page (2003), 'International Migration, Remittances and Poverty in Developing Countries', Washington, DC, World Bank, Policy Research Working Paper No. 3179.

Africa Recruit (2003), 'Submission to the HoC Select Committee on International Development', London, House of Commons, http://www.parliament.the-stationery-office.co.uk/pa/cm200304/cmselect/cmintdev/uc79-v/uc79m03.htm.

Alburo, Florian and Danilo Abella (2002), 'Skilled Labor Migration from Developing Countries: Study on the Philippines', Geneva: International Labour Office, International Migration Papers No. 51.

Amador, L. (2002), 'Mexico amplia el programa Tres por Uno. El gobierno destina dinero para acelerar las obras sociales auspiciadas por paisanos de EU', *La Opinion*, 13 February.

Banjoko, Titi (2004), 'African Diaspora: Survey on Investment', London: Africa Recruit.

Bhagwati, Jagdish (1976), 'The Brain Drain', *International Social Science Journal*, **28** (4): 691–729.

Carling, Jørgen (2004), 'Policy Options for Increasing the Benefits of Migration',Paper presented at the Metropolis International Ninth International Metropolis Conference, Geneva, 27 September–1 October.

Carrington, William J. and Enrica Detragiache (1999), 'How Extensive is the Brain Drain?', *Finance and Development*, **36** (2), 46–9.

Chami, Ralph, Connel Fullenkamp and Samir Jahjah (2003), 'Are Immigrant Remittance Flows a Source of Capital For Development?', Washington, DC, International Monetary Fund Working Paper No. 03/189.

Commander, Simon, Mari Kangasniemi and L. Alan Winters (2003), 'The Brain Drain: Curse or Boon?', Bonn, Institute for the Study of Labor (IZA) Discussion Paper no. 809.

Ellerman, David (2003), 'Policy Research on Migration and Development', World Bank Policy Research Working Paper No. 3117.

Faini, Ricardo (2002), 'Migration, Remittances and Growth', Paper presented at the United Nations University, World Institute for Development Economics Research (WIDER) conference 'Poverty, International Migration and Asylum', Helsinki, September.

Global Commission on International Migration (2005), 'Migration in an Interconnected World: New Directions for Action', Geneva, Switzerland: GCIM.

Goldring, Luin (2004), 'Family and Collective Remittances to Mexico: A Multi-dimensional Typology', *Development and Change*, **35** (4), 799–840.

Harrison, Anne, Tolani Britton and Annika Swanson (2004), 'Working Abroad: The Benefits Flowing from Nationals Working in Other Economies', Paris: OECD.

House of Commons International Development Committee (2004), 'Migration and Development: How to Make Migration Work for Poverty Reduction', Sixth Report of Session 2003–2004, Vol. 1, United Kingdom, London, House of Commons.

Igartúa, Gustavo V. (2004), 'The Temporary Mexican Migrant Labor Program in Canadian Agriculture', University of California – San Diego, Center for Comparative Immigration Studies, Working Paper No. 90.

International Organization for Migration (2003), *World Migration 2003: Managing Migration: Challenges and Responses for People on the Move*, Geneva: IOM.

Kapur, Devesh (2004), 'Remittances: The New Development Mantra', New York, United Nations Conference on Trade and Development, G-24 Discussion Paper Series No. 29.

Kapur, Devesh and John McHale (2005), *Give Us Your Best and Your Brightest*, Washington DC: Center for Global Development.

Levitt, Peggy (1996), 'Social Remittances: A Conceptual Tool for Understanding Migration and Development', Harvard University Center for Population and Development Studies, Working Paper No. 96-04.

Lowell, Lindsay B. (2002), 'Policy Responses to the International Mobility of Skilled Labor', Geneva, International Labour Organization, International Migration Papers No. 45.

Lowell, Lindsay B., Alan Findlay and Emma Stewart (2004), 'Brain Strain: Optimising Highly Skilled Migration from Developing Countries', London, Institute for Public Policy Research, Asylum and Migration Working Paper No. 3.

Lucas, Robert E.B. (2005), *International Migration Regimes and Economic Development*, Lyme, CT: Edward Elgar.

Martin, Phil (2003), 'Highly Skilled Labor Migration: Sharing the Benefits', Geneva: International Labour Organization.

Meyer, Jean-Baptiste and Mercy Brown (1999), 'Scientific Diasporas: A New Approach to the Brain Drain', Geneva, UNESCO Management of Social Transformations (MOST) Discussion Paper No. 41.

Nyonator, Frank, Delanyo Dovlo and Ken Sagoe (2004), 'The Health of the Nation and the Brain Drain in the Health Sector', Paper presented at the UNDP conference 'Migration and Development in Ghana', Accra, Ghana 14–16 September.

Ojeda, Raul H. (2003), 'Transnational Migration, Remittances and Development in North America: Globalization Lessons from the Oaxa California Transnational Village/Community Modeling Project', Washington, DC, Inter-American Development Bank.

O'Neil, Kevin (2003), 'Using Remittances and Circular Migration to Drive Development', New York: Migration Policy Institute.

——(2004), 'Labor Export as Government Policy: The Case of the Philippines', New York: Migration Policy Institute.

Psacharopoulos, George (1985), 'Returns to Education: A Further International Update and Implication', *Journal of Human Resources*, **20** (4), 583–604.

Puri, Shivani and Tineke Ritzema (1999), 'Migrant Worker Remittances, Micro-Finance and the Informal Economy: Prospects and Issues', Geneva, International Labor Organization, Social Finance Unit, Working Paper No. 21.

Ratha, Dilip (2003), 'Workers' Remittances: An Important and Stable Source of External Finance', in *Global Development Finance Report 2003: Striving for Stability in Development Finance*, Washington DC: World Bank.

Saxenian, AnnaLee (2002), 'Local and Global Networks of Immigrant Professionals in Silicon Valley', San Francisco, CA: Public Policy Institute of California.

Soerensen, Ninna N. (2004), 'The Development Dimension of Migrant Remittances', Copenhagen: Danish Institute of Development Studies.

Straubhaar, Thomas (2000), 'International Mobility of the Highly Skilled: Brain Gain, Brain Drain or Brain Exchange', Hamburg, Germany, Hamburg Institute of International Economics (HWWA) Discussion Paper, No. 88.

Suro, Roberto (2003), 'Latino Remittances Swell Despite US Economic Slump', New York: Migration Policy Institute, Migration Information Source.

United Nations (2004), *World Economic and Social Survey 2004*, New York: UN Department of Economic and Social Affairs.

Van Doorn, Judith (2002), 'Migration, Remittances and Development', *Labor Education*, **4** (129), 48–55.

Van Hear, Nicholas, Frank Pieke and Steven Vertovec (2004), 'The Contribution of UK-based Diasporas to Development and Poverty Reduction', Oxford, UK: Centre on Migration, Policy and Society.

Wehrfritz, George and Marites Vitug (2004), 'Philippines: Workers of the World', *Newsweek*, 4 October.

Winters, L. Alan (2002), 'The Economic Implications of Liberalising Mode 4 Trade',Paper prepared for the Joint WTO-World Bank Symposium 'The Movement of Natural Persons (Mode 4) under the GATS', Geneva, 11–12 April.

World Bank (2004), 'Global Development Finance Report: Harnessing Cyclical Gains for Development', Washington, DC: World Bank.

——(2005), 'Global Economic Prospects: Economic Implications of Remittances and Migration', Washington DC: World Bank.

Wyss, Brenda (2004), 'Global Poaching: Jamaica's Brain Drain', *Econ-Atrocity Bulletin*, 30 January.

7. Patterns, Trends and Government Policies: Understanding Irregular Migration from China

James K. Chin

Trafficking in human beings, also known as 'irregular migration', is one of the most pressing and complex global challenges to human security today. It reaches across borders to affect most of the countries in the world and creates common concerns for security and development that are almost impossible to manage effectively by one single country. Since 1979 Chinese migrants, particularly from Fujian, Zhejiang and the provinces of Northeast China, have constituted a major component of international irregular migration. In fact, China may provide the largest number of East Asian irregular migrants to the international labor market. This situation raises a number of questions. Why are Chinese irregular immigrants mainly from Fujian, Zhejiang and Northeast China? What amalgam of factors has motivated a huge cohort of peasants, fishermen and laid-off workers to leave China illegally? What are the major patterns and trends exhibited in China's irregular out-migration? What are the Chinese government polices towards irregular out-migration? Are there different attitudes towards irregular out-migration at various levels of the Chinese government? How could people correctly understand current irregular migratory waves from China? In this chapter, I draw upon fieldwork conducted in south China over the past decade to examine current patterns and trends in Chinese irregular out-migration. I will also present the Chinese government's response and policies toward the migratory *modus operandi*, in the hope of providing policymakers with empirical insight into the most active migration-sending regions of China.

METHODOLOGY

This research, funded by the Hang Seng Bank Golden Jubilee Education Fund for Research and the University of Hong Kong Seed Fund for Comparative Studies of Chinese Culture and Society, was conducted in coastal villages of south China with a special reference to the Fuzhou region, one of the major sources of irregular emigration in China.

The viewpoints and data presented in this chapter are mainly gleaned from my interviews, observations and informal conversations with various people involved in irregular migration activities, such as former illegal emigrants and their family members, 'snakeheads' (human smugglers), border police officials, grocery owners, peddlers, bank staff, fortune-tellers, village usurers, taxi drivers, motorcycle couriers, hotel doormen, fishermen and local residents as well as government officials at various levels. Ethnographic interviews constituted the primary interaction with respondents during my fieldwork trips.[1]

I interviewed more than 150 people in different coastal villages and towns. Such interviews were usually arranged by my local contacts with the assistance of their relatives, friends and former classmates. While my fieldwork was conducted nearly annually over the past decade, only a few representative examples and figures are selected from individual years to be examined here. The interviews were conducted face-to-face, utilizing a standardized questionnaire which I had drafted in advance and memorized. As a rule, I would not show my interviewees the long list of prepared questions, otherwise they would likely be very nervous while answering my questions or simply refuse to chat with me. I carried a digital recorder in my pocket to help me accurately document all the informal conversations.[2] All the data collected from interviews, observations and conversations would be classified before they were typed into the computer and saved. Since all of these interviews and conversations were arranged and conducted within the context of a reliable Chinese *guanxi* (personal networks), both the quantitative and qualitative data gathered for this study, I believe, should have high validity. In addition to the ethnographic research, news reports published in mainland China, Taiwan and Hong Kong were systematically read and analyzed, and this information helped identify areas for closer examination and in-depth analysis.

IRREGULAR MIGRATION FROM CHINA: PAST AND PRESENT

Illegal or irregular out-migration from China dates to at least the early days of imperial China and lasted until the late fifteenth and early sixteenth centuries, when the Ming court banned maritime trade and navigation in China's seaboard towns and villages. People continued to slip across the border for the next three hundred years, but such irregular population movements were halted by the authorities when the People's Republic of China (PRC) was established in October 1949. Nevertheless, more than one million PRC citizens still managed to illegally enter British Hong Kong in several waves from the early 1950s to 1980. Since then, a new Cantonese term, *she-tou* or 'snakehead' (illegal migration brokers), has gradually entered the modern Chinese vocabulary.[3]

South Korea and Japan

Currently, the flow of irregular Chinese out-migration is mainly directed north into South Korea and Japan; west into Siberia and then through Russia into Europe; and east and south en route to North America, Australia and New Zealand. Of the 44 000 Chinese nationals living in South Korea, almost 32 000 are there illegally. In South Korea and Japan, mainland Chinese are preferred to Bangladeshis and Indians as workers because of racial and cultural similarities (Saywell 1997, 52). In South Korea, there were 188 995 illegal migrants from other countries by 31 December 2000, according to figures released by the South Korean Embassy in Beijing. Of these, 95 625 were mainland Chinese (Li Honggu et al. 2002, 19). In other words, the number of irregular Chinese migrants in South Korea probably tripled within these three years if these two figures are reliable. In the meantime, a large number of PRC citizens tried different means to work in Japan illegally. On 22 January 1997, for example, 14 Chinese migrants from Fujian Province with fake Taiwan passports were detained by the Japanese police at Tokyo's Narita Airport.[4] In addition, according to the statistics provided by the Japanese Immigration Bureau, in 2000 there were about 250 000 illegal migrants in Japan. Of them, illegal Chinese immigrants accounted for more than 100 000, and they are regarded as the third-largest illegal immigrant group in Japan (Sasaki et al. 2000).

Southeast Asia

In Southeast Asia, the traditional destination of Chinese from southern China, irregular Chinese migrants are increasingly making their presence felt. In Manila local authorities alleged that 120 000 Chinese had illegally entered the Philippines between 1997 and 1999. Most of these Chinese went to Manila as tourists and could not speak Tagalog or English. In May 1999 Philippine immigration authorities launched three raids on the illegal Chinese immigrant community and arrested more than 100 Chinese during the operations. In mid-July 2002, 16 Chinese illegal migrants (14 males and two females) were seized at a night-time bazaar and imprisoned by the authorities in Manila (Zhuang Mingdeng 21 July 2002). The number of Chinese tourists visiting Thailand rose sharply in the late 1990s. In 1998, for example, arrivals from mainland China rose by 23 per cent over 1997 to 432995, the biggest increase for any nationality entering Thailand. While many of them are genuine tourists, a considerable number did not return to China. Instead, they chose to settle in Thailand or continue their westward journey using other people's travel documents and identity papers after inserting their own photos. In Cambodia, local police arrested 315 illegal Chinese immigrants hiding in houses owned by a high-ranking military police official in October 1999; they were subsequently repatriated to China.[5] As economic cooperation between China and Myanmar increased over the past two decades, more and more Chinese slipped into Myanmar for work. Rangoon authorities arrested 89 illegal Chinese in 2002.[6] According to statistics issued by the Malaysian Immigration Department, more than 185000 Chinese nationals overstayed their tourist visas in 2002 and 2003, becoming illegal workers. Most of these were peasants from south China and laid-off workers from northeastern China.[7]

North America

The flow of illegal Chinese migrants bound for the United States is estimated to have grown from a few thousand per year in the mid- to late-1980s to 100000 a year after 1992. A 1995 U.S. governmental interagency report on human smuggling asserts that perhaps up to 50000 Chinese nationals were being smuggled into the United States each year.[8] Most attention has focused on dramatic boat arrivals. The boats, often Taiwanese coastal freighters or traders, usually carry between 200 and 500 migrants across the Pacific. The majority, however, still complete most of their travel by airplane, using networks of Chinese communities in Latin America and the Caribbean to provide documentation and onward air or land passage to the United States. As in the nineteenth century, almost all of the irregular migrants are young men and women. According to the U.S. Department of Justice, most are advanced around $55000 to pay for the trip and thus become essentially bonded labor. My fieldwork interview data indicates that migrants usually pay a 5 to 10 per cent deposit before embarking on their journey, and the snakeheads collect the balance once the 'human cargo' successfully reaches the final destination.

Europe

Chinese migration flows to Europe are facilitated by the many Chinese bridgeheads across the continent. The snakeheads operating in Europe typically have links with criminal groups based in Hong Kong, Taiwan and mainland China.

The Chinese Embassy in Moscow reported that at the end of the 1990s over 400 000 Chinese visited Russia annually (Gelbras 2002, 100). This figure was verified in 1999 by Russian Deputy Interior Minister Valery Fedorov, who claimed that every year over 500 000 Chinese nationals visited Russia and a large number of them subsequently remain in the Russian Federation (Gelbras 2002, 102). It is estimated that some 30 000–40 000 Chinese are currently in Moscow as temporary residents (Gelbras 2002, 104), although many of them presumably are en route to their preferred countries in Western Europe. According to Russian scholars, there were 50 000–80 000 Chinese living and working in the Russian Far East and Siberia as vendors, contract workers and agricultural laborers in the 1980s and early 1990s, 100 000 in 1993 and 200 000–300 000 in 1996 (Shkurkin 2002, 86). Some 100 000 were considered illegal migrants in 1998. Vladivostok is also a staging point for Chinese migrants awaiting movement to Moscow and onward to Western Europe and the United States. U.S. Deputy Assistant Secretary of State Jonathan Winter estimated that tens of thousands of Chinese remained in limbo as of late 1998.

The Chinese who head for the Netherlands endure an arduous journey. They usually arrive in Moscow via the Trans-Siberian railway. A snakehead meets the train and takes the Chinese to a hotel and locks them in a room until another snakehead takes them by train to Prague. Next they are brought by car from Prague to the German border where another snakehead brings them across the 'green border' (an unguarded frontier) into Bavaria either on foot or by trucks. From there they proceed by train or taxi to Holland. Immigrants arriving on trains are usually dropped in front of the Central Station in Amsterdam. Those who come by taxi were, until recent changes in asylum registration procedures, driven directly to an asylum center. Thousands of Chinese have come into the Netherlands by this land route, and many try to continue their westward journey. At the Dutch port of Vlissingen, the *Marechaussee* (military police) regularly arrest Chinese who try to board boats to England or the United States with false or stolen Dutch passports. In June 1993 the Spanish police broke up a Chinese gang in Barcelona which smuggled people into the United States, Canada and Spain using presumably stolen Japanese passports.

France is a favorite destination for Chinese emigrants. While French authorities have never officially released statistics on new migrants from China, an investigative report conducted by French scholars in April 2004 indicates that more than 450 000 Chinese nationals had migrated to France over the past two decades. Of them, 250 000 are currently living in greater Paris.[9] A working group under the International Labor Organization released a report on illegal Chinese migrants in France on 21 June 2005, revealing that Paris alone is home to around 50 000 illegal Chinese migrants.[10] Such a figure probably is conservative. A Chinese journalist based in Paris quietly conducted an investigation among new Chinese migrants in 2004, discovering that about 60 000 illegal migrants from China would enter France annually, and the majority of these are from Wenzhou (Zhejiang Province), Fuqing (Fujian Province) and the Northeastern provinces.[11]

According to the United Nations, Chinese human smugglers alone earn up to $3.5 billion annually. One ring in particular, over two years, smuggled 3600 Chinese into the United States through Canada, netting approximately $170 million (U.S. INS 1998). In addition to departing from coastal areas on the mainland, Chinese use Thailand, Cambodia, Malaysia, the Philippines, Singapore, Macau, Taipei and Hong Kong as transit points to get fake passports and visas with the help of well-organized gangs. Myanmar, as well, serves as part of the illegal migrant network. Suffice it to say that illegal migration from China harms both China and the world at large, because it creates transnational human security concerns.

WHY FUZHOU, WENZHOU AND THE NORTHEASTERN PROVINCES?

Generally speaking, new irregular emigrants from China today come mainly from Fuzhou (Fujian Province), Wenzhou (Zhejiang Province) and the three provinces of Northeast China (Liaoning, Jilin, Heilongjiang). And in the greater Fuzhou region, the counties of Changle, Fuqing and Lianjiang, in particular, produce large numbers of irregular migrants. What explains this pattern?

Three important similarities can be observed in these transcontinental out-migration source regions: money, clandestine transportation channels, and international migration networks. While money to pay snakeheads or clandestine migration brokers can be borrowed from relatives, underground lenders or *biaohui* (informal credit associations), the transportation would be provided by transnational criminal enterprises. International migration networks which, as a rule, are formed on the principle of kinship, locality or dialect can be cultivated through mutual obligation and assiduous networking within linage and regional groupings.

Aside from these similarities, there are also factors unique to these sending regions which help explain the comparatively high out-migration levels. Fuzhou, the capital of Fujian Province in southeast and coastal China with a population of 6.66 million, has always been a land auspicious to emigration, as the majority of its inhabitants have always been sailors and maritime merchants.[12] The clandestine maritime activities of the people of Fuzhou have a long history, and local people are accustomed to adventure abroad. The people of Wenzhou also have a long tradition of emigrating overseas, although the first large wave of transcontinental out-migration did not emerge until the early twentieth century when the French government recruited more than 150000 laborers from Zhejiang Province.[13] Currently, Wenzhou, a city in southeast Zhejiang Province with a population of 7.43 million, is the largest concentrated source of out-migration to Western Europe.[14]

Different forces are at work in the northeastern provinces of Liaoning, Jilin and Heilongjiang. Unlike Fuzhou and Wenzhou, the people Northeast China have no tradition of emigrating overseas. The emigration phenomenon in these three provinces is actually quite new. In part it was triggered by the extensive economic reform in China in the years following 1979, when many unprofitable state-owned factories, mines and enterprises were closed, leaving a huge number of laid-off workers who had to find new means of survival. It is estimated that currently there are 40–60 million down-sized workers in China.[15] Since historically China's heavy industry had been concentrated in the three northeastern provinces and almost all the factories and companies there belong to the state-owned enterprises which have been rapidly declining over the past two decades, the majority of the laid-off workers are from the northeastern provinces. Consequently, thousands of redundant workers from northeast China have been forced to join the transcontinental migration waves – legally or not.[16]

EMIGRATORY PATTERNS AND TRENDS

There are currently at least three patterns to irregular emigration from China: organized smuggling, overstaying a legal visit and marriages of convenience.

Organized Smuggling

The first pattern is smuggling people out of China using organized human-trafficking groups. The alarming tragedy of the *Golden Venture* is a good case in point. That ship carried about 300 people from Changle, Fujian province, and ran aground offshore Rockaway Beach, Queens, New York, on 6 June 1993. Passengers drowned trying to swim to shore before the authorities arrived. Prior to 1998, the risky maritime route was the principal channel used by human-trafficking groups. Emigrants had to remain on board throughout a long journey, often lasting from 40–60 days. As more and more smuggling vessels were either captured at sea or sank en route, few Chinese now dare to sneak abroad through this method.[17]

However, human-trafficking groups have recently changed their strategies due to better enforcement by the Chinese government. Now potential new emigrants who register with snakeheads and join established smuggling operations are first divided into many small groups – each group typically has only two or three members. In order to escape the close monitoring imposed by the coast guard in Fujian and Zhejiang, illegal emigrants are often sent to northern ports before they are put into containers and shipped away from China. Sometimes irregular migrants are issued fake passports and flown abroad from remote airports inside China. While most Chinese emigrants were successfully smuggled across the Chinese border, some were not so lucky. In late April 2000, for example, three young Fujianese were detained at the Xiamen Airport. They had presented authentic PRC passports, but the original photos had been changed. A senior police officer who investigated this case told me that the three PRC passports had been bought from Guangzhou at a cost of RMB60,000 ($7500) each.[18]

> You would not believe that almost all of the passports used by human trafficking groups are authentic, only the photos of passport holders or visa pages were changed. You know, these guys possess the really advanced technology, equipment and skills needed to produce such high-quality travel documents. Some of the faked passports we seized are so perfect in quality that even our experienced experts cannot find flaws even when the photos and fibers were magnified by 100 times. According to our intelligence, such good quality passports are usually supplied in Bangkok and Phnom Penh, and the current market price for each copy of this kind of good quality foreign passport ranges from RMB170000 to RMB250000 ($21250–$31250).[19]

In the late 1990s human-smuggling groups in China adopted a new arrangement for paying trafficking fees. Unlike previous practice, that required new irregular migrants to pay a 5 per cent deposit before being spirited out of China, the new practice does not ask for a deposit. Instead, human-smuggling groups foot all up-front costs for their 'clients', including airplane tickets, meals and in-transit accommodations. These human-smuggling groups do not charge a cent until the emigrants safely reach their destination. Furthermore, migrants caught by Chinese border police could even expect that the RMB 5000 ($625) fine imposed by the Chinese government could be reimbursed by the snakeheads so long as they did not give the snakehead's name to the police.[20] Needless to say, such an attractive practice has greatly reduced the financial risks of irregular migration and encouraged new flows of young Chinese. In fact, to my surprise, local villagers highly praiseed the services provided by snakeheads:

> You urban people do not understand what is going here. You think snakeheads are blackguards who only know how to make money from us? No! Let me tell you the

truth. Here in the village, snakeheads are our true friends and they have tried their best to help our fellow villagers to meet our family members in New York. All of the financial loss incurred during the irregular migration would be paid by them until our young villagers finally arrive in America or anywhere we planned to go. Come on! Do not listen to the government propaganda. Snakeheads are good guys as they are our relatives or intimate neighbors.[21]

Overstaying a Legal Visit

The second pattern, leaving China legally but changing identity and becoming illegal migrants in transit countries, is currently the most popular one. Chinese following this route tend to fall into one of three categories: contract laborers, trade delegates and tourists.

All across China there are many companies which specialize in sending contract workers abroad. According to interviews conducted in China, many young Chinese have successfully left China and reached their destination countries in Europe through this channel.

Emigration under the cover of a trade delegation is a popular new strategy. Chinese applying for permission to travel overseas must provide proper documentation to justify their request. Observing and acquiring advanced technology overseas is a popular explanation which often receives priority from the authorities. This method, however, cannot be used often by human-trafficking groups, because it usually requires approval from Chinese government agencies. Furthermore, all the members of the trade delegation should be *Putong yingong huzhao* – ordinary citizens with regular private passports.[22]

Finally, Chinese may go abroad legally by joining a tourist group visiting countries in Southeast Asia. The most popular destinations among Chinese tourists are Thailand, Singapore and Malaysia. Rather than returning home with the group, Chinese may try to sneak into European countries with forged travel documents provided by Southeast Asian criminal groups. One travel agency manager in Fuzhou told me that sometimes the majority of the tourists in a tour group will suddenly disappear on the eve of their departure for China. The tour guide becomes scared and, with no idea of what else to do, flies back to China and reports the disappearances to the Chinese border police and to foreign embassies in Beijing.

Many Chinese travel agencies have struck deals with the embassies of Southeast Asian countries in Beijing, whereby each Chinese citizen must leave a cash deposit of around RMB5,000 ($625) with the embassy as guarantee that he or she will return home. The deposit is refunded to the Chinese tourist if he or she returns to China after the trip to Southeast Asia. If not, the deposit is confiscated by the relevant embassy as a fine. The embassies are usually happy to repeatedly confiscate the numerous deposits left by Chinese tourists, because they fully understand that the wayward Chinese tourists will not stay in their countries for long once they give up their valid PRC passports and become irregular migrants in transit countries, because their destinations are countries in Europe and North America not in Southeast Asia.

Chinese travel agencies have to pay a large fine to the Chinese border police if someone leaves their tour group and does not return to China. Consequently, Chinese travel agencies usually require potential members of Southeast Asian tour groups to pay another RMB10000–20000 ($1250–$2500) up front as an extra guarantee that the tourist will return to China. Unlike the embassies, the Chinese authorities have been placed in a quandary, since they cannot shut down the overseas tour business simply because some Chinese citizens use it as a channel to legally leave China permanently.

Marriages of Convenience

The third pattern of emigration entails international marriages of convenience. Nowadays it is quite popular among Chinese youths to legally emigrate to Europe, Taiwan and North America by entering a marriage of convenience. Such a marriage would normally be maintained for a few of years after they reach their destination countries in order to satisfy inspections by local immigration authorities. Only after the new 'spouse' pays the mutually agreed fee and is granted permanent residency status or citizenship do the couple file for an annulment.

Emerging Trends

In addition to the three patterns mentioned above, some new trends are emerging in mainland China. First, with the rapid development of economic reform in China, a huge number of workers were laid off from state-owned enterprises. The government gives them a few hundred dollars each month as a basic living allowance until they find new jobs. However, the Chinese government cannot find any ready-made way to solve this thorny problem within a short period of time. Driven by hardship and the lure of golden opportunities overseas, large numbers of redundant workers have joined the ranks of coastal peasants who seek their fortune outside of China's borders. This trend explains why more and more mainland Chinese from northeastern China can be found in the major cities of Europe, North America, Australia and South Africa.

Second, because local government officials are under pressure from their higher-level authorities to stem the flow of irregular emigration, they may ask their fellow countrymen to leave China through airports or seaports in other provinces if they are determined to emigrate. As a result, more and more Chinese irregular migrants now use passports issued by other provincial governments to apply for visas or opt to be smuggled out of China from ports far away from his or her own home province. For example, from December 1994 to April 1995, 92 irregular migrants from Fuqing, Fujian, quietly traveled to Xiangshan county, Zhejiang province, before they were smuggled to Hong Kong, Japan and South Korea (You Xianfu 1997). On 4 June 2002, the Kunming border police detained five irregular migrants from Fujian at the Kunming international airport where they were about to board a flight to Bangkok (Lu Shicheng 2002).

Third, more and more irregular migrants are trying to use authentic foreign passports to apply for visas and leave China. On 18 September 2001, for example, Mr Li from Wenzhou, Zhejiang, was detained by the Chinese border policy at the Shanghai Hongqiao international airport when he tried to fly to Europe via Seoul with an authentic South Korean passport purchased from an ethnic Chinese based in Seoul. Mr Li had paid $50 000 for the passport (Shen and Feng 2001). In October 2001 Fuzhou customs officials were surprised to find out that a large number of foreign passports had been mailed to the city to be used by human-trafficking operations. The Fuzhou Customs Agency seized 602 passports mailed from Europe, Asia and the United States in a 14-month span (Chen Mingqiang 2001).

Fourth, China's multiple human-trafficking operations are growing into an integrated network. One tragedy stands out as a prime example of the closer ties. On 1 October 2001, 60 irregular migrants set sail for South Korea. Of them, 49 were Fujianese from Fuzhou regions such as Lianjiang, Changle and Mawei, while the others were ethnic Koreans from the northeastern provinces of Heilongjiang and Jilin. The Fujian migrants had initially traveled to Liaoning in hopes of smuggling across the border from ports there, while those from Jiamusi city in northern China had taken a southward route in order to leave China from Zhejiang. Soon afterwards, these two groups of irregular migrants met in Ningbo, Zhejiang, and were merged together by the snakeheads. They were then smuggled onto a South Korean vessel as it sailed towards the open sea. In the course of this dangerous journey to South Korea, 25 of the Fujianese died and the Korean captain threw their bodies overboard (Li et al. 2002, 19–31). The fact that two separate groups of Chinese irregular migrants with different destinations could be combined to travel together indicates that a large human-trafficking syndicate with criminal connections overseas exists in China and functions quite well.

Finally, more and more Chinese teenagers have started to join the clandestine out-migration wave. In late August 2002, for example, eight Chinese teenagers (15–16 years old) from Wenzhou joined a smuggling group organized by a Wenzhou snakehead. They initially flew to Moscow via Beijing, and from Moscow they went to Yugoslavia by train. The trip became harsh and difficult when they reached Yugoslavia and were packed into a truck by the snakehead. They could not endure the risky trip and eventually ran away from the snakehead when the truck reached the suburbs of Paris. The group of Chinese teenagers went to a Paris police station by bus, where they claimed they needed assistance because their parents were Falungong disciples and had been jailed by the Chinese government (*Mingpao News* 2002).

In order to escape the attention of the international community and crackdowns by the Chinese authorities, human-trafficking groups have employed various *modus operandi*. My interviews with former snakeheads and local police officials revealed that human-trafficking groups are typically divided into five levels. The top three levels generally stay overseas and remotely control the trafficking operation with satellite phones and secret lingo. These managers would provide transportation, passports and any assistance needed, while the lower two levels are usually made up of local residents who are in charge of recruitment among their fellow countrymen. This multilevel management structure makes it difficult for the Chinese provincial authorities to find effective ways to completely eliminate irregular migration in coastal China. In fact, internal reports submitted by local police departments admit that there is no point in arresting these 'small fish' or putting them in jail. Very quickly, new snakeheads would move up from lower levels. And the invisible top snakehead would remain untouched overseas to control the trafficking operation.

Finally, another organizational form common in Fujian is joint-share cooperatives. According to police reports, sometimes three or four friends with limited funds collaborate to plot and organize irregular migration runs. They would first work out a business plan and decide how the shares were to be distributed among them, then divide the profit achieved afterwards in accordance with the shares as agreed at the beginning. This kind of collaboration, however, would not be stable or function continuously. Very likely, the next endeavor would take place among a different group of people and different share holders.

The human-trafficking group is augmented by its own vast international criminal network. Strictly speaking, this network is composed of several different transnational networks. Those based in coastal China would be responsible for recruiting potential emigrants, and those in Taiwan would usually be in charge of providing transportation, while others in Southeast Asia are mainly local ethnic Chinese who act as transmitters. After each operation is successfully carried out, each part would get what it deserves according to their internal agreement. More details concerning their internal transactions, however, remain confidential.

WHY EMIGRATE IRREGULARLY?

Contrary to what Western media frequently report, new migrants smuggled from China are almost all economic emigrants, although many claim to be political refugees. According to local police records in Pingtang, an island geographically approximate to Taiwan and a hot spot for illegal emigration from China, one unlucky villager has failed 19 times in his effort to emigrate, although most of his relatives and friends have successfully reached their destinations overseas. When asked if they keep trying to smuggle themselves out of China, these young 'snakes' always replied, 'yes'.[23] But why? What are the real motivations behind their persistent efforts to keep moving towards countries overseas? The following frank confession from a former smuggled emigrant may help explain the drive to go abroad:

> You asked me why I have to try my luck overseas? And why should I spend such a big sum money and risk my life in the clandestine migration journey? We youths of course could lead a good life here [i.e. Changle] in the home villages, and each month we could earn something around RMB500 to RMB1000 ($62.50–$125) easily. But it is not enough, you know. We want to have a decent life with our own villas and cars, and maintain a high level income, definitely it cannot be realized here in China. And it can only be achieved in New York, in Japan, and in London. China is such a vast country with too many people to struggle for survival or to be rich. And we do not need to compete with them in this regard. People like you from the city would not understand. We need money. We need to make more money, and make money quickly overseas.[24]

Obviously, improving individual economic positions is one of the key factors when weighing the pros and cons of going abroad illegally. In addition, the traditional Chinese cultural value of reputation – 'to keep one's face' – to some extent contributes to the exodus of the younger generation of Chinese. Throughout coastal Chinese villages there are successful villagers who were smuggled overseas years ago and then returned to the homeland with a large sum of money. They built luxurious houses in south Fujian and their lavish daily lives were noted by others who had remained in China, encouraging them to place their fates in the hands of human-trafficking groups. Cao Xianxin, a peasant in Cangxi Village of Fuqing County, Fujian, had told his wife before he embarked on his fatal journey to the United Kingdom with a Yugoslav passport, 'Let's try our luck in Europe. I just cannot accept the fact that many of my friends and fellow villagers are able to make money in Europe and built luxurious villas in our village with the money earned while I am mocked by people for not being able to do the same' (*Liu Zhiwu* 3 July 2000). Thus, the traditional value which devotes particular care to 'face' and self-respect has lured more and more young Chinese to try their luck in far off countries.

Another factor that needs to be taken into account is the local maritime history along the coastal villages of south China. Fujian, as briefly depicted above, is a very telling example in this respect. Unlike other parts of China where residents historically have been inward-oriented, Fujianese have been well aware of the danger and the difficulties their neighbors and families faced when seeking fortune overseas. Probably because the Fujianese have their particular historical background related to travel, they usually believe that what they did previously or are doing at present in terms of irregular migration is nothing wrong. Instead, they ask why governments, either the Chinese government or any foreign government, do not provide them with a legal channel to go overseas and be reunited with their families.

CHINESE GOVERNMENT POLICIES TOWARDS IRREGULAR EMIGRATION

The anti-irregular emigration policies enacted at different levels of the Chinese government are consistent and they are made up of a three-tier set of policies. Generally speaking, the policies and regulations issued by the central government in Beijing serve as broad principles which provide local governments with a foundation from which to deal with this thorny issue. A general principle or requirement may be put forward by the central government, but the provincial-level and county-level governments must work out the details. Usually, lower levels of the government have more concrete, detailed regulations, and their policies are outlined in their internal party documents.

Central Government

Confronted with blame and pressure from the international community, the Chinese government, especially the central government in Beijing, has maintained a very clear stance toward irregular emigration from the very beginning. In fact, the first set of policies and laws specifically addressing the issue of irregular emigration came into being as early as 1979, when Beijing unveiled the Criminal Law of the PRC. Articles 176 and 177 of the 1979 Criminal Law clearly state that it is illegal for PRC citizens to smuggle themselves across the border or to organize clandestine emigration operations, and the ringleaders of such illegal activities will be severely punished (Zhongguo fazhi chubanshe 1979). Six years later, in November 1985, the Chinese president promulgated the first set of PRC immigration laws, that included a comprehensive set of regulations relating to border control and passport procedures. Probably because irregular emigration was not a major problem in China at that time, the migration law did not specify stringent punishments. Unless the laws were seriously violated, ordinary irregular migrants would only be detained for ten days (*Shiyong xingfa canzhao falu he xingzheng fagui leibian bianji weiyuanhui* 1997, 1720–21).

In July 1991 the Ministry of Public Security convened a police chiefs' meeting regarding the issue of irregular emigration, and police chiefs from seven coastal provinces and municipalities attended the conference in Beijing (Guowuyuan qiaowu bangongshi 1993). Soon afterwards, a document aimed at curbing irregular Chinese migration was drafted and jointly issued by the Overseas Chinese Affairs Office under the State Council, Ministry of Foreign Affairs, Ministry of Public Security, Ministry of Foreign Trade and Economic Cooperation as well as the Ministry of Labor on 1 April 1992. It was the first official Chinese document to clearly depict the grim situation of irregular emigration then confronting the Chinese government (Zhonggong zhongyang bangongting 1992). Apart from emphasizing the role the provincial police departments would play in disseminating the new government policies, the central government ordered the police departments in five provinces (Fujian, Zhejiang, Guangdong, Yunnan and Guangxi) to tighten their control over the border regions and coast line (Zhonggong zhongyang bangongting 1992). Moreover, the Chinese central government has changed its passport-issuing policy since late 1999.

The Beijing authorities eventually realized that they cannot simply close the door and prevent their people from traveling overseas. If Chinese people want to go overseas legally, then let them go. After all, it is a basic human right for citizens to have their own travel documents. At least in theory, all PRC citizens can legally be granted a private passport if he or she applies for one. Nevertheless, each province or city has its own regulations for issuing passports. While citizens in Shanghai, Beijing and Guangdong will find it relatively easy to acquire a private passport for themselves, residents in Fujian and Zhejiang provinces still face local regulations to better control the process. For example, an applicant might need to deposit a certain amount of foreign currency (e.g., $5000) at the Bank of China. Females younger than 35 normally would not be granted a private passport to travel overseas, as young female Chinese have frequently been discovered to be providing sexual service in cities overseas.[25] Clearly, there is still a long way to go before the Chinese authorities fully release their control over passport issues.

In the meantime, in order to consolidate control over the border and combat irregular emigration, the Standing Committee of the Chinese National People's Congress, China's legislative body, issued a supplementary law on 5 March 1994 to address the issue of irregular emigration. In March 1997, the National People's Congress amended the Criminal Law accordingly and four articles concerning irregular emigration were added into the Criminal Law which detailed the punishments for human-trafficking crimes (Jianming xingshi ban'an shouce 1999, 1746–47; *Zhonghua renmin gongheguo xingfa* 2000, 264–70). Taken together, these laws provide law-enforcement authorities with necessary legal basis, but they also demonstrate that the central government has actively sought to perfect the legal system to help suppress the irregular emigration wave.

Provincial Governments

For many years, irregular emigration was not an issue that attracted the attention of local governments. When a series of tragedies occurred and prompted intervention from Beijing, the provincial government started to take this issue very seriously. A number of working meetings were consequently organized in order to discuss the problem and possible solutions. Accompanied by a large group of senior government officials, the governor of Fujian Province, for example, visited coastal villages in the three counties noted above, together with delegations from the Ministry of Public Security in Beijing. In addition, a large sum of funds was subsequently allocated to help local governments purchase powerful searchlights to be installed at every key coastal port and dock which had been used to smuggle Fujian migrants out of China, as well as to better equip the border police.

The provincial government frequently organized operations to combat local irregular emigration activities. From 1 April to 31 July 2002, more than 200 snakeheads and potential irregular migrants were arrested in Fujian by the border police. On 5 March 2002, 75 Fujianese who had planned to be smuggled overseas were imprisoned in Fuzhou. Of them, four were snakeheads. At the same time, provincial governments along the coast launched several rounds of propaganda to educate villagers about the dangers of human trafficking in hopes of slowing the pace of irregular out-migration (Fujian Provincial Government 2002).

Counties and Villages

At the county-government level, the strict regulations combating irregular emigration did not come into being until the mid-1990s. Apart from laws previously drafted and issued by the central and provincial governments, local county governments drafted and enacted their own policies and regulations which usually are much more demanding and harsher than those issued from Beijing and provincial authorities. For example, in the greater Fuzhou region, every year the municipal party secretary, mayor or head of the relevant county must sign an agreement with all the local leaders to ensure that no irregular migrant would be found in any of the towns under his administration. The town leaders will, in turn, sign a similar agreement with all the village heads under his jurisdiction and require the same pledge from those village heads. Once a human smuggling case is reported, the leader of the relevant village or town will be fired, while the mayor or local party secretary will receive an internal warning issued by his superior. In addition the disgraced government officials will be deprived of any awards and bonuses he or she may have received previously. This punishment is due to a local government policy called *Yipiao foujue zhi* or 'Failure to Combat Irregular Migration'. The punishment policy not only applies to local government officials, but it is also frequently used to encourage local border police to work harder. In Changle, for example, the head of the coastal *paichusuo* (border police station) would be punished and fired if irregular migrants or snakeheads were found in their administrative zones (Zhonggong Changle shiwei, 1999).

To closely watch coastal villagers and to prevent them from becoming new irregular emigrants, local Chinese governments even adopted some stern measures that dated to imperial China. *Lianbao zhidu* or the 'Collective Guarantee System' is such a case in point. As occurred during the Ming and Qing dynasties, every ten families of a village are organized as one collective guarantee unit. If a member of one family is found guilty of smuggling overseas, the other nine families will have to face punishment from the local government. The local government in Changle created individual files for the 1695 sailing vessels and for the 5669 sailors registered with them. No sailing license would be issued unless the vessel, its captain and sailors pass a screening procedure jointly enacted by the border police and local shipping authorities. Yet another approach is for local governments to provide a bonus for villagers who help the authorities to launch a crackdown on planned human trafficking activities. For example, anybody who provides tips to border police that lead to the arrest of major irregular migration organizers will be awarded RMB10000 ($1250). For small-time snakeheads, the prize ranges from RMB3000 to RMB5000 ($375–$625). Meanwhile, the various levels of the

Chinese government will launch propaganda campaigns in the local media, in the hope of persuading coastal villagers to give up their dreams of searching for better opportunities overseas.[26]

Nevertheless, despite the best efforts of local officials, new irregular migrants continue to flow out from China as evidenced by the annual statistics compiled by local government. The real reason that the Chinese government is still unable to curb or eliminate these diverse flows after so many efforts is that local governmental cadres at the village level actually are willing to defy orders from the central and provincial governments. As local residents, they themselves share the benefits gained from the out-migration flows. In Houyu village (Monkey Island), for example, new buildings with luxurious decorations can be seen everywhere. All of these were built with money remitted from overseas. However, the whole village seems dead. Only small children, old men and old women can be seen in the village, because for several decades all the males and young women have gone overseas. The entire village stands almost empty now, all shops have closed and the majority of the villagers have either moved to the provincial capital, Fuzhou, or overseas. The few remaining local residents must walk 20 minutes to Langqi village to have their meals. It is widely recognized at the grassroots level that outflows of new Chinese migrants are good for local economic development, as almost all of the families and villages there largely subsist on annual remittances sent from their fellow villagers overseas.

One local town head told me that irregular emigration is 'Very good indeed for us, you know'. At the very least, he said, 'I could name three advantages brought by the irregular emigration'. He continued:

First, the local economy has been greatly improved and the living standard of my fellow countrymen has been enhanced a lot over the past two decades with the huge number of remittances flowing back from overseas. Second, the phenomenon of unemployment which has harassed us for many years has finally disappeared because almost all of our young men and women have gone overseas and are earning foreign currencies now. Third, the social order is becoming better as compared with what we had previously since our teenagers do not fight in the street anymore. Instead, following the examples set by their parents, they are now trying their best to smuggle [themselves] to countries in the West.[27]

In fact, ordinary people in the countryside support and protect snakeheads. They even offered fancy titles for these operatives, such as *minjian laogong buzhang* (Ministers of Nongovernmental Labor) and *minjian yinhang hangzhang* (Directors of Nongovernmental Banks). In other words, neither ordinary villagers nor village-level cadres hate snakeheads.

CONCLUSION

Admittedly, the current policies adopted by both Western countries and China cannot effectively address – much less stop – the waves of irregular emigration from China. To remedy this trend and to purposely direct the irregular migration wave into controlled channels, constructive policies and relevant regulations are needed from both sides.

First, there needs to be a regular working mechanism and closer working relations between Western countries and China to enable both sides to negotiate relevant issues on a regular basis. Ideally there would be a high-level official representative in charge of migration affairs from the European Union and the United States stationed in Beijing to facilitate exchanging information and sharing views with their Chinese counterparts.

Second, there needs to be a memorandum of understanding between relevant Western countries and China. Details related to collaboration in migration affairs should be listed, such as sharing information, establishing liaison offices, training personnel and creating labor recruitment agents to facilitate the legal import of qualified Chinese workers.

Third, the United States and receiving countries of the European Union should be more careful in granting political refugee asylum rights and not continue to accept those illegal migrants who claim that they are political refugees under the cover of Falungong followers or as victims of China's one-child policy. Such misleading messages sent from Western countries without doubt further encourage the human flows from mainland China.

Fourth, a detailed survey should be conducted as soon as possible among Western countries to identify service sectors which might need foreign workers. Once such detailed information is ready, Western countries could start to identify target countries and negotiate with them to import legal workers.

Fifth, government authorities on both sides should launch joint information and education campaigns about the realities of illegal emigration. Apart from pamphlets and posters, a series of television documentaries which vividly depict the real life of illegal Chinese migrants overseas and their many hardships would educate and possibly dissuade potential illegal migrants in China. Such an effort could effectively reduce the wave of illegal emigration from mainland China.

Sixth, illegal migration is a transnational crime, and therefore it is imperative to seek international cooperation among the law-enforcement agencies of East Asia and Southeast Asia. If possible, major Western countries should set up liaison offices in key cities of the region, such as Hong Kong, Bangkok, Tokyo and Taipei. Such a measure could help to curb the irregular Chinese emigration tide at China's gateways.

Last but not the least, to better understand the current social situation in mainland China and to facilitate appropriate policymaking in the future, international organizations such as the United Nations, European Union or International Organization on Migration should allocate a large sum of money to establish a long-term research team to monitor China's migration activities and to regularly provide Western leaders with updated summaries and policy suggestions.

Unless the economic disparities that now exist between China and Western countries reduce greatly or China's economic development reaches the same level as that of North America or most EU countries, the Chinese irregular migration flows will not end anytime soon. In fact, in the years ahead the endless stream of illegal Chinese emigrants is likely to continue. In other words, human migration is a natural human flow which cannot be forcibly stopped by governmental administrative means. Nevertheless, with continued economic reform in mainland China and further collaboration between Beijing and receiving countries in Europe, China's illegal human flows hopefully could be reduced or at least controlled in the near future.

NOTES

1. Ethnography draws on different methodologies, including in-depth interviews, participant observation and secondary analysis of documents and archives. Ethnographic interviews play a very important role in my research. While the informal conversation with my interviewees is similar to story-telling in the sense that it is unstructured, I do have guide questions and a questionnaire designed and prepared in accordance with my research requirements.
2. Hidden recording of informal conversations without previous consent of interviewees is normally not allowed in Hong Kong. Nevertheless, given the sensitivity and difficulties involved in the current analysis of clandestine activities, hidden recording seems to be the only option for a researcher to conduct his or her interviews in the Chinese mainland.
3. For detailed studies on irregular migration from mainland China to British Hong Kong, see Wong Chung-kwong (1995), 'Chinese Illegal Immigrants: Their Effects on the Social and Public Order in Hong Kong', M.Phil. thesis, University of Hong Kong; Li Ruojian (1997), 'Xianggang de Zhongguo dalu feifa yimin yu feifa rujingzhe wenti', [Illegal migrants from the Chinese Mainland in Hong Kong and the Issue of Illegal Migration], Renkou yanjiu [*Journal of Demographic Studies*], 21 (1), 44–7; Lin Jiezhen and Liao Bowei (1998), 'Yimin yu Xianggang jingji' [Migration and Hong Kong's Economy], Hong Kong: Commercial Press; Gu Du (2000), 'Toudu Xianggang jinxitan', [Illegal Migration to Hong Kong: Past and Present], *Kaifang zazhi* [*Journal of Openness*], (August), 48–50.
4. Chinese Border Police, internal newsletter (February 1997).
5. 'Toudu chuguo mengsui taxiang', [Citizens who Illegally Emigrated to Countries Overseas Ended with Failure], *Qianjiang Evening News* (6 March 2000).
6. Chinese Border Police, internal newsletter (November 2002).
7. Information provided by Vice Consul Ning Jun, Chinese Embassy to Malaysia. Also see CCTV news report, 'Malaixiya qianfan 180 ming Zhongguo laogong', [180 Chinese Laborers were Repatriated by Malaysia] (16 April 2004).
8. 'Presidential Initiative to Deter Alien Smuggling: Report of the Interagency Working Group',

Washington, DC, 1995. See also Paul J. Smith (ed) (1997), *Human Smuggling: Chinese Migrant Trafficking and the Challenge to America's Immigration Tradition*, Washington DC: Center for Strategic and International Studies, pp. viii–xv.

9. Agence France-Presse (11 April 2004).
10. China News Agency News, 'Faguo feifa huagong baogao gongbu' (Investigation Report on Illegal Chinese Laborers in France is Released), 23 June 2005.
11. Chinese Border Police, internal newsletter (February 2004).
12. 'Population Statistics of Fuzhou 2005', *Bulletin of Fuzhou Municipal Bureau of Statistics* (February 2006).
13. For a detailed account on Chinese emigration to Europe, the Wenzhou people in particular, see Minghuan Li (1999), *We Need Two Worlds: Chinese Immigrant Associations in a Western Society*, Amsterdam: Amsterdam University Press.
14. 'Population Statistics of Wenzhou 2004', *Bulletin of Wenzhou Municipal Bureau of Statistics* (January 2005).
15. Research Department, Chinese State Council, 'Woguo de jiuye xingshi yu duice yanjiu' [A Study on Current Employment Situation of China and Relevant Policies], Beijing: State Council, Internal Working Report (March 2000).
16. For detailed studies on migration from China's northeast provinces, see Galina Vitkovskaya, Zhanna Zayonchkovskaya and Kathleen Newland (2000), 'Chinese Migration into Russia', in Sherman W. Garnett (ed.), *Rapprochement or Rivalry: Russia–China Relations in A Changing Asia*, Washington DC: Carnegie Endowment for International Peace, pp. 347–70; Vilya G. Gelbras (2002), 'Contemporary Chinese Migration to Russia', in Pál Nyíri and Igor Saveliev (eds), *Globalizing Chinese Migration: Trends in Europe and Asia*, Burlington, VT: Ashgate, pp. 100–07; Marc Paul, 'The Dongbei: The New Chinese Immigration in Paris', in Nyíri and Saveliev, *Globalizing Chinese Migration*, pp. 120–28; Elizabeth Wishnick (2004), 'Chinese Migration to the Russian Far East: A Human Security Dilemma', Paper presented at the University of Hong Kong, Asian Studies Center workshop 'Illegal Migration and Non-Traditional Security: Processes of Securitization and Desecuritization in Asia', Beijing, 10 – 11 October.
17. Interviews by author, Changle and Lianjiang, 26 – 28 December, 1999 and 8 October 2004.
18. There has been an internal and stable exchange rate between China's RMB and U.S. dollars over the past two decades in the Chinese mainland; and $1 converts to 8 RMB dollars. Such an exchange rate is adopted throughout this chapter.
19. Interview by author with senior police official, Fuzhou, 10 July 2001.
20. Interview by author with villagers in Tangtou Town, Changle, 5 April 2000.
21. Interview by author with villagers in Houyu, Changle, 14 October 2002.
22. Three types of passports are currently being used in China, including diplomatic passports for diplomats and senior government officials, ordinary public passports for ordinary civil servants, and private passports for normal citizens.
23. Interviews by author with former smuggling immigrants in Fuqing, 7 May 1998 and Lianjiang, 25 July 2002.
24. Interview by author with a former smuggling immigrant in Langqi Island, Changle, 3 June 2004.
25. Interview by author with senior police official in Fuzhou, 28 August 2002.
26. Internal Fujian government report dated 30 April 2000; also, series of internal special reports prepared by the border police department and Fuzhou Anti-irregular Migration Office dated from 1990 to 2001.
27. Interview by author, Guantou Town, Lianjian County, 29 September 2002.

BIBLIOGRAPHY

Chen Mingqiang (2001), 'Fuzhou haiguan chahuo daliang sheji feifa yimin jiahuzhao jiazhengjian' [A Large Number of Faked Passports and Certificates have been Detained by the Fuzhou Custom], *Fuzhou wanbao* (13 October).

China News Agency (2002), 'Nanfang qi-shengshi lianshou fantoudu, chengpi haishang toudu jiben ezhi' [Joint Efforts among the Seven Provinces of South China to Combat Human Trafficking and Large Groups of Irregular Emigration have Basically been Curbed], (23 May).

Fujian Provincial Government (2002), 'Fujiansheng jinqi fan toudu gongzuo qingkuang baogao' [Report on the Recent Development of Combat against Illegal Emigration Activities in Fujian], Internal government working report.

Gelbras, Vilya G. (2002), 'Contemporary Chinese Migration to Russia', in Pál Nyíri and Igor R. Saveliev (eds), *Globalizing Chinese Migration: Trends in Europe and Asia*, Burlington, VT: Ashgate, pp. 100–07.

Guowuyuan qiaowu bangongshi (1993), 'Guowuyuan qiaoba deng liuge bumen guanyu luoshi zhongbanfa [1992] sanhao wenjian caiqu youli cuoshi zhizhi woguo gongmin feifa yiju guowai de tongzhi' [On implementing the No. 3 document issued by the Office of the Central Committee of the CPC in 1992 and adopting effective measures to curb the illegal emigration of PRC citizens, jointly issued by six ministries under the State Council), No. 1].

Jianming xingshi ban'an shouce bianxuanzu (1999), *Jianmin xingshi ban'an shouce* [A Concise Manual for Criminal Cases Judgement], Beijing: Renmin fayuan chubanshe.

Li Honggu, Jin Yan, Lei Jing and Zen Fangjie (2002), '10.8 Toudu'an' [The case of 8th October Human Trafficking], *Sanlian shenghuo zhoukan*, nos. 6–7 (February),18–31.

Li, Minghuan (1999), *We Need Two Worlds: Chinese Immigrant Associations in a Western Society*, Amsterdam: Amsterdam University Press.

Li Ruojian (1997), 'Xianggang de Zhongguo dalu feifa yimin yu feifa rujingzhe wenti', [Illegal migrants from the Chinese Mainland in Hong Kong and the Issue of Illegal Migration], Renkou yanjiu [*Journal of Demographic Studies*], 21 (1), 44–7.

Lin Jiezhen and Liao Bowei (1998), 'Yimin yu Xianggang jingji' [Migration and Hong Kong's Economy], Hong Kong: Commercial Press.

Lintner, Bertil (1999), 'The Third Wave: A New Generation of Chinese Migrants Fans Across the Globe', *Far Eastern Economic Review* (24 June), 28–29.

Liu, Zhiwu (2000), 'Zhiqingren jieshao toudu neimu', *News Daily* (3 July).

Lu, Shicheng (2002), 'Wu touduke buxi zhongjin ban jiahuzhao Kunming jichang shiti' [Five Irregular Migrants who Spent Lots of Money to Purchase Faked Passports were Arrested at the Kunming Airport], *Yunnan ribao* (10 June).

Mingpao News (2002), 'Zhongguo ba shaonian toudu wang faguo' [Eight Chinese teenagers smuggled into France], Hong Kong (27 August).

Nyíri, Pál, and Igor R. Saveliev (eds) (2002), *Globalizing Chinese Migration*, Burlington, VT: Ashgate.

Paul, Marc (2002), 'The Dongbei: The New Chinese Immigration in Paris', in Nyíri and Saveliev, *Globalizing Chinese Migration*, pp. 120–28.

Sasaki, Shoko, Randy Houston and Lola Parocua (2000), 'Combating Illegal Migration', internal working report presented at U.S. Immigration and Naturalization Service

Regional Alien Smuggling Conference, Bangkok, Thailand, 1–3 August.

Saywell, Trish (1997), 'Workers' Offensive: China joins the league of major labour exporters. Sending workers overseas brings in foreign exchange and helps relieve unemployment at home – a little,' *Far Eastern Economic Review* (29 May), 50–52.

Shen Guobin and Zhu Feng (2001), 'Waiji huaren guonei bingshi, youren mai qi huzhao maochong shiren toudu beiqin' [An Ethnic Chinese Died of Illness in China but his Passport was Purchased by an Irregular Migrant who Planned to Pretend to be the Dead Man and Smuggle Himself out of China], *Wenzhou ribao* (23 September).

Shiyong xingfa canzhao falu he xingzheng fagui huibian: zhonghua renmin gongheguo gongmin churujing guanlifa (1997), [Classified Collection of Criminal Laws, Relevant Laws and Administrative Regulations: Immigration Law of the People's Republic of China], Beijing: Falu chubanshe, pp. 1720–21.

Shkurkin, Anatolii M. (2002), 'Chinese in the Labour Market of the Russian Far East : Past, Present, Future', in Pál Nyíri and Igor R. Saveliev (eds), *Globalizing Chinese Migration: Trends in Europe and Asia*, Burlington, VT: Ashgate, pp. 74–99.

Smith, Paul J. (ed.) (1997), *Human Smuggling: Chinese Migrant Trafficking and the Challenge to America's Immigration Tradition*, Washington DC: Center for Strategic and International Studies.

U.S. Immigration and Naturalization Service, Department of Justice (1998), Press Release, 'U.S. Cripples Major International Chinese Alien Smuggling Operation', Washington DC (10 December).

Vitovskaya, Galina, Zhanna Zayonchkovskaya and Kathleen Newland (2000), 'Chinese Migration into Russia', in Sherman W. Garnett (ed.), *Rapprochement or Rivalry: Russia–China Relations in A Changing Asia*, Washington DC: Carnegie Endowment for International Peace, pp. 347–70.

Winer, Jonathan M. (1998), 'Address to Forum on Transnational Crime at Amerika Haus', Vienna, Austria (27 April).

Wishnick, Elizabeth (2004), 'Chinese Migration to the Russian Far East: A Human Security Dilemma', Paper presented at the University of Hong Kong, Asian Studies Center workshop 'Illegal Migration and Non-Traditional Security: Processes of Securitization and Desecuritization in Asia', Beijing, 10 – 11 October.

Wong Chung-kwong (1995), 'Chinese Illegal Immigrants: Their Effects on the Social and Public Order in Hong Kong', M.Phil. thesis, University of Hong Kong.

You, Xianfu (1997), 'Ren Dianman deng yunsong taren touyue guobianjing Wang Meiqing wozhang'an', [Case of Ren Dianman who smuggled people across the border and Wang Meiqing's case for laundering money earned from organizing irregular emigration], in Zhongguo renmin daxue faxueyuan (ed.), *Zhongguo shenpan anli yaolang* [Selected Key Cases of China: Criminal Case Volume 1996], Beijing: Zhongguo renmin daxue chubanshe, pp. 436–40.

'Zhonggong Changle shiwei, 'Changle shi renmin zhengfu guanyu jiaqiang fantousidu gongzuo lingdao zerenzhi de jueding', [Regulations drafted by the Chinese Communist Party Committee of Changle and municipal government on strengthening the combat illegal emigration in the Changle region], (1999) Internal document No. 6.

Zhonggong zhongyang bangongting (1992), 'Guowuyuan qiaowu bangongshi waijiaobu gong-anbu jingmaobu laodongbu guanyu jinyibu fangfan he zhizhi woguo gongmin feifa yiju guowai de yijian' [Document jointly issued by the Overseas Chinese Affairs Office under the State Council, Ministry of Foreign Affairs, Ministry of Public Security, Ministry of Foreign Trade and Economic Cooperation and Ministry of Labour Forces on Further Preventing and Prohibiting PRC Citizens from Illegally Emigrating Abroad], Document No. 3.

Zhongguo fazhi chubanshe (ed.) (1979), *Zhonghua renmin gongheguo xingfa* [Criminal Law of the People's Republic of China], Beijing: Fazhi chubanshe.

Zhonghua renmin gongheguo xingfa [Criminal Law of the People's Republic of China] (2000), Beijing: Fazhi chubanshe, revised version.

Zhuang, Mingdeng (2002), 'Fei yiminju xianling feifa waiqiao benyuenei zishou', [The Philippine Immigration Authorities Set a Deadline for the Illegal Migrants to Voluntarily Surrender Themselves to the Authorities by the End of July), *Lianhe zaobao* (Singapore) (21 July).

8. Regionalism and Migration in West Africa: Do Polar Economies Reap the Benefits?

Adama Konseiga

In recent decades multilateral trade and financial negotiations have focused on globalization, specifically how to expand and strengthen the multilateral trade system and how to prevent the recurrence of disruptive financial crises in emerging markets. However, the international labor market remains completely absent in the agenda of the international economic system. Instead, migration policies have shifted to where migration flows are viewed as a challenge to the social stability and economic growth for both the receiving and the sending countries. In response to the growing shortages of skilled labor, industrialized receiving countries have increasingly adapted immigration policies to favor the entry of skilled workers, while continuing to penalize unskilled flows. However, international migration continues to account for an important part of poor countries' livelihoods. Benefits for the developing countries traditionally include remittances, increased trade and capital flows and migrants who return with new skills and knowledge. Remittances alone add up to $100 billion each year – more than double the total public aid devoted to development issues in 2000.

While in the nineteenth century migration flows played a key role in fostering income convergence between Europe and the United States, today restricted labor migration is increasingly gaining recognition as being a direct impediment to trade, particularly in the service sector. This chapter examines the convergence[1] role of migration because an important achievement of the regional arrangements in West Africa has been to promote the free movement of persons, creating important international migration flows in the region. From 1960 to 1990, nearly 12 per cent of the total population of West Africa (excluding Nigeria) moved away from their homeland. In 1993 the Network of Surveys on Migration and Urbanization in West Africa (NESMUWA) carried out an important study in seven countries: Burkina Faso, Côte d'Ivoire, Guinea,

Mali, Mauritania, Niger and Senegal. The results confirmed the importance of migrations in West Africa and the diversity of patterns at the country level. Between 1988 and 1992, more than 6.4 million migratory movements were recorded among the seven countries of the network (Konseiga 2005a). Among these migrations, 2.3 million were international, while 1.3 million were inside the network. The most important flows were recorded between Côte d'Ivoire and Burkina Faso. The exchange between Côte d'Ivoire and Burkina Faso (508 000 movements) represents about 40 per cent of all migrations in the network. The flows between Côte d'Ivoire and Mali (283 000) and between Côte d'Ivoire and Niger (114 000) are much smaller. The high level of intra-African migration flows appears to be the best argument for regional integration efforts.

Yet the consequences of migration in the departing and arriving countries have not been fully studied. The focus of the new economics of labor migration (NELM) approach is the determinants of migration and the characteristics of migrants at micro levels. At the macroeconomic level, the basic neoclassical model of growth assumes that the population and the labor force grow together at the exogenous rate n. The latter assumption holds only in the context of a closed economy. When the economies can trade, under perfect labor or capital mobility, per capita outputs and wages immediately converge, therefore the neoclassical model cannot explain the kind of slow convergence documented in the literature. Blanchard (1989) suggests that human migration may be responsible for restoring the kind of convergence observable in empirical studies. This chapter examines the possibility of immigration and emigration in response to economic opportunities within the eight countries of the West African Economic and Monetary Union (WAEMU) [2] for given mortality and fertility rates. Therefore, the migration of persons becomes the main mechanism for change in an economy's population and labor supply. However unlike natural population growth, gains in population for the destination economy may represent corresponding losses for the source economy (labor force and possibly human capital), and this brings into the debate the brain drain issue. While there is a consensus that the gains from migration to the home country accrue in the form of remittances, new business and trade networks (Diaspora effects) and migrants returning home with amplified skills acquired abroad, the net benefits rely on the extent of the brain drain. This extent is measured as the ratio of the number of immigrants in the host country at a given level of educational attainment to the total number of individuals in the labor-exporting country with the same level.

In the remainder of the chapter, I examine the total macroeconomic effects of labor mobility inside WAEMU, where Côte d'Ivoire – with 25 per cent of all sub-Saharan African intraregional exports – represents the main attraction for migrants from landlocked countries (e.g. Burkina Faso, with less than 0.9 per cent of Sub-Saharan Africa's regional exports). As the richest country in the regional bloc, Côte d'Ivoire is the most attractive economic pole, and its performance has important effects on the other regional partners. Decaluwé, Dumont, Mesplé-Somps and Robichaud (2001) show that the trade benefits mainly accrue to Côte d'Ivoire because the country has the capacity to attract foreign direct investment (FDI), assuming a stable macroeconomic environment. However the economic interdependence suggests that the expected benefits for Côte d'Ivoire may likely spill over to Burkina Faso because of the stake Burkina Faso has in Côte d'Ivoire via its migrant population. While Burkinabè exports of goods to Côte d'Ivoire represent only 0.07 per cent of the total exports (1996), Burkinabè represent the majority of foreigners living in Côte d'Ivoire (56 per cent of the foreign population in 1998, and 14 per cent of the total population in the receiving country).

The next sections present a quick review of both the conventional brain drain approach and the new brain gain versions. After that overview I present the dataset built for the subsequent empirical analysis and then proceed with the econometrics of growth convergence. The empirical strategy consists of comparing the performance of an economy without migration to the counterpart economy. Following this strategy, I consider Burkina Faso to be the most important sending country to Côte d'Ivoire, relative to Mali and the other WAEMU countries. Simultaneously I consider an opposite case, France. Compared other WAEMU countries, Burkina Faso has fewer migrants heading to France. The findings suggest that there are different forces in play which make migration a force for both economic divergence and convergence, depending on the parameters and the destination choice.

CONVERGENCE OUTCOMES IN THE RECEIVING COUNTRY

I use the neoclassical growth model[3] as a framework to examine whether migration plays an important role in the process of regional convergence. In the closed neoclassical economy, the per capita growth rate tends to be inversely related to the starting level of output or income per person. This leads to convergence; that is, the growth rate of an economy is a decreasing function of the distance between its initial conditions and its own steady state.

The structural estimating convergence equation is easily expanded to include migration and human capital in the same way as it is done with physical capital, leading to the augmented Solow model (for more details, see Barro and Sala-i-Martin 1992, 1995). In the empirical literature, the included regressors are usually the initial level of GDP per capita, the log of the investment ratio minus the population growth rate and the stock of human capital. Time-specific dummies can be also included when using this procedure. Including human capital in an empirical implementation of the Solow growth model reduces the point estimate of the coefficient associated with physical capital, that is ordinarily held to be much too high in light of the mean value of labor's share in GDP across countries and across time periods. Finally, the likely effect of human migration is to accelerate growth convergence dynamics in a neoclassical setting.

WELFARE EFFECTS IN SOURCE COUNTRIES: BEYOND REMITTANCES AND RETURN MIGRATION

The literature on the growth effects of migration has so far ignored the sending countries, and the typical finding actually tends to argue that migration has a negative growth effect in the receiving country, unless migrants have a similar – or higher – capital value per person than natives.[4] Because the converse is expected for the sending country, migration becomes a powerful force working toward income convergence between capital-rich and capital-poor countries (Faini 2002). These results largely explain current restrictive immigration policies in the traditional receiving countries – the United States, members of the Organization for Economic Cooperation and Development (OECD) and the Arab Gulf countries – and account for the more marginal role of migratory flows in multilateral trade negotiations. However Hamilton and Whalley (1984) estimated that the liberalization of world labor markets could double world income and that the highest gains would be for developing countries.

Recently the international mobility of skilled labor has become a key component of the global-based economy, especially in industrial countries. Highly talented workers are essentially becoming more globally mobile as goods, services and capital have become more globally mobile over time. Under this brain-circulation perspective, the international mobility of skilled workers can generate global benefits by improving knowledge flows and satisfying the demand for highly skilled workers where the demand is strongest (Harris and Schmitt 2003). The location of FDI, research and development (R&D) programs and skilled professionals are jointly determined: success in attracting one resource draws more of each. There is a growing literature on skilled migration from developing countries as well. When productivity is fostered by both the individual's human capital and by the average level of human capital in the economy, individuals underinvest in human capital (Lucas 1988). In the presence of such externalities, Stark (2003) showed that a strictly positive probability or prospect of migration, by raising both the level of human capital formed by optimizing individuals in the home country and the average level of human capital of non-migrants in the country, can enhance welfare and nudge the economy toward the social optimum. Therefore under a well-controlled restrictive migration policy which matches the optimal level of the signaling, the welfare of all workers is higher than under any alternative policy. Migration is a powerful policy tool to achieve such goals despite the apparent loss of human capital through the migration leakage commonly known as 'brain drain'.

The preceding results of brain drain accompanied by brain gain can be easily included in the neoclassical growth model (Beine, Docquier and Rapoport 2003). The alternative conventional view on highly skilled emigration from developing to developed countries is extremely negative and tends to present the emigration of their skilled labor as a curse for source countries (Bhagwati and Hamada 1974). Beine, Docquier and Rapoport (2003) concluded that emigration has two opposite effects: first, migration opportunities increase the expected return from education and therefore induce more people to invest in education (the 'brain effect'); second, emigration reduces the stock of human capital left in the sending country (the 'drain effect'). Therefore, the net benefits rely on the extent of the brain drain.

In the specific context of WAEMU member countries, existing sources (Zanou 2001) and a survey conducted in 2002 (Konseiga 2005b) revealed the poor educational attainment levels of migrants from Burkina Faso. This makes the question of the leakage of this meager resource even more crucial. The empirical research question is formulated as follows: do highly educated professionals from landlocked WAEMU countries living in Côte d'Ivoire or elsewhere represent a sizable proportion of the pool of skilled workers in their countries of origin or is it too small figure to worry about? Data on the importance of brain drain inside WAEMU are estimated in the next section and the main findings in the skilled migration literature are then examined in the convergence equation estimations.

ECONOMETRIC APPROACH AND ESTIMATIONS

While there are a few studies on brain drain, most of them are not econometric assessments and did not have data on any of the WAEMU countries. The most recent data set includes only those developing countries which received more than $500 million in official worker remittances in the year 2000. The following sections try to bridge this research gap by estimating brain drain data using the perpetual inventory method.

BRAIN DRAIN ESTIMATES AND EMPIRICAL ANALYSIS

I use the perpetual inventory method to generate the human capital dataset. Adams (2003) used the same methodology, but he made the strong assumption that the two receiving regions considered (OECD and United States) have the same educational distribution of migrants from each labor-exporting country, that does not allow a comparative econometric study of the different destinations. To compare the two destinations which have very different development levels (Côte d'Ivoire and France), the human capital and brain drain data need to be estimated more accurately.

Schooling Capital of Migrants in Côte d'Ivoire

Three types of raw data are needed to estimate the quinquennial schooling capital of migrants living in Côte d'Ivoire: benchmark data on schooling attainment, school enrolment data and the ratio of migrants aged 15–19 and 20–24 to the total population above 15 years old. Data were obtained from different sources, mostly national censuses or surveys.[5] The quinquennial data generated using the perpetual inventory method were compared and adjusted with annual data generated using the multiple imputation method. The latter procedure retains the assumption that data were missing at random. Multiple imputation reflects the uncertainty of the estimates and a value is assigned for each missing measurement using maximum likelihood parameter estimates.

Schooling Capital of the Domestic Population

The same techniques were applied for each country's local human capital estimations. These estimates are less error-prone because the benchmark data were easier to gather for the countries thanks to both national and international sources (UNESCO 1992, 2000; Barro and Lee 2000; United Nations Development Programme 2003; and World Bank 2000, 2002, 2003a). Data are readily available for the yearly values of school enrolment rates over the period considered (1970–2001) as well as for the population share. The estimates are again tested by comparing the five-year data from the perpetual inventory method to the replicates built using multiple imputation applied for each year. To check for the accuracy of the data generated, sample countries which are similar were compared: Niger, Mali and Burkina Faso.

Schooling Capital of Migrants to France

Migration to France is the only case where estimations were not needed, because data are available for migrant educational attainment for the seven countries covering the period 1925–99. Detailed information on gender and age at arrival of the migrants were also recorded in the data set (INSEE 1999). Finally, additional data on migrant stocks for the years 1968, 1975, 1982, 1990 and 1999 and a time series of migrant flows were used (Thierry 2004). However, unlike the preceding cases, no information exists for the no-schooling category; that will be a constraint on the variables used in the regressions. The data generated for destination France were also cross-checked using information on the sending country's number of students in France under the assumption that the latter constitutes a good proxy for brain drain at the tertiary level.

STATISTICAL ANALYSIS OF BRAIN DRAIN ESTIMATES

Tables 8.1 and 8.2 present estimated migration rates by educational category for each labor-exporting country. For all levels of education, Burkina Faso shows a higher incidence of brain drain to Côte d'Ivoire, relative to the other WAEMU countries, whereas the opposite picture holds concerning migration to France.[6] This confirms the position of Côte d'Ivoire as the main destination for Burkina Faso while France is a relatively more important destination for Mali. Therefore, Mali can serve as a reference group, because both source countries are Sahelian with similar macroeconomic characteristics.

Focusing on secondary and tertiary levels of education, the results in Table 8.1 suggest that the migration to Côte d'Ivoire is causing a significant brain drain for both Burkina Faso and Mali; more than the conventional threshold of 10 per cent of the group with at least a secondary education has migrated. The very high migration rate (74 per cent) of the best educated from Burkina Faso simply indicates that the number of migrants with a tertiary education who leave this country represents a very high proportion of the local capital stock available with the same level of education. This constitutes an important pressure on a meager resource. Even though the estimated figure for tertiary-educated migrants from Burkina Faso may overstate the true size of the brain drain from the country, revealing some measurement error that the econometric estimations should account for, this important leakage calls for further explanations.

First, putting aside the problem of measurement error, the calculations of brain drain for the migrant subgroup are affected by definitional problems. Côte d'Ivoire defines immigrants as all persons born abroad who moved to the country, no matter if they subsequently acquired citizenship (Zanou 2001). The latter portion of immigrants who acquired citizenship in the host country can

Table 8.1   Average Migration Rates to Côte d'Ivoire by Level of Educational Attainment (age 15 years and above)

Immigrants in Côte d'Ivoire as fraction of the individuals in the labor-exporting country, with the specified schooling level of educational attainment*

	Primary	Secondary	Tertiary
Benin	0.01	0.03	0.05
	(0.003)	(0.02)	(0.03)
Burkina	0.07	0.20	0.74
	(0. 01) (–) (—)	(0.05) (–) (—)	(0.65) (–) (—)
Mali	0.02	0.12	0.21
	(0.015)	(0.18)	(0.13)
Niger	0.004	0.01	0.030
	(0.003)	(0.005)	(0.013)
Senegal	0.004	0.004	0.005
	(0.001)	(0.003)	(0.0035)
Togo	0.01	0.008	0.014
	(0.0003)	(0.005)	(0.005)

Notes:

*standard deviation in parentheses.

(–) (—): outcome of mean comparison for brain drain at the specified school level using two-sample t test with unequal variances. (–) indicates significant brain drain from Burkina Faso relative to Mali; (—) indicates significant drain from Burkina Faso relative to all other WAEMU countries; (+) and (++) if the respective opposite holds.

Source: Author's calculations using the perpetual inventory method.

overestimate the 'effective' migrant population.[7] Some data appears to confuse the concepts of 'immigrants' and 'foreigners'. The latter group includes descendants of immigrants born in Côte d'Ivoire, who are likely to be better educated than their peers.

Second, during the period under study, Côte d'Ivoire developed the most successful educational policy inside WAEMU – while 76.9 per cent of foreigners living in the country are illiterate, this ratio dropped to 57 per cent in the Ivorian native population (Zanou 2001).[8] This policy may have attracted many students from Burkina Faso who then acquired their education in Côte d'Ivoire, which has better education infrastructure compared to Burkina Faso (7 per cent and 1 per cent of enrollment rates at the tertiary level are

Table 8.2   Average Migration Rates to France by Level of Educational Attainment (age 15 years and above)

Immigrants in France as fraction of the individuals in the labor-exporting country with the specified schooling level of educational attainment*

	Primary	Secondary	Tertiary
Benin	0.002	0.007	0.35
	(0.007)*	(0.003)	(0.91)
Burkina	0.0004	0.003	0.023
	(0.00015) (+) (++)	(0.0005) (+) (++)	(0.01) (+) (++)
Mali	0.007	0.045	0.05
	(0.002)	(0.052)	(0.016)
Niger	0.0003	(0.002)	0.014
	(0.0002)	(0.005)	(0.004)
Senegal	0.005	0.021	0.055
	(0.002)	(0.006)	(0.016)
Togo	0.0005	0.012	0.14
	(0.0001)	(0.012)	(0.19)
Côte d'Ivoire	0.0006	0.003	0.024
	(0.0002)	(0.001)	(0.01)

Notes: See Table 8.1.

the respective 1998 levels for Côte d'Ivoire's and Burkina Faso's educational systems, according to the 2003 World Development Indicators). However, this second source of bias may have changed over time and needs additional investigation, because one of the channels of the recent increasing return migration is through students sent home to study in Burkina Faso as result of its relatively cheaper school fees.

Third, the pool of tertiary-educated individuals in the poorest source countries of WAEMU (Burkina Faso and Mali) is much smaller in absolute terms than the corresponding pool in the richer countries (Senegal, Benin and Togo). Nevertheless, the percentage share of the best educated in the total stock which migrated is probably much higher in the poor countries because they were more attracted by the stable development in Côte d'Ivoire during the period under study. Poor Sahelian countries rely more on migration as a self-insurance mechanism, and the consequences may be that poorer countries retrieve more from their meager educational resources inside the free movement zone of WAEMU.

Finally a brain drain incidence above 70 per cent is not unusual. It is actually interesting to compare with other findings. Using the Carrington and Detragiache dataset and ranking countries according to the reliability of the data source, Beine, Docquier and Rapoport (2003) found the following impressive brain drain toward all destinations: Guyana (77.5 per cent), Jamaica (77.4 per cent), Ghana (25.7 per cent), Gambia (61.4 per cent), Tunisia (63.3 per cent), Algeria (55 per cent) and Senegal (47.7 per cent).

Both Table 8.1 and Table 8.2 indicate that the relative proportion of low-skilled migration from WAEMU countries is not very high. All the countries have a migration rate for those with a primary school education which is less than 10 per cent of their important domestic stock. The highest figure for primary school migrants is that of Burkina Faso (7 per cent), followed by Mali (2 per cent) in Table 8.1.

It appears from this descriptive statistical analysis that recorded legal migration from WAEMU countries involves relatively more movement of better educated people, people who are more educated than those who remain at home. Overall, these statistical patterns are in line with previous studies. Carrington and Detragiache (1998) confirmed that migration rate distribution is heavily skewed toward educated people. Sub-Saharan Africa lost 30 per cent of its skilled personnel between 1960 and 1987. Jamaica has to train five doctors in order to keep one (Faini 2002), representing a leakage of 80 per cent of the national resources allocated. For Ghana alone, more than 15 per cent of the home country population with a tertiary education has migrated to the United States.

ECONOMETRIC ANALYSIS

The link between migration and growth in sending countries is complex at the empirical level. A major link between migration and output growth in the home country is the positive externalities which the new brain gain model endogenized through the prospect of migration. The migration literature suggests three additional positive effects: better distribution, new skills and new networks.

Todaro (2000) argues that the significance of migration lies in its implications for economic growth in general and for the character of that growth, particularly its distributional consequences. Migration flows may be associated with equally large flows of remittances. At the micro level, remittances affect household welfare. In the short run, the direct impact of remittances is to diminish the budget constraint on rural and urban households while in the longer run the transfers will indirectly improve household total income through a reallocation of resources. In the context of missing credit and insurance markets, the latter effect works through higher capital or input investments in the small businesses and agriculture sectors, as well as household human capital investments. At a more macro level, remittances represent an important source of foreign exchange which reduces the deficit of the balance of payments. In 1980 remittances equaled total exports in Pakistan, and were equal to 60 per cent of exports in Egypt, Turkey and Portugal. In Burkina Faso remittances are currently as important as the principal export product (cotton), namely one-third of export revenues. Migrants may return home after having acquired a set of productive skills which will benefit the growth prospects of their home country. Finally, diaspora externality creates business and trade networks and promotes technology diffusion as well as FDI.

In contrast to these benefits, the conventional approach argues that any depletion of a country's stock of human capital is detrimental to its current and future economic performance, and brain drain is basically a negative externality imposed on those left behind. At the origin-country level, the positive externalities of skilled migrants toward home-country production, the education costs paid by the home country and the education benefits are all lost. This argument makes brain drain a zero-sum game, with the rich countries getting richer and the poor countries getting poorer.

Having this in mind, the econometrics of growth convergence analysis consists of comparing the performance of an economy without migration to the counterpart economy. This is achieved by comparing Burkina Faso – the most important sending country to Côte d'Ivoire – to Mali and the other WAEMU countries. The reverse holds when I consider France as receiving country, as it is the least popular destination for Burkina Faso.

In this section I use the brain drain data for an econometric analysis of the augmented Solow model. Faini's approach was based on a pooled OLS regression, that poses enormous problems of countries' unobserved heterogeneity. Both Nerlove (2002) and Arcand and d'Hombres (2002) argue that most of the recent investigations of growth convergence and the rate of convergence are flawed by their failure to account for the inconsistencies of single cross-section or panel studies in a dynamic context.[9] In the current study, a growth convergence estimation which highlights the key role of labor migration and brain drain (Table 8.3) is carried out using panel data methods. I accounted for existing sources of biases which relate to the problem of low variability resulting from estimations in first differences, the usual problem of measurement error in human capital as well as endogeneity problems. Concerning the suitability of the set of instruments, I conducted a preliminary descriptive analysis of correlation and variability. The results show that the

Table 8.3   Growth Convergence: Brain Drain Impact

	(1) Fixed effects (within) with correlated panels corrected standard errors	(2) Fixed-effects (within) IV regression	(3) Fixed-effects (within) IV regression, GMM estimation
	Annual per capita GDP growth (constant local currency)	Annual per capita GDP growth (constant local currency)	Annual per capita GDP growth (constant local currency)
Initial GDP per capita	−0.032 (−6.13)***	−0.030 (−4.14)***	−0.032 (−3.84)***
Log of the investment minus population growth rate	1.912 (1.04)	3.829 (1.89)*	5.856 (2.88)***
Brain drain Côte d'Ivoire (no schooling)	−114.429 (−2.81)***	−82.005 (−1.58)	−122.322 (−3.17)***
Brain drain Côte d'Ivoire (secondary)	−77.754 (−1.88)*	34.029 (0.36)	−151.215 (−3.83)***
Brain drain Côte d'Ivoire (tertiary)	5.585 (0.60)	−6.389 (−0.51)	7.282 (1.21)

correlations among all variables are strong enough, and it can be expected that the instruments are suitable for the estimations. Because the test indicated sufficient correlations, the instruments can be expected to allow for identifying the coefficients of the endogenous variables (Stock, Wright and Yogo 2002). The variables were then inspected to see if they exhibit sufficient within-panel variation to serve as their own instruments. Finally, the output presented in

Table 8.3   continued

	(1) Fixed effects (within) with correlated panels corrected standard errors	(2) Fixed-effects (within) IV regression	(3) Fixed-effects (within) IV regression, GMM estimation
	Annual per capita GDP growth (constant local currency)	Annual per capita GDP growth (constant local currency)	Annual per capita GDP growth (constant local currency)
Brain drain France (tertiary)	−34.432 (−0.89)	−56.385 (−1.34)	190.238 (3.00)***
Brain drain France (secondary)	−350.579 (−2.02)**	−551.462 (−1.92)*	145.499 (1.66)*
Constant	45.383 (5.73)***	40.135 (3.84)***	21.770 (3.20)***
Observations	120	125	55

Notes:

z statistics in parentheses.

* significant at 10%; ** significant at 5%; *** significant at 1%.

Instrumented variables: brain drain to Côte d'Ivoire, initial GDP.

Hansen J statistic (over identification test of all instruments): 12.843

Chi-sq(9) P-val = 0.16984.

Table 8.3 passes the Hansen-Sargan test for over identifying restrictions.[10]

The results in Table 8.3 represent a standard convergence equation in which national GDP growth (in per capita terms) depends on the previous year's level of national per capita GDP (Kaufman, Swagel and Dunaway 2003). An additional control variable is the log of the investment ratio minus the population growth rate, that reveals the impact of investment and population growth (Arcand and d'Hombres 2002). Finally, the estimation of convergence in a context of open economies should include migration effects for all countries considered. Therefore, the estimated brain drain variables are included. The brain drain variables are derived from the estimations of human capital as indicated in the previous section. The convergence equation tested a number of country-specific factors as well, but these results are not shown here.

Before interpreting the final outputs in the last column (regression three), I need to examine the first results in Table 8.3. The first regression (fixed effects with correlated panels corrected standard errors) indicates strong convergence effects. However, the investment becomes significant only when instrumental variables with generalized method of moments (GMM) estimation are used (regressions two and three). In the final outputs (see regression three using GMM estimation), the brain drain effects appear significantly negative when the migration destination is Côte d'Ivoire, while the reverse holds when the destination is France. Therefore, brain gain appears to happen only when migrants from WAEMU countries choose an industrialized country as their destination. This seems to support the Venables (1999) conclusion that an African country should prefer a 'north-south' type of integration agreement. However, unlike Venables there are strong income convergence effects inside the WAEMU, that simply support the argument that the advanced economies are not the only ones to see benefits from the Union.

Migrants with no schooling who leave their home country for Côte d'Ivoire have a negative impact on regional growth, as these people might be more productive in their country relative to the more human-capital intensive economic sectors of Côte d'Ivoire. As discussed earlier, the schooling rate is markedly higher in Côte d'Ivoire across all levels, as compared to the source countries (Eyssen 1996). In the source countries, the illiteracy rate is above 75 per cent, that is, nearly 50 per cent higher than in Côte d'Ivoire. These results suggest that the least costly migration for the Sahelian countries might be seasonal. The Sahelian countries did not incur labor loss, as the pattern is compatible with rain-fed agriculture. Another implication is that source countries may want to develop irrigation and agricultural investments which will optimize the impact of their important rural unskilled labor force at home. However, the regional brain drain at the secondary schooling level appears to have a strongly negative impact, supporting the argument that intraregional brain drain may not favor growth. There is no brain gain when the movement of skilled migrants is toward the polar economy, Côte d'Ivoire. Unlike regional skilled migration, for the countries whose migration is directed toward France, the positive effect of a well-controlled policy of brain drain appears at the higher and secondary schooling levels, as shown in regression three of Table 8.3. These two results do not contradict the brain-gain theory. As shown earlier, for the level of welfare of the sending country to increase, the destination should be very attractive in terms of expected gains, and the source country's migration policy should be designed so that the probability of migration is not above a certain threshold, estimated at around 10 per cent (Adams 2003). Under the latter conditions part of the education investment in the source country would actually act through those who migrate to advanced countries, send back remittances and increase incentives for investing in human capital in the sending country. The negative outcomes of regional brain drain will primarily affect a country like Burkina Faso, because the statistical tests indicate that it has the highest brain drain to Côte d'Ivoire. Tables 8.1 and 8.2 clearly show that the brain drain to Côte d'Ivoire of the best educated from Burkina Faso is above the conventional threshold, whereas the other WAEMU countries do not suffer a severe brain drain toward France, where their migration is concentrated.

Existing estimates in the migration literature suggest that remittances alone more than offset the net welfare loss usually derived from the welfare impact of migration. However, I did not find any significant effect of remittances in my regressions (results not shown), that may indicate that its effects are captured through the investment variable. The non-significant effect of remittances may also reveal some of the negative effects of the Ivorian political crisis during the 1990s. Doré, Benoît and Engmann (2003) established that the spillover effect of current and past Ivorian crises on neighboring countries could take place through trade channels (depending on the size and the geographical proximity of the neighbor) and also through capital flows and current transfers, much as happened during the Asian economic crisis.[11] In Burkina Faso, workers' remittances fell from 50.3 billion to 30 billion CFA francs in 2002, mainly as a consequence of the repatriation[12] of economic migrants from Côte d'Ivoire and the worsening economic situation in the latter country.

CONCLUSION

Over the past ten years there has been an increasing amount of attention paid to the ambiguous relationship among international migration, brain drain and economic growth, but few studies have analyzed the growth impact of skilled migration. This study filled the research gap by building the first data set on brain drain concerning seven countries of the Western African Union (WAEMU) and highlighting the size of the brain drain toward Côte d'Ivoire and France. The study has gone beyond the usual descriptive analysis and evaluated the implications on growth convergence.

The positive message is the finding that there exists a convergence path inside WAEMU which leads to the conclusion that polar economies are not the only beneficiaries of the Union under conditions of the free movement of persons. However, the migration of skilled personnel speeds up this process of convergence only when it is outward-oriented; that is, toward developed countries like France. Therefore, migration can be used as a powerful force working toward income convergence between capital-rich and capital-poor countries. If the traditional receiving countries (the United States, other OECD countries and Arab Gulf countries) care about the welfare of poor countries, they should collaborate to design carefully controlled immigration policies (monitoring the size of brain drain) which match the optimal welfare level and include the migratory policy in the globalization arena. It appears that when the best and brightest professionals leave, the dream of emulating them motivates many others to follow them abroad. The most difficult role of policymakers remains ensuring that the second effect outweighs the first, so that the welfare of the source countries strengthens more than it otherwise would. The policy can be twofold, influencing both push and pull factors. If the prospect of getting a visa to OECD countries is strong enough, then it will motivate more people to invest in education, but if the chances of landing a visa is too low, the poor sending country might gain more qualified personnel than it loses. However, sending countries can strengthen research capacities to keep students home while ensuring better conditions for achieving personal welfare. The latter trend is illustrated by a June 2005 survey conducted in Kenya by the Africa's Brain Gain (ABG) association. Results indicated that 70 per cent of students wanted to leave Kenya soon after graduation, but their plans to do so were not determined by the political climate, a lack of patriotism or a sense of responsibility. Instead, the reasons were linked to dim economic and employment prospects at home. The desire to leave Kenya stems from a perceived lack of adequate employment opportunities and salary levels to facilitate economic well-being. The ABG findings are applicable to all of the WAEMU countries.

The current study has highlighted the lack of official statistics on brain drain in the WAEMU and in sub-Saharan Africa in general. To be able to reap benefits from brain drain, African governments should first develop a database of citizens abroad. As globalization allows goods and people to become more mobile, good statistics on expatriates can facilitate policy formulation toward circulation patterns which enable Africans abroad to invest their vast knowledge back into the continent. This can be facilitated by offering short-term visiting positions to Africans abroad, strengthening partnerships and collaboration through student and faculty exchanges, encouraging centers of excellence with comparable international remuneration rates and pursuing other comparable incentives structures.

This study also found that Burkina Faso is the main exporter of labor to Côte d'Ivoire. Furthermore, the analysis shows that Burkina Faso out performs only Niger, that does not have migrants flows directed to France. Burkina Faso seems to lose a critical proportion of its meager pool of skilled workers through migration to Côte d'Ivoire. But the brain loss is as important as the unskilled year-long migration, because the unskilled migrations signifies a loss of agricultural earnings, suggesting that policymakers should invest in the rural sector to promote agricultural innovation, truck farming during the off season and local off-farm activities. The results suggest that the most effective migration for the Sahelian countries is seasonal. When migration is seasonal, the increased migration flow will translate into higher liquidity which enables households to overcome credit and insurance market failures and to invest in their main agro-pastoral activities. At the same time, households are able to smooth their consumption, that typically is subject to high uncertainty under local conditions. Households actually have higher incentives to invest in their farm plots because they can easily monitor the behavior of family members left behind. One characteristic of seasonality is that very often the migrant who is head of the household brings part of the remittances when returning home. This enables the migrant to control for a situation of rent or misuse which often arises when migration is permanent and the migrant has to delegate supervision of his home investment to those who stay behind. In the Sahelian context, seasonal migration to Côte d'Ivoire is made possible because the main economic activities are extensive livestock raising and rain-fed agriculture, which require an important labor force and therefore the presence of migrants in the short rainy season from July through September.

NOTES

This is a revised version of a paper presented at the sixth annual GDN meeting in Dakar. The author is grateful for comments and suggestions provided by Jean-Louis Combes, Jean-Louis Arcand, Susanna Wolf, Béatrice d'Hombres and the Macroeconomic and Trade Research Group at the Center for Development Research, University of Bonn, Germany. He also acknowledges the important support during data collection from Philippe Bocquier and Xavier Thierry. However, the usual disclaimers apply.

1. Convergence is understood here as the tendency of poor economies to grow faster than rich ones. This is conditional to the economy's steady state.
2. The West African Economic and Monetary Union (WAEMU or UEMOA the French acronym) comprises eight countries: Benin, Burkina Faso, Côte d'Ivoire, Guinea Bissau, Mali, Niger, Senegal and Togo.
3. Other justifications of the use of the Solow framework in empirical analysis are given in Arcand and d'Hombres (2002). Despite the popularity of endogenous growth theories as theoretical constructs within which the determinants of growth can be understood, it is difficult to test them structurally.

4. Borjas (1999) found that immigrants are in average less skilled than US natives.
5. For enrolment rates, averages over the periods were considered due to extreme scarcity of statistics for some countries of interest. This assumes the enrollment likelihood for an average migrant of the sending country in Côte d'Ivoire. For schooling attainment, the nearest year available was retained in some cases like in the Barro and Lee dataset. In a few cases, the methods of multiple imputation or interpolation were applied.
6. Recall that the calculations for the brain drain to France are based on French Census data. Other calculations based on stocks of students as proxy for the tertiary level human capital provide similar ranking of the countries regarding the brain drain phenomenon.
7. Stark (2003) explained how the integration of migrants as nationals of the host country may affect negatively their saving capacity and their willingness to remit. The migrants who acquired citizenship may have easier access to school and health facilities as well.
8. School enrolment in official school is markedly higher in Côte d'Ivoire on all levels, whereas in the Burkinabè Sahel, kuranic education is nearly the only existing one (survey 2002). This makes a relative disadvantage on the Ivorian urban labor market for the unskilled migrants (Eyssen 1996).
9. The authors proposed new methods of estimation. Nerlove (2002) devised a new method of maximum-likelihood estimation based on the density of the observations unconditional on the starting values of the dependent variable, and he argued that the usual procedures for doing feasible generalized least squares (GLS) or for obtaining starting values for maximum likelihood (ML) are seriously flawed. Arcand and d'Hombres (2002) proposed a new estimator which solves the problem of low variability resulting from estimations in first differences.
10. The descriptive statistics of all variables used in the study and the complete set of econometric tests are available upon request.
11. See Ades and Chua (1997) for some theoretical foundations of the negative impact of regional instability on the economic growth of neighboring countries and Guillaumont, Guillaumont and Brun (1999) about the negative effects of domestic instability.
12. In the aftermath of the 1999 Coup d'Etat, several thousands of migrant agricultural workers – mainly Burkinabe and Malians – had to leave Tabou (in the South) because of ethnic clashes with indigenous Krou population. The surge in forced return migration is currently an important regional issue.

BIBLIOGRAPHY

Adams, Jr, Richard H. (2003), 'International Migration, Remittances and the Brain Drain: A Study of 24 Labor-Exporting Countries', Washington, DC, World Bank, Policy Research Working Paper No. 3069.

Ades, Alberto and Hak B. Chua (1997), 'Regional Instability and Economic Growth: Thy Neighbor's Curse', *Journal of Economic Growth*, **2** (3), 279–304.

Anderson, T.W. and Cheng Hsiao (1981), 'Estimation of Dynamic Models with Error Components', *Journal of the American Statistical Association*, **76**, 598–606.

Arcand, Jean-Louis and Béatrice d'Hombres (2002), 'Explaining the Negative Coefficient Associated with Human Capital in Augmented Solow Growth Regressions', Clermont-Ferrand, France, Centre d'Etudes et de Recherches sur le Développement International, Etudes et Documents No. E 2002.27.

Barro, Robert J. and Xavier Sala-i-Martin (1995), *Economic Growth,* Cambridge, MA: MIT Press.

——(1992), 'Regional Growth and Migration: A Japan-United States Comparison', *Journal of the Japanese and International Economies,* **6** (4), 312–46.

Barro, Robert J. and Jong-Wha Lee (2000), 'Data Set on Educational Attainment of the

Total Population Aged 25 and Over', Cambridge, MA: Harvard University, Center for International Development.

Beck, Nathaniel and Jonathan N Katz (1995), 'What To Do (and Not to Do) with Time-Series Cross-Section Data', *American Political Science Review,* **89** (3), 634–47.

Beine, Michel, Frédéric Docquier and Hillel Rapoport (2003), 'Brain Drain and LDCs' Growth: Winners and Losers', Stanford, CA, Stanford University, Center for Research on Economic Development and Policy Reform Working Paper No. 129.

——— (2001), 'Brain Drain and Economic Growth: Theory and Evidence', *Journal of Development Economics,* **64** (1), 275–89.

Bhagwati, Jagdish N. and Koichi Hamada (1974), 'The Brain Drain, International Integration of Markets for Professionals and Unemployment', *Journal of Development Economics,* **1** (1), 19–42.

Blanchard, Olivier J. (1989), *Lectures on Macroeconomics,* in Barro and Sala-i-Martin (eds) *Economic Growth.*

Borjas, George J. (1999), *Heaven's Door: Immigration Policy and the American Economy,* Princeton: Princeton University Press.

Braun, Juan (1993), 'Essays on Economic Growth and Migration', Ph.D. diss. Harvard University, Cambridge, MA.

Carrington, William J. and Enrica Detragiache (1998), 'How Big is the Brain Drain?' Washington, DC, International Monetary Fund Working Paper No. WP/98/102.

Decaluwé, Bernard, Jean-Christophe Dumont, Sandrine Mesplé-Somps and Véronique Robichaud (2001), 'Union Economique et Mobilité des Facteurs: Le Cas de l'UEMOA', in Messaoud Boudhiaf and Jean-Marc Siroën (eds), *Ouverture et Développement,* Paris: Economica, pp. 281–307.

Doré, Ousmane, Anne Benoît and Dorothy Engmann (2003), 'Regional Impact of Côte d'Ivoire's Sociopolitical Crisis: An Assessment', Washington, DC, International Monetary Fund Working Paper No. 03/85.

Eyssen, Hans (1996), 'Are West-African Immigrants Discriminated in Côte d'Ivoire?', Washington, DC, World Bank Regional Program on Enterprise Development Working Paper No. 75.

Faini, Riccardo (2002), 'Migration, Remittances and Growth', Paper presented at the United Nations University, World Institute for Development Economics (WIDER) conference 'Poverty, International Migration and Asylum', Helsinki, 27–28 September.

Guillaumont, Patrick, Sylviane Guillaumont and Jean-François Brun (1999), 'How Instability Lowers African Growth', *Journal of African Economies* **8** (1), 87–107.

Hamilton, Bob and John Whalley (1984), 'Efficiency and Distributional Implications of Global Restrictions on Labour Mobility: Calculations and Policy Implications', *Journal of Development Economics,* **14**, 61–75.

Harris, Richard G. and Nicholas Schmitt (2003), 'The Consequences of Increased Labor Mobility Within an Integrating North America', in R. Harris (ed.), *North American Linkages: Opportunities and Challenges for Canada,* Calgary: University of Calgary Press, pp. 313–52.

Institut National de la Statistique et des Etudes Economiques (1999), *Recensement de la Population,* Paris: INSEE.

International Monetary Fund (several years), *Balance of Payments Statistics Yearbook,* Washington, DC.

Kaufman, Martin, Philip L. Swagel and Steven V. Dunaway (2003), 'Regional Convergence and the Role of Federal Transfers in Canada', Washington, DC,

International Monetary Fund Working Paper No. 03/97.

Koenker, Roger (2001), Panel Data. 'Lecture 13', mimeo, University of Illinois at Urbana-Champaign, Department of Economics.

Konseiga, Adama (2005a), 'New Patterns in the Human Migration in West Africa', *Vienna Journal of African Studies*, **8**, 23–46.

Konseiga, Adama (2005b), *Regional Integration beyond the Traditional Trade Benefits: Labor Mobility Contribution, The case of Cote d'Ivoire and Burkina Faso*, Frankfurt: Peter Lang.

Lucas, Robert E. (1988), 'On the Mechanics of Economic Development', *Journal of Monetary Economics*, **22** (1), 3–42.

Nerlove, March (2002), *Essays in Panel Data Econometrics*, New York: Cambridge University Press.

Stark, Oded (2003), 'Rethinking the Brain Drain', Bonn, Center for Development Research (ZEF) Discussion Papers on Development Policy No. 71.

Stock, James H., Jonathan H. Wright and Motohiro Yogo (2002), 'A Survey of Weak Instruments and Weak Identification in Generalized Method of Moments', *Journal of Business and Economic Statistics*, **20** (4), 518–29.

Thierry, Xavier (2004), 'Recent Immigration Trends in France and Elements for a Comparison with the United Kingdom', *Population*, **5**, 635–72.

Todaro, Michael (2000), 'Urbanization and Rural-Urban Migration: Theory and Policy', in Michael Todaro (ed.), *Economic Development*, 6th edn,, New York: Addison Wesley, pp. 291–325.

UNESCO (1992), *Educational Data*, Statistical Institute.

UNESCO (2000), *Statistical Yearbook*.

UNDP (2003), Population data.

Venables, Anthony J. (1999), 'Regional Integration Agreements: A Force for Convergence or Divergence?', Washington, DC, World Bank Policy Research Paper No. 2260.

—— (2003), 'Spatial Disparities in Developing Countries: Cities, Regions and International Trade', mimeo, London School of Economics.

Wooldridge, Jeffrey M. (2001), 'Applications of Generalized Method of Moments Estimation', *Journal of Economic Perspectives*, **15** (4), 87–100.

——(2002), *Econometric Analysis of Cross Section and Panel Data*, Cambridge, MA: MIT Press.

World Bank (2000), *World Development Indicators*.

World Bank (2002), *World Development Indicators*

World Bank (2003a), *World Development Indicators*.

World Bank (2003b), *Global Development Network data*.

Zanou, Benjamin (2001), *Migrations. Rapport d'Analyse du RGPH-98*, Institut National de la Statistique Côte d'Ivoire.

Index